DOUBLE DEATH

DOUBLE DEATH

The True Story of Pryce Lewis,
the Civil War's Most Daring Spy

GAVIN MORTIMER

WALKER & COMPANY
New York

Copyright © 2010 by Gavin Mortimer

Published by Walker Publishing Company, Inc., New York

All papers used by Walker & Company are natural, recyclable products made from wood grown in well-managed forests. The manufacturing processes conform to the environmental regulations of the country of origin.

LIBRARY OF CONGRESS CATALOGING-IN-PUBLICATION DATA HAS BEEN APPLIED FOR.

ISBN: 978-0-8027-1769-6

Visit Walker & Company's Web site at www.walkerbooks.com

First U.S. edition 2010

1 3 5 7 9 10 8 6 4 2

Typeset by Westchester Book Group
Printed in the United States of America by Worldcolor Fairfield

For Margot and Sandy

CONTENTS

PRYCE LEWIS WAS a Welshman, born in Wales to Welsh parents. Yet Britain in the mid-nineteenth century was a country indifferent to racial distinction, and Lewis was happy to call himself an Englishman (by which he meant Briton) regardless of whether he was playing a role in his work as a Civil War spy or discussing his background. Allan Pinkerton also described Lewis as an Englishman, even though he, a Scot, would have been aware of the difference. As Lewis is described in contemporary newspapers and military communiqués as "an Englishman," I refer to him throughout the book as an Englishman and not a Welshman. This is for the sake of clarity, not because I want to receive sacks of letters from Welsh nationalists accusing me of being a narrow-minded Englishman!

ACKNOWLEDGMENTS

I FIRST CAME ACROSS Pryce Lewis in the summer of 2008 while researching my previous book, *Chasing Icarus*. As I sat in the New York Public Library scrutinizing the city's newspapers from 1911, I chanced upon a report describing his wartime career. "Now that," I thought to myself, "is a great story. I do hope my agent and editor agree." They did, fortunately, although unsurprisingly. Both George Gibson at Walker Bloomsbury, and Gail Fortune of the Talbot Fortune Agency, have exceedingly good noses when it comes to stories. Jackie Johnson was an assiduous editor with a deft touch for smoothing down rough edges and rooting out superfluity, so I doff my cap in thanks that they all supported, encouraged and guided me so wholeheartedly from the outset, even during the moments when my dark artistic temperament got the better of me.

My research for *Double Death* began in Sussex, the birthplace of Timothy Webster, and the English county where my parents live. So while I toiled away at the East Sussex Archives in Lewes, I was able to retire at the end of each day to the house of my parents (David and Sheila), where not only was I supplied with good food and fine wine, but my mom even did my laundry! Thanks to them, and to the staff of the East Sussex Archives.

In London I was assisted in my research by the staff of the National Archives in Kew, the British Library in St. Pancras and the National Newspaper Library in Colindale. And Dawn Gill of the Powys Archive in Wales unearthed some crucial information about Pryce Lewis and his family. Not so long ago a visit to any British archive was always a trying experience, mainly because of the antediluvian facilities, but sustained investment in recent years has transformed most British archives into wonderfully user-friendly establishments.

Lastly as far as British thanks go, I owe an immeasurable debt to Mary Oldham and David Pugh of the Newtown Local History Group. David in particular was the personification of patience as I sent him long, rambling e-mails about Pryce Lewis and his early life in Newtown, mid-Wales. Without fail he replied to all my badgering, not just with courtesy but with much invaluable information. David, I am most grateful.

During my research trip on the other side of the Atlantic I—as always—walked into a barrage of kindness. The staff at the Library of Congress and the National Archives in Washington, D.C., assisted me in every way possible, as did the employees of the New York Public Library. My epic voyage north from New York City to St. Lawrence University in Canton, New York, close to the Canadian border, involved a lot of snow, a lot of Amish (that's a story for another day) and many long hours in a bus. But my reward was the incredible Pryce Lewis Collection and a few days on the beautiful campus of St. Lawrence. Everyone was unfailingly generous in their hospitality but none more so than Mark McMurray, the archivist, Darlene Leonard, his assistant, and Tish Munt, one of the librarians. Thank you so much.

Other people went out of their way to help me in researching and writing *Double Death*. Patty Goff was good enough to send me complimentary copies of her books, *Allan Pinkerton and the Larch Farm* and *Timothy Webster: The Story of the Civil War Spy and His Family*. As usual, Tom Schoff opened the door of his Manhattan B&B and made sure there was always a good bottle of red close at hand, which was usually finished as we put the world to rights. Zoe Lucas and Lyall Campbell of Halifax, Nova Scotia, answered some questions I had regarding emigration routes between Britain and Canada; similarly Claudia Cheely and Kevin Nelson of the Western Virginia Planning Department furnished me with some information about Hanover County in the Civil War. The astonishingly knowledgeable Bob Krick of the National Park Service, Richmond National Battlefield Park, fielded some important questions. Leo Lawton did likewise on the subject of Hattie Lawton.

But the people I have most to thank have been dead for decades.

On November 15, 1888, David Cronin, in his introduction to *Pryce Lewis: His Adventures as a Union Spy During the War of the Rebellion,* wrote, "The narrative of Pryce Lewis is published chiefly because it is believed that it will be found interesting to the general reader as well as to students of our late Civil War."

Alas, despite the best efforts of Cronin, himself a veteran of the Civil War and the editor of Lewis's memoirs, no publisher was found. In the early years of the twentieth century Cronin and Lewis tried once more to get the manuscript published but again without success. In due course the pair died, and the three books of memoirs, together with a dense wad of wartime correspondence, lay forgotten at the bottom of a trunk in the small apartment of Mary Lewis, Pryce's daughter, a pottery teacher in Manhattan.

In the winter of 1928 a history graduate from New York's Columbia University named Harriet Shoen enrolled in one of Mary Lewis's night classes. During the months that followed the pair struck up a warm friendship, though the teacher sometimes wounded the pupil's artistic pride with frank criticisms of Shoen's pottery skills.

One day during a discussion about the Civil War (in which Shoen's grandfather had fought), Lewis mentioned that her father had been a Union spy. Pressed for more details, Lewis clammed up and Shoen imagined they were just yarns not suitable for a serious student of history such as herself. It was only in the 1940s, as the unmarried Lewis contemplated the end of the family lineage, that she revealed to Shoen the true extent of her father's espionage activity. "One day early in 1945 Miss Lewis came to my Forty Second Street Office in New York with a large package under her arm," wrote Shoen a few years later. "That night I took the three time-worn notebooks that contained the handwritten memoirs of Pryce Lewis as a spy for the Union home with me. I read all night and on into the morning . . . I was amazed and delighted, also somewhat chagrined by my lack of enthusiasm in past years."

Mary Lewis agreed to sign the notebooks over to Shoen, who then spent several months typing up the memoirs and conducting further research into their content. A two-year posting as associate professor of history at Davis and Elkins College in West Virginia distracted Shoen, but in 1950 she embarked upon a third attempt to get the Pryce Lewis story into print.

In August of that year she approached the Ann Watkins literary agency in New York, providing a brief history of the memoirs: "Mary Lewis says the obituaries [of her father] were awful, that they were all written without any reporters consulting her, Lewis's nearest relative at the time. It is a very sad subject for her, and she is so feeble that I don't like to ask her too much."

But when Mary Lewis died four years later, her father's memoirs remained nothing more than a grimy, dog-eared manuscript returned by a dozen New York publishing houses. Shoen kept going, however, out of loyalty to her friend "Lewie," as much as her desire to see the memoirs in print, but the file of rejection slips grew ever thicker. Eventually ill health forced Shoen to admit defeat, and she died in 1967. Whoever cleared the spinster's New York apartment and stumbled across the Pryce Lewis material must have wondered what should be done. The trash can was the simple solution, but instead this historical hero contacted the History Society of St. Lawrence County, New York, explaining that Harriet Shoen, born in the county seventy-one years ago, had recently passed on and left reams of documents about the Civil War. Interested? Thankfully the society said yes, and so this priceless piece of history was saved. In later years the society donated the Pryce Lewis Collection to the nearby university of St. Lawrence in Canton, where the documents are now carefully guarded by Mark McMurray and Darlene Turner, the institution's archivists. So I say thank you to David Cronin, to Mary Lewis, to Harriet Shoen, to that unknown person who sifted through Shoen's papers after her death, to the St. Lawrence Historical Society and to St. Lawrence University.

But most of all, it's Pryce Lewis I must thank. It's taken 122 years to get your story into print, and I do hope the wait was worthwhile.

"There Goes a Big Slide of Snow"

O N THE EVENING OF DECEMBER 5, 1911, an old man named Pryce Lewis shuffled along Jefferson Avenue in Jersey City, New Jersey. Snow was banked high on the edge of the sidewalk, but in the center it had turned to a foul slush that seeped through the old man's scuffed leather shoes. His dark blue suit was threadbare, and he wore a frayed boater above a creased face that sported a ragged white mustache. Lewis stopped at 83 Jefferson Avenue and let himself into the modest boardinghouse. His landlady heard him return and emerged from a door on the ground floor. She handed him a letter, and his weary brown eyes flickered when he saw the Washington postmark. Lewis opened the envelope in the hallway and said nothing as he read the letter inside. Then he shook his head and mumbled, "My God!" Without another word he climbed the stairs to his small room at the top of the house.

The next morning, Wednesday, December 6, Lewis rose early. He put on the same dark blue suit and the same scuffed leather shoes from the night before. For a final touch he fastened a black bow tie to his white cotton shirt. It had stopped snowing, and the sky was a deep clear blue. Lewis sat at a table and wrote a short note to his landlady. It said, "Look for my body in the garret."

Not long after he had folded the note into a small brown envelope and left it on the table, Lewis changed his mind about where he would die.

He removed two business cards from his wallet and slipped them into the pocket of his suit. On one card was written "Isaac D. White, World editorial rooms" and on the other "William Davidson, M.D., 139 Clark Street, corner of Carteret Avenue, Jersey City." He also withdrew two dollar bills and left the wallet on the table next to the envelope addressed to his landlady.

At midmorning Lewis left the house unseen, covering his bald head with his boater, and made his way to Jersey City station. He had a short wait before boarding a train that took him through Penn tunnel and into New York City. At Penn Station he caught a streetcar and headed south from Seventh Avenue toward City Hall.

He alighted close to City Hall and began walking along the sidewalk. In front of him, towering into the unblemished sky, was the tallest skyscraper in New York City, the World Building, built twenty-two years earlier on the orders of Joseph Pulitzer, owner of the *World* newspaper. The building's façade was red sandstone, and a dome of burnished copper marked the highest point of the 370-foot-high structure. As Lewis approached the World Building he was swept along by the wave of humanity that pulsed back and forth from the Park Row entrance to the Brooklyn Bridge, situated next door to the newspaper headquarters. He entered the building under the bronze torchbearers mounted above the doorway and asked a receptionist for directions to the observation platform.

Lewis took an elevator to the sixteenth floor. As he emerged from the elevator he saw the short flight of stairs that led to an observation platform situated at the top of the dome. In one of the filing rooms on the sixteenth floor an employee of the *World*, Oscar Corbett, sat at his desk. He watched the old man climb the stairs, pause halfway, hesitate and then continue up.

It was bitterly cold on the platform. The only noise was the breeze whipping the flag back and forth. Lewis stooped under the iron railing that encircled the platform and inched his way toward the edge of the platform.

A few seconds later Oscar Corbett heard a rushing sound. Not bothering to look up from his desk in the filing room, he remarked to a colleague, "There goes a big slide of snow."

For several days Lewis's broken body lay unclaimed in a city morgue.

Newspapers wondered who he was, this old man who had ended his life in such abject fashion. Then, day by day, piece by piece, his story took shape. The following month an article appeared in *Harper's Weekly* under the headline: A REPUBLIC'S GRATITUDE: WHAT PRYCE LEWIS DID FOR THE UNITED STATES GOVERNMENT, AND HOW THE UNITED STATES GOVERNMENT REWARDED HIM. The paper explained that Lewis was a Civil War hero, a spy who had "habitually imperiled his life for the United States . . . one who had achieved more than a hundred soldiers." Yet his reward, continued *Harper's Weekly*, was to be abandoned by the government. How shameful, for "it was the sum of his achievements for the country that makes the country's neglect of him seem so sordid . . . the government in dire need used him. The government at ease coldly drove him to death."

CHAPTER ONE

"Little Molehills from the Green Sea"

IN 1849 THE AUTHOR Samuel Lewis published his *Topographical History of Wales*. Few of the places he visited on his extensive tour of the country had enchanted him as much as Newtown, a small town nestling in a beautiful valley on the banks of the river Severn in North Wales, approximately 180 miles northwest of London, and sixty miles north of Cardiff, the Welsh capital. Newtown was able to trace its origins back to the thirteenth century, but for centuries it had been nothing more than a pretty but insignificant settlement of a few hundred souls. Then at the end of the eighteenth century Newtown began to prosper thanks to the wool that came from the sheep feeding on the valley grass. The Industrial Revolution enabled Newtown's workers to produce more wool, and by 1841—the year of Britain's first official census—the town's population had exploded to 4,550.

Eight years later, in 1849, Samuel Lewis visited Newtown and found it to be flourishing with its substantial bridge, its gas lighting and its good soil. That didn't stop him from putting down Newtown on a couple of points, namely, the town's rather shoddy paving and the pervasive whiff of soot that came from all the coal burning. But they were minor cavils; all things considered, the author found Newtown delightful.

That same year a tall young man, eighteen years of age, was working in Newtown as a flannel weaver. He had bold brown eyes and wore his thick brown hair wavy at the sides, in part to hide his oversized ears. Handsome, healthy and quick-witted, perhaps he already sensed that one day his personality would outgrow Newtown and demand fresh stimulation.

But for the time being his attention stretched to not much more than pretty girls and foaming ale.

The young man's name was Pryce Lewis (he and the author were unrelated), born in 1831,* the fourth son of John and Elizabeth Lewis. On the surface they were an ill-suited couple; John was thirty years older than his wife, and while she could read and write, John could do neither. When they married in November 1825, he signed his name with a cross. Elizabeth came from the village of Berriew, nine miles northeast of Newtown, and her father, Thomas Nock, was a farmer. It might have been that John Lewis was employed by Nock as a weaver in the winter and a harvester in the summer, and that one day he wooed the farmer's daughter as they toiled side by side. Another possibility, however, is that John and Elizabeth were doing things in the field other than harvesting, things that necessitated a sudden wedding. Six months after their marriage Elizabeth gave birth to twins, George and Arthur.

When Britain undertook its census of 1841, the fifteen-year-old twins had four brothers: Richard, thirteen, Pryce, ten, Thomas, seven, and the runt of the litter, five-year-old Matthew. That year the Lewis family was living in the south of Newtown, in one of the cramped dwellings built in the backyards of existing houses to accommodate the woolen weavers and their families. John Lewis gave his occupation as "woolsorter"—a skilled job that required separating the various grades of wool from the fleeces to ensure that only the best quality was used—but in 1841 he was sixty-five, bent double by a lifetime of grind. Fortunately he had the twins to carry on the family tradition. "Woolen weavers," replied George and Arthur, when the census taker asked their occupation.

But the twins would have little wool to weave before the censor reappeared in 1851. Newtonians called the ensuing decade the "Hungry Forties" as the woolen industry suffered a severe depression. While northern

---

* Parish records show that Pryce Lewis was baptized on February 13, 1831, and although his exact birth date was not recorded, his birth year in the 1841 census was given as 1831.

English cities such as Bradford, Rochdale and Leeds produced flannel more cheaply than their Welsh rivals, the wealthy manufacturers in Newtown continued to increase the rent of the weavers' cottages.

So while the author Samuel Lewis might have been charmed by what he found in Newtown in 1849, he probably saw only what the town's officials wanted him to see. He made no mention in his book of the poverty, the inequality, the squalid living conditions endured by hundreds of the town's inhabitants or the regular cholera outbreaks that swept through Newtown.

John Lewis died in the winter of 1850 at the age of seventy-three. He was laid to rest on December 2, and the burial record stated that he had been living with his family above the White Lion public house in Penygloddfa. Perhaps it was cholera that claimed him, or maybe just the ravages of time and toil. Whatever the reason, his demise threw the Lewis family into turmoil. Approximately six miles to the southwest was the Newtown workhouse, dubbed the "Bastille" by locals, who likened its high walls and barred windows to the infamous French prison. It was home to 350 wretched paupers, and Elizabeth Lewis was determined that she and her family wouldn't add to the numbers. The fifty-year-old mother of six found work as an assistant in a grocer's store on Commercial Street, took in a lodger and secured a position for seventeen-year-old Thomas as a junior clerk with a Newtown attorney.

When the census taker returned in 1851 he found the Lewis family well situated. One of the twins, twenty-five-year-old George, had emigrated to the United States, and the other, Arthur, had also left home, though he hadn't headed west with his brother. Richard, twenty-three, was a groom, Thomas a clerk, and fifteen-year-old Matthew a schoolboy. The only one of the six brothers who seemed unsure of what to do with himself was twenty-year-old Pryce. He told the census taker he was a flannel weaver, but Mrs. Lewis must have sighed at the description.

She knew Pryce was the most gifted of her brood. He had excelled at the school he attended in a room above the Green Tavern in Ladywell Street. The teacher, Edward Morgan, was also the innkeeper of the tavern, but he never touched a drop hence his nickname, "the teetotaler." He was a good teacher, but Pryce was also a good learner, a boy with a boundless curiosity, a robust humor and a love of reading. He could be a little opinionated, but that was offset by his abundance of charm.

The aimless Pryce continued to test his mother's patience well into the 1850s. At some point Matthew Lewis joined George in America, and Richard headed to London to learn the butcher's trade, but Pryce remained in Newtown. One can only speculate why he stayed in this remote rural town while one by one his brothers broadened their horizons. Perhaps it was a love affair, or perhaps Pryce was the son who didn't wish to desert his mother. Elizabeth Lewis was clearly a remarkable woman; tough (not only did she survive six labors, but none of her children died young, a rare accomplishment in working-class Victorian Britain) but intelligent, resourceful and resilient. She was a survivor, and though in some measure she passed on her genes to all her children, it was Pryce who most inherited his mother's vigorous character.

But in the early summer of 1856 Pryce decided it was time to fly the family nest. He was now twenty-five, and life was passing him by. George and Matthew were well settled in America—both in Connecticut but leading separate lives—and an increasing number of Newtonians were making the trip across the Atlantic in search of a better life. A great many ended up in Blackinton, near North Adams in western Massachusetts, trading an ailing woolen industry for a burgeoning one. But Pryce Lewis had no intention of working in one of Blackinton's many woolen factories, grinding out long hours for low pay. He saw America as the opportunity to start afresh, create a new identity for himself, one that was more purposeful than the dreary existence he had hitherto led in Newtown.

In May 1856, Pryce Lewis kissed his mother good-bye. Through the tears and the hugs there would have been whispered promises of return, but neither would have been fooled. Elizabeth Lewis was in her late fifties, while her son was embarking on a voyage fraught with peril. In just the first two months of 1856 three ships, each crammed with excited emigrants, had perished in the pitiless Atlantic. The largest of the three, a clipper ship called the *Driver*, had sailed from Liverpool bound for New York on February 12 with 370 passengers and crew. Somewhere en route it sank to the bottom of the ocean.

The name of the ship on which Lewis sailed from Liverpool in May 1856, is unknown but it wasn't the *Thornton*, which departed the same month and arrived safely six weeks later. But as there was a rich diversity of emigrants on board the *Thornton*, so there would have been on Lewis's vessel.

Irish, Scottish, Welsh, English, a few Scandinavians, the odd German. They were young and old, male and female, mainly poor. The *Thornton*'s passengers included farmers and masons, carpenters and clerks, makers of dresses and makers of shoes, a confectioner, a milliner and a dozen or more laborers. Different trades but the same dream: a new life in America.

In the final hours before their ship sailed, passengers would spend the last of their pence on a hot meal of the best possible quality, for during the next few weeks they would have to survive on a diet of stale bread, bad meat and a foul, watery soup.

Then came the harrowing moment of departure, in many cases the eternal severance of a familial bond. A reporter for the *Illustrated London News* witnessed one such moment in 1850. "As the ship is towed out, hats are raised, handkerchiefs are waved, and a loud and long-continued shout of farewell is raised from the shore, and cordially re-sponded to from the ship. It is then, if at any time, that the eyes of the emigrants begin to moisten . . . the most callous and indifferent can scarcely fail, at such a moment, to form cordial wishes for their pleasant voyage and safe arrival."

The last link to be severed between the emigrants and their previous life was the tow boat's rope. Once that was gone, it was out into the open sea and a voyage of discomfort and, more often than not, rank terror. Sixteen years before Pryce Lewis sailed for New York, a thirty-year-old Charles Dickens had undergone a similar journey. Dickens was then at the height of his powers, but when he found himself in a mid-Atlantic storm he would have willingly traded all his fame and wealth for the security of dry land. "The laboring of the ship in the troubled sea on this night I shall never forget," he wrote in his account of his American odyssey. "Thunder, lightning, hail and rain, and wind, are all in fierce contention for the mas-tery . . . every plank has its groan, every nail its shriek, and every drop of water in the great ocean its howling voice . . . Words cannot express it, thoughts cannot convey it. Only a dream can call it up again, in all its fury, rage and passion."

But Dickens survived, as did Lewis, who must have stood on deck and witnessed his new home take shape before his eyes. Perhaps Lewis had read Dickens's *American Notes* and was familiar with the author's descrip-tion of his first glimpse of America resembling "little molehills from the green sea." But perhaps Lewis's memory failed him at such a fantastic moment, and instead he just gawked with his fellow passengers. There before them was the United States of America, a young and dynamic country with so much more to offer than jaded, bitter, played-out Britain. There one needed money and influence to succeed, but in America all men were created equal.

CHAPTER TWO

"A Detective! Me?"

P RYCE LEWIS ARRIVED IN AMERICA with only his leather valise. He was twenty-five years old, a good age to begin again. He wasn't sure what he wanted to do, except he knew he wanted nothing to do with the burgeoning community in Massachusetts that was intent on re-creating Welsh life in a little plot of northeast America. He hadn't crossed an ocean for that. Nor was Lewis particularly attracted by Connecticut and the prospect of building a life alongside his two brothers: thirty-year-old George, who now had a family of his own, and lived in Torrington; and twenty-year-old Matthew, who resided in Litchfield, six miles south of his brother. Matthew was working and living on a farm owned by the Hoig family, James and Eliza and their three young children. Nonetheless Pryce traveled to Connecticut and caught up with George and Matthew. Doubtless there were letters to pass on from their mother, and gossip, too, of dear friends and old sweethearts.

While browsing a Connecticut newspaper one day, Pryce saw an employment notice that took his fancy. The London Printing and Publishing Company was soliciting responsible men to sell its publications across the country. As instructed in the notice, Pryce mailed a letter to Samuel Brain at the company's headquarters in New York, and received in return further information along with a catalog of its books.

He was asked to attend an interview with Mr. Brain at the company's office on Dey Street. The well-read Lewis got the job and for nearly two years sold the books of the London Printing and Publishing Company throughout northeastern America. The job entailed a lot of traveling, endless hours on the railroad, so Lewis became intimately acquainted with his employer's products: he was an expert on the British problems in India thanks to Charles Ball's *History of the Indian Mutiny*, and he became something of a grammarian after plowing through Thomas Wright's *Universal Pronouncing Dictionary and General Expositor of the English Language: Being a complete literary, classical scientific, biographical, geographical and technological standard*. But the book he liked best was the company's most recent acquisition, Henry Tyrrell's three volumes of the *History of the War with Russia: Giving full details of the operations of the Allied Armies*.

The Crimean War of 1854–56 had captured the imagination of the British people, and the Victorians had appropriated the war for themselves. The roles of France and the Ottoman Empire in helping to defeat the Russian forces had been all but dismissed. In their place was Florence Nightingale, "the Lady with the Lamp," as the *Times* of London christened the nurse whose devoted care had alleviated the suffering of the wounded British soldiers, along with the glorious and futile cavalry charge during the Battle of Balaclava, immortalized in Alfred, Lord Tennyson's poem "The Charge of the Light Brigade." Within weeks of the poem's publication in 1855, there were few people in Britain unable to recite it by heart. Henry Tyrrell's three volumes might have been less florid than Tennyson's poem, but running to nearly 1,100 pages they were considerably more substantial. Pryce Lewis devoured them with gusto as he traveled through Illinois, Wisconsin, Iowa and as far west as the Mississippi River.

But by the spring of 1859, Lewis had grown tired of this job and its monotonous routine. He quit and moved to Chicago, where he found employment as a clerk in a grocery store run by David Erskine and his wife, Grace. David Erskine was a thirty-six-year-old Scot who, before coming to America, had lived in the West Indies, where two of his three children were born. Lewis lasted a year with Erskine, but by early 1860 his feet were feeling restless. It was nearly four years since he'd left Wales, yet here he was, twenty-nine years old, a grocery clerk in a small Chicago store. Hardly the life he'd imagined when he crossed the ocean.

And yet all around him in Chicago there was tantalizing evidence of what was possible, the rewards on offer for those immigrants who embraced their new home with both hands. Since 1840 the population of Chicago had ballooned from 4,450 to 109,260. In 1842 it had been just a dirty dot on the shores of Lake Michigan, too insignificant for Charles Dickens, whose extensive itinerary had stretched from Lake Erie in the North to Richmond in the South. But by 1860 Chicago was a booming city, the economic epicenter of northwest America. The Illinois and Michigan Canal connected Lake Michigan to the Mississippi and enabled Chicago to overtake St. Louis as the wheat industry's major transporter, but it was the railroads that transformed the city. The first railroad had arrived in Chicago in 1848 (the Galena & Chicago Union), but twelve years later there were fifteen, and with the trade the companies also brought development. The railroads purchased large tracts of land on which to build their lines, but they also constructed breakwaters and dikes to prevent the routes being flooded by Lake Michigan. Safe from the threat of inundation, more companies constructed factories and warehouses—some as high as six stories—and effluence no longer flowed through the streets of Chicago.

Lewis was anxious to accomplish something in Chicago, not just for the financial enrichment, but because he yearned for a little adventure in his life. Then one day he read in one of the city's seven daily newspapers of the Pike's Peak gold rush of 1859; not long after, the city began swelling with returning "Fifty-Niners," who brought back tales of the riches to be had in the gold regions of Pike's Peak country, a hostile expanse of territory that stretched from southwestern Nebraska to western Kansas.

Lewis listened to their stories and decided he'd try his luck in the summer of 1860. He gave his notice at Erskine's grocery store, and to all his friends who asked, he told them he was heading west to mine for gold. "Pike's Peak or bust!" he boomed, repeating the slogan of the day.

Shortly before he was due to leave Chicago Lewis encountered a man he had met during his days as a traveling salesman. The last time he'd seen Mr. Charlton was in Detroit, where they'd passed an agreeable few hours discussing literature, the Crimea, America and a host of other topics. Charlton never forgot a face, and when he passed Pryce Lewis in the street he pumped his hand and asked how he was doing. When Lewis told him of his intention, Charlton looked aghast.

Don't believe the miners' stories, he advised Lewis, they were nothing more than fiction fueled by a combination of powerful liquor and
wounded pride. There was barely any gold to be had in Pike's Peak,
and what little there was had long since been mined. Disease and depri-
vation were all that lay out West, said Charlton, who then invited Lewis
for a drink.

For a while they swapped small talk, until Charlton leaned in a little
closer and told Lewis his boss was on the lookout for good men. Lewis
realized that Charlton had never revealed what line of work he was in.
Now he did. Charlton lowered his voice and told Lewis he was a detective.
What's more, he reckoned Lewis could be one too. Lewis laughed. "A
detective! Me?"

Charlton nodded, and explained that not only was it an easy profession to master, but the pay was pretty good. Lewis balked at the idea.
He couldn't imagine himself as a detective. Charlton persisted, and a
couple of hours later Lewis was standing before Charlton's superior,
George Henry Bangs.

Bangs was the deputy head of the detective agency, and like Lewis he
was twenty-nine. They also shared a similar prepossessing physique, but
Bangs sported an abundant salt and pepper beard that compensated for
the hair he lacked on top. He invited Lewis to take a seat, offered him a
coffee, then asked to hear a little bit of his background. As Lewis talked
Bangs scrutinized his face and head as he did with every potential employee. It was orders from the boss, the head of the agency, who was a
firm believer in the science of phrenology.

In the mid-nineteenth century it was widely believed that a person's intelligence and character could be deduced from the examination of the
shape and size of the skull. The larger the head, so the phrenologists believed, the more intelligent the person, while the stouter the torso, the more
stupid one was. When Bangs's boss underwent a "Phrenological Description" in Chicago by Professor O. S. Fowler, the good professor concluded
in his expensive report that the detective chief's dominant characteristics
were "earnestness, enthusiasm, heartiness, whole-souledness, impetuosity
and excitability . . . your name ought to be 'whole soul' because you throw
so much soul into everything you do."

In fact the chief's name was Allan Pinkerton, and it was he who had
the final say on whether Pryce Lewis became the latest recruit to the

detective agency he'd established ten years earlier. Bangs would have given Pinkerton a detailed physical account of Lewis, as well as describing his intelligence, his deportment and his initiative. He would also have mentioned something of Lewis's life in Wales, and this was probably as important to Pinkerton as anything else in deciding whether or not to hire Lewis.

Allan Pinkerton was an exceptional man with many admirable qualities. He was brave, physically and morally; he was loyal, diligent and hardworking. He could be generous, thoughtful, and to the oppressed he was a staunch supporter. But Pinkerton also had his flaws. He was insecure, dogmatic, humorless and authoritarian, a man who saw the world through a narrow prism. People were either good or bad; he lacked the nuance of mind to grasp the complexities of human nature. So his munificence extended only to those who yielded to his iron will; to those who crossed him—even if they were justified in doing so—he bore a lifetime of malice. Allan Pinkerton had another outstanding trait: his moral ambiguity. He told the truth only when it suited him; when it didn't, he lied.

Pinkerton was born in the Gorbals district of Glasgow on July 21, 1819, the fourth (though second surviving) son of fifty-two-year-old William and his second wife, Isabella. Allan later claimed his father had been a policeman, but he was nothing of the sort; William Pinkerton made his living as a handloom weaver until he lost his job not long after Allan's birth. Unlike many of his former workmates, William found further employment as a warder in a Glasgow jail, a position he held until his death in the early 1830s.

Years later, when Allan Pinkerton was well established in America, he let it be known that his father, the "policeman," had been murdered while on duty. It was another lie, though he told the truth about his seven-year apprenticeship as a cooper. His role with the Glasgow Chartists, however, he bent like a stave of one of his barrels to fit his own ends

Pinkerton had joined the Chartist movement following the end of his apprenticeship in 1838 when his master, William McAulay, gave the job of cooper to his own unqualified son.

Pinkerton set out to find work elsewhere in Scotland, and during his travels the impressionable nineteen-year-old attended his first Chartist meetings. Here he listened to the impassioned arguments between those

Scottish Chartists who favored action through peaceful means, "Moral Force" Chartists, and those who favored more robust methods, the "Physical Force" Chartists.

Pinkerton supported the latter, as did most Glaswegian Chartists, and such was the fervor with which Pinkerton embraced the movement that in September 1839 he was elected one of six members of the Glasgow Universal Suffrage Association. That same month, at the Chartist National Convention, it was decided that the time had come for a national uprising. The catalyst for the insurrection was the arrest and incarceration the previous May of four Welsh Chartists, and it was intended that Chartists from around Britain would descend on Newport in south Wales and demand their release. The date chosen for the attack was the first week of November, but what had been envisaged as a nationwide uprising dwindled to a regional protest. Men's ardor cooled as the day approached and the realization dawned that this was revolution, and everyone knew the penalty for that. The tens of thousands of Chartists expected to converge on Newport was in reality no more than five thousand, the majority from south Wales, and armed only with pikes and clubs.

The Newport Rising of November 4, 1839, was a bloody fiasco for the Chartists. Five hundred special constables and a regiment of soldiers waited for the rebels, and in the ensuing violence twenty-two Chartists were killed. The ringleaders were hunted down and sixty-two of their number transported to Australia. Never again would the Chartists rise up in such force. In later life Pinkerton claimed he'd been present at the Newport Rising, but in all probability this was another distortion of the truth. Contemporary reports made no mention of a contingent of Glasgow Chartists, and none of those wounded or transported came from the city.

For the next two and a half years Pinkerton continued to work for the Chartist cause, but it was more a hobby than a belief. There were rallies and meetings and assemblies, all opportunities to rattle the Chartist tail, but the government had drawn the movement's venom. Nevertheless it was at a Chartist fund-raising concert in the summer of 1841 that Pinkerton's life turned upside down. There on stage, a vision in white, was Joan Carfrae, whose voice and beauty and whole being captivated the twenty-two-year-old Pinkerton. But he wasn't one of life's romantics, nor was he physically attractive. The young Allan Pinkerton was five foot eight with an upper body that resembled one of his barrels. He had the face of a fire-and-brimstone preacher, cold blue-gray eyes, a crude dark beard and a mouth that rarely smiled.

But Pinkerton was nothing if not persistent, and he "got to sort of hanging around her, clinging to her, so to speak," during the months that followed. Eventually Joan succumbed, and the courtship resulted in marriage, along with another Pinkerton fabrication. The legend he promulgated in America was that he had fled Glasgow because he "had become an outlaw with a price on his head" and that he'd married Joan in a secret ceremony hours before friends spirited them onto a vessel bound for North America. The truth, as was often the case with Pinkerton, was more prosaic. He and Joan married on March 13, 1842, in one of Glasgow's most prominent churches, and it wasn't until April 3 that they boarded the *Kent* bound for Montreal. Allan Pinkerton was one of 63,852 Britons who emigrated to the United States in 1842, the highest annual total to that point. He might have told his fellow passengers, in hushed tones, that he was running from the law, but in reality the only thing he was fleeing was the powerlessness of the British workingman.

CHAPTER THREE

"Murdered in the Most Shocking Manner"

NONE OF THIS WAS TOLD to Pryce Lewis during his interview with Pinkerton's deputy. It was he who had to impress George Bangs, which he evidently did because he was offered a position with the agency. Bangs "praised Lewis's appearance and was confident that he was adapted to detective work, would learn it easily and would like it." Lewis remained unconvinced, even when he was informed that he could start immediately "with a good salary which would be increased as he became proficient."

Lewis asked for time to think. He left the Pinkerton offices in the company of Charlton and over supper interrogated him about the agency and its founder. Charlton told Lewis how Pinkerton had worked his way from Scotland to Chicago, via Montreal, nearly twenty years earlier, before opening a cooperage in Dundee, a Scottish settlement forty miles northwest of Chicago. So how did a cooper become a detective? inquired Lewis. Charlton explained that in 1846 Pinkerton had helped track down a gang of counterfeiters in Dundee, an exploit that brought him fame among his fellow citizens. Storekeepers enlisted his aid to snare other petty criminals, and soon his name began to ripple across the state. In 1847 he was invited to become deputy sheriff of Cook County in Illinois. Two years later, as Chicago's crime rate increased in line with its population, Pinkerton was appointed the city's first detective by Mayor Levi Boone.

But the following year he quit to become a mail agent for the United States Post Office, chasing thieves who stole checks and postal orders. That same year, continued Charlton, Pinkerton and a man named Edward Rucker rented a small office at 89 Washington Street and opened the Pinkerton & Co. Detective Agency.*

Rucker soon left the business to his partner, and for a while Pinkerton combined his work for the post office with running his agency. But the latter demanded more and more of his time as Chicago's flourishing railroad network brought in troublemakers from across the country. Soon Pinkerton had expanded his agency. Charlton ran through the recruits: Lewis had already met George Bangs, the first detective hired by Pinkerton; then there was Sam Bridgeman, who liked his liquor but was good at his work; Adam Roche, a German whose only vice was tobacco; the canny John Fox; and finally there was Timothy Webster, not only the star of the agency but the most popular. Charlton was sure Lewis would find the British-born Webster agreeable. They were all fine detectives, said Charlton, but none had been born to the role. Bangs was a former reporter, Bridgeman a soldier, Fox a watchmaker, Roche a lumberman and Webster a tinsmith. Pinkerton had given them a few pointers at the start, but most of what they learned they acquired on the job, as Lewis would surely do.

Next Charlton told Lewis about some of the cases they solved, most of which centered on the network of railroads. Since 1855 Illinois Central had been paying the agency ten thousand dollars per annum to protect its six railroads and their employees: Michigan Central, Michigan Southern and Northern Indiana, Galena and Chicago Union, Illinois Central, Chicago and Rock Island, and Chicago, Burlington and Quincy.

There had been murders to crack, robberies to solve, outlaws to catch, and at this very moment Pinkerton and most of the team were in Alabama, waiting to give evidence at the trial of Nathan Maroney, the charismatic manager of the Montgomery branch of the Adams Express

---

* There is confusion as to the exact year the agency was founded. On one occasion Allan Pinkerton gave 1850 as the date and on another 1852. The agency probably began on a small scale in 1850 but took off two years later, the year Pinkerton appeared to part company with Rucker and go it alone.

Company, who had been charged with stealing forty thousand dollars of the company's money. The crime had riveted the Southern states, and there was outrage in some quarters that a Yankee like Pinkerton had accused so prominent a man as Maroney of criminal activity.

Charlton had said enough. This was the life of adventure Lewis craved. The next day he accepted Bangs's offer. Once the paperwork had been dispensed with, it was down to work. First, Lewis was to consider himself an "operative," not a detective, the latter having connotations of corruption, at least in Chicago, where venality was rife among law enforcers, uniformed or otherwise. It was emphasized to Lewis that he was to adhere scrupulously to the Pinkerton's operating guidelines (later published in pamphlet form under the title *General Principles of Pinkerton's National Detective Agency*). Failure to do so would result in instant dismissal. For example, operatives were not to accept rewards or bonuses, nor were they to tail any public official while he was executing his duty; the agency would not accept cases that involved divorce or other scandalous affairs, and it would refrain from prying into a woman's morals. This was because in Pinkerton's view the role of detective was a "high and honorable calling . . . he is an officer of justice, and must himself be pure and above reproach." Thus it was unacceptable for any of Pinkerton's operatives to resort to nefarious means to ensnare their prey; this was to be done by stealth and guile. "It cannot be too strongly impressed upon detectives that secrecy is the prime condition of success in all their operations," stated Pinkerton, which meant that every operative had to be, to some extent, a performer, an actor, a master of disguise, with the "player's faculty of assuming any character that his case may require, and of acting it out to the life, with an ease and naturalness which shall not be questioned."

Bangs taught Lewis how to shadow a target, how to wear a disguise (there was reportedly a large closet in the agency's office full of costumes and accessories) and how to pull off the new persona without arousing suspicion. Bangs would also have introduced Lewis to the agency's gallery of rogues, a Pinkerton innovation that soon caught on worldwide. Wanted men were described in detail—their accents, physique, dress and distinguishing features—and these descriptions were often accompanied by sketches or daguerreotypes of the suspects, along with examples of their handwriting.

Bangs's last point was his most emphatic: be careful. Many of the men they pursued were violent desperadoes for whom human life was cheap. Cornered, they'll come out fighting. Satisfied that Lewis had a strong command of the basic tenets of detective work, Bangs sent him out onto the Chicago streets to shadow a suspect. Lewis trailed the man for several days, closely, unobtrusively, skillfully. But it was boring work, and when Lewis reported to Bangs at the end of the assignment, he was ready to resign. Detecting wasn't all it was cracked up to be. Bangs laughed and told him it had been a trial run, that the "suspect" was in fact a fellow operative and that another Pinkerton man had been tailing Lewis to see how he got on. His report had been glowing, and Bangs was delighted to welcome him into the fold.

For the next few months Lewis roamed the western and eastern states, tailing and tracking. He lived out of a valise, and whenever he had a few days off he returned to Connecticut and lodged with his brother George in Torrington. It was in the Constitution State that Lewis helped bust a gang of express robbers, a success that won him a salary hike. Toward the end of 1860 he was invited by Pinkerton to work with him on a case in New York.

The affair was quickly solved, so the two men had time to become acquainted. Their common ground was Chartism, and though Lewis had been only a boy during the movement's heyday, in manhood he embraced the ideology. Delighted that Lewis had been a supporter of the Chartists, Pinkerton wanted to know if Lewis's social conscience had made the journey across the Atlantic; was he now an abolitionist? Lewis looked down at Pinkerton and replied that he was "an out-and-out Abolitionist."

They must have made a strange pair as they walked along a New York sidewalk, the graceless Pinkerton with his scowling, overgrown face, and the debonair Lewis, described by a contemporary as being "in the vigor of early manhood, tall and erect with an affable presence, regular features, a healthful complexion, and pleasant enough, though penetrating, black eyes . . . he was naturally light-hearted and possessed a keen sense of humor."

Suddenly Pinkerton turned to Lewis and asked if he was familiar with Edward Bulwer-Lytton's book *Eugene Aram*. Lewis replied that he was not. "Procure it, and read it on your return to Chicago," instructed Pinkerton. "I'll have something further to say on the matter when I next see you."

The pair parted, and Lewis sought out a copy of *Eugene Aram*, his interest piqued by the strange demand. Not that he was particularly surprised. In the eight months since he'd started working as one of Pinkerton's operatives Lewis "had come to regard him as a man of original, not to say eccentric, methods."

He found the book in the salesroom of Harper & Brothers, the grandiose office block in Franklin Square, and the next day boarded a Chicago-bound train. During the journey northwest Lewis barely looked up from his lap, so engrossed was he in the fate of Daniel Clark, a shoemaker from Knaresborough in central England, who had vanished one foggy night in the winter of 1745. Bulwer-Lytton had reconstructed the true story with haunting accuracy, from the day Clark disappeared to the day, thirteen years later, when the schoolteacher Eugene Aram was arrested and accused of murdering his former friend. The evidence was weak—an unidentified skeleton in a cave and the testimony of a man whom Aram said was the real murderer—but the defendant was found guilty and sentenced to hang. On the eve of his execution, Aram wrote a confession and then slashed his wrists.

Lewis had finished the book by the time he was back in Chicago, and the tale of Eugene Aram left a deep impression on him. In particular, he was "fascinated by the descriptive analysis of Aram's mental condition after he had committed a great crime. He suffered from remorse, somewhat as Macbeth did after the murder of Banquo."

When Pinkerton returned the following week he summoned Lewis to his office and asked if he had read the book. He had, and enjoyed it very much. They discussed the book's contents for a while, and then Pinkerton came to the point. A murder had been committed in Jackson, Tennessee, the previous year, and the culprit was still at large. It was rumored that the suspected murderer was a respected citizen in Jackson, and Pinkerton's plan was that Lewis should go there "as a gentleman of leisure and gradually form an intimacy with him. In time he should be able to detect the mental characteristics which were developed in Eugene Aram and obtain clues that might lead to the full exposure of the criminal." Lewis was soon on his way to Jackson, scrutinizing the case notes of what the *New York Times* had called "a most atrocious murder."

On the morning of Friday, February 4, 1859, George Miller, head cashier of the Jackson branch of the Union Bank of Tennessee, failed to open the bank, a most unusual occurrence for a most diligent man. Friends visited his lodgings, which were connected to the bank by a passageway, but found no trace of him. They forced the door to the bank, and there he was, "murdered in the most shocking manner." He was seated at a table, a checkbook before him and a pen in his hand, the back of his head caved in by two mighty hammer blows. "Two or three leaves had been torn from the check-book," reported the *New York Times*, "and either destroyed or carried away. The bank was robbed of some $16,600 in coin, and a very considerable quantity of small coin scattered over the floor. The murderers unbarred the front door and passed out, and pulled the door after them." The *Times* added that Miller was considered a "worthy and exemplary" young man, always exceedingly careful not to admit anyone into the bank at improper hours. He had last been seen at eight P.M. the previous evening; thus it seemed likely that Miller knew his killer, or at least his accomplice, and was in the process of writing a check when he was struck from behind.

Lewis arrived in Jackson in January 1861 "and stopped at the principal hotel and mingled freely with the people, adopting the role of an English gentleman looking for an opportunity to invest capital in business." Lewis soon discovered that a man awaiting trial for horse stealing was boasting that he knew the killer. An interview was arranged, and the prisoner told Lewis that one of the murderers lived in Memphis and called himself "the doctor." Lewis relayed the information to Chicago, but Bangs replied in a telegram of February 18 that he didn't believe the horse thief's claims; one of the early suspects in the case had been a man named Dr. Gibbs, but he'd been cleared of any involvement. Bangs proceeded to say that he had communicated with Pinkerton, who was out of town, and the latter remained convinced that the guilty party was the "leading citizen" first suspected. "He [Pinkerton] reviews the life of the man since the murder which every act goes to show that there is a load of guilt upon his mind, almost too much for him to bear, and like Macbeth with his diseased mind and vision he sees *Blood, Blood, Blood,* whichever way he turns, upon everything—and scents it everywhere. And like Aram he seeks vent for his thoughts, and consequently fears to trust himself in contact with others. He fears the face of man, having in his soul the brand of Cain, and its effects are daily visible, controlling every act of his life and embittering every movement of his existence."

Nevertheless Lewis persevered in the case, although day by day it became harder to make any headway. What now concerned the good citizens of Jackson, Tennessee, wasn't the fate of the unfortunate Mr. Miller but the fate of the Union. There was rebellion in the air, and in the town's hotels and saloons "fire-eating Southerners boasted of their superiority to the 'mudsills of the North' and predicted that the Southern States would easily establish a separate independence." Lewis considered himself lucky not to be a Yankee in such circumstances, and when accosted in a bar or saloon, he raised his glass and promised that the English people would stand side by side with their Southern brethren if war broke out. He soon found that "he readily fell in with the ways of the warm-hearted Southerners and liked them socially irrespective of their political notions." As Lewis toasted the Southern states and damned the Federal government, his boss was eight hundred miles east in Baltimore, attempting to break up a gang of Southern assassins intent on murdering president-elect Abraham Lincoln.

CHAPTER FOUR

"A Plan Had Been Laid for My Assassination"

T HE YEAR THAT PRYCE LEWIS had arrived in New York, 1856, coincided with the election of Democrat James Buchanan as the fifteenth president of the United States. As Lewis traveled the eastern states selling books, he would have read in the newspapers of the demands of the Buchanan administration to extend the slave area. Since the Missouri Compromise of 1820 the states north of the Mason-Dixon Line (the boundary between Pennsylvania and Maryland) had been "free states," but by the early 1850s the Southern states wanted to expand slavery into these free states. In particular they had their eye on Kansas and Nebraska, two states west of the Mason-Dixon Line, and throughout the 1850s the states were at the center of a tug-of-war between the antislavery states and the Southern states. The citizens of Kansas in particular were opposed to slavery, but their attempts to be recognized as a free state were continually blocked by Buchanan and the Democrats, although the issue proved to be the rock on which the Democratic Party was smashed during the stormy run-up to the 1860 election.

The Northern Democrats knew that if they acceded to demands from their Southern brothers to extend slavery into Kansas and Nebraska they would be voted out of office, so they (with the support of some Southern Democrats) nominated Illinois's Stephen Douglas as their presidential candidate, a man who believed that it was for the people of a state to decide for themselves whether they should be free or slave; the enraged Southern Democrats held their own convention and elected the pro-slavery John Breckinridge of Kentucky as their nominee. By doing so the two bitter factions knew they had all but handed the presidency to the Republicans—the "Black Republicans" as they called their hated adversaries—but such was the divisive nature of the slavery issue that the Democrats were unable to work together to save their party.

The Republicans, however, whose ultimate aim was to abolish slavery, still had to choose a candidate who would appeal to voters in all the free states, from New Jersey to Illinois to California. The belligerent William Seward had been an early front-runner but was seen as too much of a rad-ical; the fiery manner in which he denounced slavery alarmed senior Republicans, who knew that many voters in the North were indifferent to slavery. There was also a whiff of scandal around Seward, corruption emanating from his political manager, Thurlow Weed.

But who else was there? Simon Cameron and Salmon Chase were tal-ented, but both had as many weaknesses as strengths. Which left only Abraham Lincoln, the Illinois "rail-splitter" who had been born in a log cabin fifty-one years earlier. He was opposed to slavery, but less forcefully than either Seward or Chase, and he was popular among immigrants, who saw him as the personification of the American dream: a man from the backwoods who had risen to become a lawyer and a politician. Perhaps, most significant of all, Lincoln's integrity was indubitable. He was known as "Honest Abe," and his reputation was untainted by scandal.

Lincoln won the Republican nomination and in November 1860 claimed the presidency, carrying every free state bar New Jersey. But he won only 40 percent of the popular vote (54 percent in the North), and in the Southern states news of his election was greeted with despair. A young English governess named Sarah Jones was staying at the Ex-change and Ballard Hotel in Richmond, Virginia, on election day and witnessed the effect of the result on the population.

> From early morning voting was going on at several public build-ings in the neighborhood . . . at every corner men were comparing notes and hourly bulletins were issued respecting the various polls throughout the country . . . long and continued shouts and huz-zahs assailed one's ears from time to time till towards midday.

Success seemed to gleam around. By and by the shouts became less frequent. News from more distant regions must have changed the aspect of affairs and chilled their hopes. Next one perceived a depression in the looks of passers-by, more so and so, then the groups dispersed in silence. By dusk a funeral cloud seemed to hang over the city. By nine o'clock the town seemed hushed in sleep. The night before the hotel had been noisy with tramping and merriment, serenaders outside and hopeful politicians within had prolonged the revels to a late hour. Now the disappointment seemed too great for utterance.

It took a while for the result to sink in, and for the Southern states to formulate a response. The first to do so was South Carolina, which called a convention to vote on whether to secede from the Union and form an independent republic. The result of the vote was announced on December 20, 1860: 169–0 to secede. The correspondent of the London *Times* was shocked at the depth of feeling he witnessed at the convention, commenting that "there is nothing in all the dark caves of human passion so cruel and deadly as the hatred the South Carolinians profess for the Yankees." The surprise of the *Times'* reporter at the depth of American feeling was indicative of his country's unpreparedness for the impending conflict. Immediately after the election of Lincoln, Lord Lyons, the British minister in Washington, sent a dispatch to Lord John Russell, the foreign secretary, in which he predicted that the fallout from the election result was a storm that would soon blow over. In Russell's reply to Lyons, dated January 10, 1861, he expressed the opinion that "the best thing now would be that the right to secede should be acknowledged . . . I hope sensible men will take this view." Lyons had assured Russell that Lincoln was "no Radical," so it seemed likely to the British that the president-elect would grant the Southern states their wish in order to avoid conflict. That was certainly the view taken by the *Economist* journal in its January edition when it wondered why the North hadn't already taken the opportunity to "shake off such an incubus and to purify [itself] of such a stain."

But in January 1861 more states followed South Carolina's example, and by early February Mississippi, Florida, Alabama, Georgia, Louisiana and Texas no longer belonged to the Union. On February 8 representatives of the rebel states convened in Montgomery, Alabama, to form a Confederacy totaling 2,287,147 free citizens and 2,165,651 slaves. The next day Jefferson Davis of Mississippi, erstwhile secretary of war in the Federal government, was elected president. The mood was buoyant, the excitement palpable, and delegates laughed off talk of civil war. "A lady's thimble will hold all the blood that will be shed" was how people summed up the possibility of conflict.

Allan Pinkerton had first met Abraham Lincoln in February 1855 when the detective agency was asked to protect Illinois Central's railroad system. The Springfield legal firm of Lincoln and Herndon drew up the contract, and Pinkerton signed it in Lincoln's towering presence.

Pinkerton would have approved of Lincoln's ascetic personality as he would the lawyer's opposition to slavery. Four months earlier, in October 1854, Lincoln had given his famous speech at Peoria during the state and congressional elections when, as a member of the dying Whigs, he railed against the "monstrous injustice of slavery" and asked how it was possible that 'near eighty years ago we began by declaring that all men are created equal; but now from that beginning we have run down to the other declaration, that for some men to enslave others is a 'sacred right of self-government.' "

Lincoln never wavered from this ideology throughout the turbulent years that followed, as he left the Whigs and joined the Republicans. At times he tempered his language—he disavowed the firebrand abolitionist John Brown in 1859—but he never tempered his convictions. Pinkerton, on the other hand, under no such political constraints, was unyielding in his support of the abolitionist cause in both words and deeds.

While John Brown was an embarrassment for a Republican politician like Lincoln, he was a martyr to Pinkerton, who "detested slavery . . . this institution of human bondage." He labeled it a "curse to the American nation" and believed that John Brown was the man to rid the nation of its curse. The pair's paths first crossed sometime in the mid-1850s, and though Pinkerton took no part in such infamous incidents as the Pottawatomie Massacre (when Brown and his followers murdered five pro-slavery settlers in Kansas), he knew Brown well enough to let him into his house on March 11, 1859. Brown came with a price on his head, a $250 reward to be paid by the U.S. government, but that wasn't all he had with him that night. There were also eleven runaway slaves. Brown asked Pinkerton to help him find the money to get the slaves to Canada. Pinkerton did as asked, and the party made it into Canada.

Eight months later Brown attempted to seize the Federal arsenal at Harpers Ferry with a private army. During his planning for the raid Brown had talked of 4,500 men marching with him, first into the arsenal and then into the Southern states to put an end to slavery once and for all. In the end Brown had with him twenty-one men. Though they took possession of the lightly guarded arsenal, Brown and his men were over-run by a company of marines thirty-six hours later.

Brown was tried in a Virginia court on charges of murder, treason and conspiracy to rebel, and found guilty. On December 2, 1859, an emotion-less Brown was hanged at Charleston in front of 1,500 soldiers and 1,000 Virginians. A reporter for *Harper's Weekly* wrote that the crowd displayed neither sympathy nor satisfaction. They just stood "mute and motionless" as Brown danced on the end of the rope.

Pinkerton alleged later that he'd tried to rescue Brown, and "had it not been for the excessive watchfulness of those having him in charge, the pages of American history would have never been stained with the record of his execution." There was no evidence of such an attempt.

The execution of Brown hardened Pinkerton's determination to abol-ish slavery, and the election of Lincoln made his dream a probability. But the Scot was aware, more so than Lincoln's coterie of political advisers, of the lengths to which some secessionists might go to prevent the president-elect reaching Washington. The London *Times* had talked of the "dark caves of passion" in South Carolina, and Pinkerton understood the meta-phor. In his dozen years of fighting crime he'd seen the extent of men's "passion," their propensity to murder, rape and rob. Then in January 1861 word reached him that a coven of fanatic secessionists were plotting to seize Maryland and cut off Washington from the Union.

Following Lincoln's presidential victory rumors of dastardly deeds about to be committed by rebel Southerners had swirled across the Eastern states like snowflakes in a storm. Most were attributed to men in snug taverns carrying nothing more dangerous in their hand than a bot-tle of hard liquor. Nevertheless Samuel Felton, president of the Philadel-phia, Wilmington and Baltimore Railroad, felt concerned enough to ask Pinkerton to visit his New York office. As Pinkerton soon discovered it wasn't the president's well-being that kept Felton awake at night, more the thought of what would happen to his railcars, bridges and tracks should armed men from the Southern states march on Washington. Felton had nightmarish visions of his line from Pennsylvania to Maryland being seized by the rebels and used to transport men into the capital.

Felton had asked the government to send troops to protect his line but the request had been refused, hence the call to Pinkerton. The Scot doubted there was much his agency could do, he hadn't the resources to guard a railroad, but he traveled to Philadelphia and made some discreet inquiries. Finding no evidence of a conspiracy, Pinkerton dispatched Felton a reassuring telegram and returned to Chicago. A few days later, on January 30, Felton sent a telegram of his own urging Pinkerton to reconsider: a plot was afoot, he was sure of it. Pinkerton mulled it over and then cabled his response—he would take the case.

Why Pinkerton changed his mind is unclear. Perhaps he had got wind of a serious plot, or perhaps Felton's persistence had paid off, or maybe he simply realized that here was a wonderful opportunity to promote the Pinkerton & Co. Detective Agency.

He and a team of operatives left Chicago on February 1. There were eleven in total, including Pinkerton, and among their number were two women, Kate Warne and Hattie Lawton.

Warne had appeared at Pinkerton's office one day in 1856, recently widowed and looking for a purpose to life. The thought of employing a female detective had never crossed Pinkerton's mind, but the brown-haired Warne suggested that a woman could "worm out secrets in many places to which it was impossible for male detectives to gain access."

Lawton was a more recent addition to the agency, a beautiful woman in her mid-twenties, according to Pinkerton, who described her thus: "Her complexion was fresh and rosy as the morning, her hair fell in flowing tresses of gold, while her eyes, which were of a clear and deep blue, were quick and searching in their glances."

Pinkerton paired Lawton with Timothy Webster and dispatched them to Perrymansville, in the north of Maryland. They were to act as a married couple while Webster insinuated himself into a local militia that was rumored to be fomenting insurrection against the Federal government. The rest of the team dispersed throughout Baltimore, in bars, brothels and billiard halls, an ear to the ground and an eye on the crowd, gathering scraps of information that might give credence to Felton's concerns. Pinkerton adopted the alias of John H. Hutchinson and rented some office space opposite the premises of a man suspected of harboring rebel sympathies.

But after a week of undercover work neither Pinkerton nor his operatives had dug up any hard evidence of a plot corresponding to the one envisaged by Felton. What there was, however, was plenty of gasconade, threats from men of what they would do to Lincoln if ever he dared cross their path. It was bluster, but it gave Pinkerton an idea, one which appealed to Samuel Felton.

The year 1861 had not started well for Felton; not only was he convinced his railroad was the target for Southern insurgents, he was despondent at the itinerary of the president-elect during his twelve-day inauguration tour. Lincoln was scheduled to depart from Springfield, Illinois, on February 11 and head east to Cincinnati, then on to Columbus, Buffalo and New York. From New York he would travel south through Philadelphia, Harrisburg, Baltimore and on to Washington, where he would deliver his crucial inaugural address on March 4. Felton had hoped Lincoln would ride his railroad from New York to Washington, but instead he was to take the Northern Central Railroad from Harrisburg to Baltimore. It was an excruciating prospect for Felton, particularly as his own Philadelphia, Wilmington and Baltimore Railroad was the sworn enemy of the Northern Central.

Now the only plot in Baltimore was the one conceived by Pinkerton and Felton, who agreed that it would be most unfortunate if it was discovered that elements hostile to Abraham Lincoln were lurking along the Northern Central route. It would entail a change of plan, a rerouting of the president's journey, removing him from the "dangers" of the Northern Central Railroad to the safer Philadelphia, Wilmington and Baltimore line.

The poor wretch selected by Pinkerton to be Lincoln's putative assassin was a thirty-eight-year-old Corsican named Cipriano Ferrandini, who worked as a barber at Barnum's Hotel. Not unusually for someone in his line of work, Ferrandini liked to talk, and he made no secret of his support for secession. Pinkerton later tried to depict Ferrandini as a Latin revolutionary, impetuous and hot-blooded, still seething with rage at the fate of Felice Orsini, the Italian political activist executed in 1858 for trying to murder Napoleon III.

In reality, Ferrandini was a married man who had been living in Baltimore since the 1840s. Although he had served in the Maryland National Guard, his interests now lay more with his three young children than with armed uprisings. But that didn't matter to Pinkerton, who now had his revolutionary figurehead (and the fact he was a Catholic to boot was wonderful news for Pinkerton, who, like many Scottish Protestants of the time, had an innate dislike of all things papal). He dashed to Philadelphia to warn the unsuspecting Lincoln. Meanwhile the mayor of Washington, James G. Berret, had caught wind of the rumors and demanded to know of John Garrett, president of the Baltimore and Ohio Railroad, if there was a grain of truth to be had in them. Garrett gave a scornful laugh and told the mayor they were "the simple inventions of those who are agents in the West for other lines, and are set on foot more with a hope of interfering with the trade and travel on the shortest route to the seaboard than with any desire to promote the safety and comfort of the President elect."

Pinkerton arrived in Philadelphia on February 21. That evening in the St. Louis Hotel he revealed to Norman Judd, one of the presidential party, that Ferrandini and his cohorts intended to strike when the president-elect arrived in Baltimore two days hence, traveling westward past the waterfront in a carriage between President Street depot and Camden Street (where trains to Washington departed). Several assassins would line the three-mile route, mingling with the crowds, and any one of them would strike when he was sure of success. Judd requested that the detective come to the president's hotel (the Continental) and repeat the plot. Lincoln later recalled, "[Pinkerton] informed me that a plan had been laid for my assassination, the exact time when I expected to go through Baltimore being publicly known. He was well informed as to the plan, but did not know that the conspirators would have pluck enough to execute it. He urged me to go right through with him to Washington that night. I didn't like that. I had made engagements to visit Harrisburg, and go from there to Baltimore, and I resolved to do so."

Despite the efforts of Pinkerton and Felton, Lincoln insisted on sticking to his schedule. He left the room, leaving Pinkerton to convince Judd and the other advisers that Lincoln's life was in danger. He succeeded, and the next day, February 22, it was decided that Lincoln would visit Harrisburg, but instead of continuing on to Baltimore as scheduled, on the Northern Central line, he would make a clandestine return to Philadelphia that same evening and from there catch a night train, one that belonged to the Philadelphia, Wilmington and Baltimore railroad, to Baltimore. In that way Lincoln would be in and out of the city hours ahead of his scheduled time, thus denying Ferrandini the chance to plunge a dagger through his heart.

The change of plan was effected without incident—aided by the disabling of the Harrisburg telegraph wires to Baltimore to prevent any rebel alerting the conspirators—and Lincoln arrived in a deserted Washington at six o'clock on the morning of February 23. Two days later an editorial in the *Philadelphia Inquirer* praised "the determination of the officers of the Philadelphia, Wilmington and Baltimore Railroad that nothing should be done to endanger the safety of . . . Mr. Lincoln." Felton had the publicity he craved, and Pinkerton was sure his role in preserving the life of the president-elect would be rewarded over time. Lincoln, however, soon realized he had exercised rare poor judgment in heeding "the solicitations of a professional spy and of friends too easily alarmed." Many newspapers and a great swath of public opinion ridiculed his timid passage through Baltimore, disguised in "scotch cap and cloak," as behavior unworthy of an American president.* The *Baltimore Sun* did "not believe the Presidency can ever be more degraded by any of his successors than it has by him, even before his inauguration."

In its edition of February 27 the *New York World* treated the whole incident with skepticism. It described Pinkerton as "a gentleman of Vidocquean repute in the way of thief-taking" and mockingly alluded to the "Italian barber [who] wanders vaguely through this shadowy surmise, a leader of the Baltimore carbonari." Yet in the wake of the alleged plot Cipriano Ferrandini wasn't even arrested by the authorities, let alone charged with any assassination plot. He continued at Barnum's, charging six cents for an easy shave and spinning more yarns for his clients.

---

* In fact Lincoln wore an old overcoat and a soft felt hat given to him by a friend in New York, as much for warmth as for disguise. Ward Lamon, one of the presidential party, also offered Lincoln a pistol and knife for his protection, but Pinkerton brusquely rejected the suggestion.

CHAPTER FIVE

"Set a Price on Every Rebel Head and Hang Them"

IN THE SPRING OF 1861, to complement his cover story of being an English gentleman seeking business opportunities in Jackson, Pryce Lewis had cultivated a splendid set of "Dundrearies," luxuriant sideburns as worn by the dim-witted Lord Dundreary in *Our American Cousin*. This play had been a success on both sides of the Atlantic two years earlier, and a good many Americans were under the impression that an extravagant pair of Dundrearies were de rigueur for the more well-bred Englishman.

Unfortunately for Lewis, his whiskers were the only things developing well in Jackson. He had won the confidence of Pinkerton's prime suspect in the case, the "leading citizen," but the friendship had so far proved fruitless. Lewis reported to Chicago, "After the closest observation during many conversations carefully planned to lead up to subjects which might cause the betrayal of symptoms similar to those which marked the conduct of Eugene Aram, I failed to detect the slightest trace of remorse or mental trouble of any unusual kind." In short, either the man was a killer without a conscious, or he "was entirely innocent of the murder."

As the days lengthened and the trees blossomed Lewis and his new companion conversed about little else other than the rapidly deteriorating relations between the Confederate and Federal governments. Lincoln may have told the Southern states in his inaugural address that "we must not be enemies," but in Jackson the plea had fallen on deaf ears. Lewis noted that with every day that passed the town was "in a fever of preparation for war . . . troops were being enrolled and camps of instruction established in the vicinity of the town. Marching, drilling, drum beating and band playing were features of every day life." Lewis regularly cabled Chicago for advice, but each time he was told to carry on as best he could.

Six hundred miles to the east, in Fort Sumter at the entrance to Charleston Bay, Major Robert Anderson found himself in a similar predicament. Anderson and eighty-five men had been stranded in South Carolina since the previous December, hunkered down behind the pentagonal fort's twelve-foot-thick brick walls. Encircling Anderson's garrison were hundreds of Southern militiamen and a disconcerting number of coastal guns. On his election as president of the Confederacy, Jefferson Davis made it clear that his government prized the fort, but upon his inauguration as president of the Federal government, Lincoln was equally adamant that he wouldn't be bullied into capitulation.

Yet Lincoln had to act quickly for the men inside the fort were running out of food. For six weeks the new president agonized over his course of action; if he sent a supply convoy into Charleston Bay, it would precipitate a war for which he would get the Southern blame, but if he yielded to Davis's demand the North would pillory him as a poltroon. He received little help from his cabinet, particularly the Machiavellian secretary of state William Seward, who saw Sumter as his chance to fatally undermine Lincoln and seize the presidency for himself. Cede the fort, he advised Lincoln, as a gesture of goodwill. But Seward had underestimated Lincoln's strength of character, and the more he meddled the more the president stiffened. On April 5 he dispatched a fleet of supply ships to Fort Sumter, but with a proviso that was relayed to Jefferson Davis. The vessels would be unarmed, their only cargo was "food for hungry men." If, therefore, Confederate forces chose to open fire on defenseless ships, it would be construed by the Federal government as an act of war.

Now it was Davis perched on the horns of a dilemma: did he allow the fort to be resupplied and lose face in the South, or did he open fire and provoke war with the North? On Tuesday, April 9, he held a cabinet meeting, and the outcome was unequivocal: war. Three days later, a few hours before the fleet of supply ships was scheduled to arrive in Charleston Bay, the Southern forces unleashed a storm of fire on Fort Sumter. Major Anderson and his men endured for a day and a half before they lowered the Stars and Stripes. The rebel flag was hoisted, and the Charleston bells began to peal.

As the South reverberated to the sweet sound of bells, the noises in the North were of a far more martial tone. "Set a price on every rebel head and hang them as fast as caught," thundered the *Philadelphia Inquirer*, while the *New York Times* warned the South that what it had started the North would finish. The rebellion, it said in its editorial of April 13, "must be trampled under foot and extinguished forever [and] the president will be false to his oath, as well as to his nature, if he hesitates an instant as to the course which he must pursue."

Two days later Lincoln authorized the mobilization of seventy-five thousand troops, and men were soon marching to the strains of "Yankee Doodle," but only in those states above the Mason-Dixon Line. In the South the rebellion appeared to be infectious. Kentucky refused to comply with Lincoln's order, as did Tennessee.

In Virginia the sentiments were just as strong, or at least they were in the eastern and southern sections of the state, and in the capital, Richmond, where Sarah Jones, the English governess, recorded how a "convulsion seized the public mind, and 'To arms! To arms!' was now the sudden cry." A one-hundred-gun salute blasted out in honor of the Sumter victory, and the Stars and Bars flew from above the capitol building. Inside delegates voted on whether to secede, the more pusillanimous being swayed by the chest-thumping rhetoric of ex-governor Henry Wise—the man who had hanged John Brown—who told a hushed chamber that he had ordered armed men to seize the Federal arsenal at Harpers Ferry and they were doing so as he spoke, and that anyone present who failed to support these "patriotic volunteer revolutionists" was not fit to call himself a Virginian. On April 17 the secessionists carried the day, 88–55, much to the chagrin of Virginians to the west of the Shenandoah Valley. They resented being ruled from Richmond, a city they saw as effete and unrepresentative of the state. In western Virginia few people owned slaves, and even fewer wished to leave the Union.

Having arrogated the Federal arsenal, Virginian forces then seized the country's predominant naval base near Norfolk. To consolidate its reputation as the heart of the Confederacy, Virginia invited President Davis to move his government to Richmond, an altogether more salubrious location than Montgomery. Davis accepted, and there was more reason to celebrate in early May when the Virginian-born Robert E. Lee, the most outstanding officer in the American army, turned his back on the Union and joined the Confederacy. It had been a torturous decision for Lee, and he accepted command of the Virginian army with little glee. While callow young men marched through the state to the tune of "Dixie's Land," cheered on their way by Southern belles, Lee feared "that the country will have to pass through a terrible ordeal, a necessary expiation perhaps for our national sins."

On the day Lee foresaw an impending catastrophe, Sunday, May 5, Allan Pinkerton was in Washington waiting for an interview with Abraham Lincoln. Pinkerton had written to the president on April 21 to tell him that he had in his agency "sixteen to eighteen persons on whose courage, skill and devotion to their country" he could rely. Pinkerton was also anxious Lincoln should know that if his detective agency could "be of any service in the way of obtaining information of the movements of the Traitors or safely conveying your letters or dispatches or that class of Secret Service which is the most dangerous, I am at your service." The letter was hand-delivered to Lincoln by Pinkerton's most trusted operative, Timothy Webster, who returned to Chicago with a presidential message secreted in his walking cane. The note invited Pinkerton to Washington to discuss his proposal, and the Scot arrived on May 2. He found the capital greatly changed since his last visit, a bewildering juxtaposition between those who were loyal to the Union and those who weren't. He passed down streets "filled with soldiers, armed and eager for the fray; officers and orderlies were seen galloping from place to place . . . [but] here too lurked the secret enemy, who was conveying beyond the lines the coveted information of every movement made or contemplated." He didn't comment on the proliferation of groggeries and bawdy houses, the destination for thousands of Lincoln's volunteers, but Pinkerton would have visited neither; he disapproved of liquor, and he was devoted to his darling Joan and their four children.

The next day, Friday, May 3, Pinkerton arrived at the White House, in the early throes of a twenty-thousand-dollar refurbishment under the stern direction of Mrs. Lincoln, and was escorted inside, where after a short wait he was granted an audience with the president and his cabinet. Pinkerton was informed that the administration "had for some time entertained the idea of organizing a secret-service department of the government, with the view of ascertaining the social, political and patriotic status of the numerous suspected persons in and around the city." However, Pinkerton was told, nothing further had yet been done about the matter, and thus his suggestions were eagerly awaited. He furnished the cabinet with his ideas "as fully and concisely as I was able to do . . . and, after I had concluded, I took my departure, with the understanding that I would receive further communications from them."

But he didn't, so in a sulk he left Washington, muttering dark oaths about the government's "confusion and excitement." But Pinkerton's spirits were soon lifted by a letter he found waiting for him at the post office in Philadelphia, where he'd briefly stopped en route to Chicago. The letter had been written nearly two weeks earlier in Columbus by General George McClellan, who signed himself "Major General, commanding Ohio Volunteers."

McClellan was a West Point graduate and former railroad president whose privileged life had left his character flabby and unformed. He had no experience of adversity or hardship, only of success, which had nourished his ego but not his resolve. McClellan was thirty-four when war broke out, and though a Democrat and apathetic to slavery, he accepted a military command in the Union army. McClellan and Pinkerton had known each other for several years, having met through the Illinois Central Railroad, of which McClellan was vice president at the time. It was a curious friendship for McClellan was as extravagant as Pinkerton was austere, but the common thread that ran through both men was their gargantuan conceit.

When McClellan called, Pinkerton came running, and the pair sat down in Cincinnati, the former's headquarters, in the second week of May. In between sending Pinkerton the letter and receiving him at his headquarters, McClellan had been promoted to commander of the Department of the Ohio, which comprised the forces of Ohio, Illinois and Indiana. Now he asked Pinkerton to establish a secret service within the department. By the end of May Pinkerton had transferred the seat of his detective agency from Chicago to Cincinnati, and most of his agents were out in the field on assignment. Timothy Webster brought back important information concerning rebel troop activity in Memphis and Clarksville, and Pinkerton—operating under his nom de guerre of Major E. J. Allen—reported from behind the enemy lines in Kentucky.

In Virginia, meanwhile, the growing tension between those in the south and those to the west of the Allegheny Mountains was coming to a head. On May 23 a referendum was held on whether the state should secede; 128,884 people agreed with their political masters and voted to leave the Union. Thirty-two thousand Virginians elected to remain loyal to the Union, and most of them lived in the western part of the state. As rebel militia began to take up positions in the recalcitrant region, the loyalists appealed to Lincoln's government for help. But Washington had no troops to spare; they were all needed to guard against the expected rebel assault on the capital. Fortunately for the Virginian Unionists, help was at hand from another source, just across the Ohio River. Governor William Dennison of Ohio instructed McClellan to take an army across the river and drive back the Confederate troops.

Toward the end of June McClellan had twenty thousand men in Virginia, but there now emerged a trait that was to bedevil the young general during the coming months: hesitancy. He lacked the killer instinct of the great commanders, and instead of striking out to destroy the small ragtag army of General Robert Garnett, McClellan asked Pinkerton to find out the strength and condition of the rebel forces in Charleston. As Pinkerton pondered who to send on the dangerous mission, Pryce Lewis arrived in Cincinnati, carrying some valuable information concerning the Confederate army in Tennessee, as well as his report of the Jackson murder.

In fact the murderer of the bank cashier was the horse thief Lewis had interviewed in jail. The man subsequently confessed and was hanged. But neither this revelation, nor that of the rebel troop strength, held Pinkerton's attention in quite the way Lewis's whiskers did, and they gave him an idea.

CHAPTER SIX

"An English Nobleman Travelling for Pleasure"

P RYCE LEWIS HAD LEFT Jackson on June 9, the day after Tennessee became the eleventh and last state to officially secede from the Union and join the Confederacy. The announcement had been greeted with "great excitement among the people and troops were coming and going in all directions as if they were marching to actual battle." Lewis traveled from Jackson to Cairo, Illinois, where he found that "the Northerners were foolishly self confident" in believing the insurrection would soon be quelled, and thence on to Chicago. There he discovered that the agency had relocated to Cincinnati. Thus it wasn't until mid-June that he finally came face-to-face with Pinkerton at his headquarters in the Broadway Hotel at Broadway and Second Street.

While Lewis's reports on the Tennessee army were passed to McClellan, who, impressed with their contents, forwarded them to Simon Cameron, the secretary of war, Pinkerton briefed his operative on the situation in Virginia. They pored over maps, familiarizing themselves with the regions that lay on either side of the Allegheny Mountains, the state's crooked spine that ran from the northeast to the southwest. Pinkerton pointed out Charleston, the county seat of Kanawha County, and told Lewis that there were rumored to be one thousand rebel troops in and around the town. There were also known to be Confederate camps at strategic points along the Kanawha River, which flowed west from

Charleston into the Ohio River. Lewis's job was to get into Charleston, assess the strength and state of the forces in the town and then get out. In theory, it didn't sound too difficult, but in reality it was a mission fraught with danger. The Kanawha Valley was in turmoil, a region fissured by suspicion and hostility. Neighbor had turned against neighbor, father against son, so the appearance of a stranger would send Virginians reaching for their guns, regardless of whether they were loyalists or secessionists. In addition, rebel patrols swarmed across the valley arresting anyone whose face didn't fit, while the *Richmond Dispatch* warned its readers to be on the lookout for spies and fire starters, such as those who had recently tried to burn down the nearby iron foundry. The best way to deal with such "scoundrels," advised the paper, "consists in suspending the offender by a rope, with his feet at an inconvenient distance from the ground."

Pinkerton turned to his operative and revealed his brilliant idea: Lewis would adopt "the character of an English nobleman travelling for pleasure." Pinkerton's stern face flushed with excitement as he elaborated his plan. Lewis already had the whiskers, and in the coming days all the other accoutrements of the English aristocracy would be purloined to embroider the ruse. Once that was done, Lewis would set off for western Virginia on a sightseeing tour of the region. If he was stopped by rebel soldiers, all he had to do was feign indignation and say the world had come to a pretty pass when an Englishman couldn't even enjoy his vacation without fear of molestation. With Great Britain openly sympathetic to the Southern cause, Pinkerton was sure Lewis "would thus escape a close scrutiny or a rigid examination should he, by an accident, fall into the hands of the rebels."

Lewis thought the plan was feasible, though he had a couple of points to make. First, while he was confident he could play the part of the blue-blooded aristocrat, there could be no scrimping on the trappings; they had to be authentic. There was a strong bond between Virginia and England, and the better-bred Virginian would find it odd were a nobleman from the old country to appear attired in anything other than garments of the highest quality.

That led Lewis to his second point: who was he to be? He couldn't simply gallivant across Virginia claiming to be the Duke of Westminster, or some other celebrated aristocrat; he would surely be unmasked.

That was a problem, agreed Pinkerton. They had to come up with a very minor aristocrat, someone whose blood was of the thinnest blue. Then a name sprang to Lewis's mind: Lord Tracy.

Four miles north of Newtown lay Gregynog Hall, a centuries-old home that came with a history. As a boy Lewis had heard stories from his father of Arthur Blayney, master of Gregynog, and his peculiar habits. The bachelor preferred the company of farmers and weavers to people of his own rank. He had a particular hatred of lawyers and studied law only so he would never fall victim to what he saw as the innate duplicity of the profession. He threw lavish parties, overflowing with good wine and rich food, and he fed the leftovers to his pack of hounds. So fat did the animals become that when Blayney hunted, his huntsmen had to carry the enormous hounds across streams and ditches. He died childless in 1795, stating in his will that he was to buried in a plain and perishable coffin and bequeathing Gregynog Hall to a relative, the eighth Lord Tracy of Toddington, in the English county of Gloucestershire. Tracy had possession of the twenty-thousand-acre estate for a mere two years before he too died, so Gregynog passed to Tracy's daughter, Henrietta, who in 1798 married her cousin, Charles Hanbury. He became the proud owner of both the Toddington and the Gregynog estates, and celebrated by assuming the name Charles Hanbury-Tracy. In 1838, to mark the coronation of Queen Victoria, he was raised to the peerage with the title Baron Sudeley of Toddington.

Rather convoluted, don't you think? asked Lewis. Pinkerton agreed. It had been something of a struggle to keep up. Exactly, so perfect for what they had in mind. He would call himself the ninth Lord Tracy. It would require an exceedingly well-informed Virginian who knew that the Tracy bloodline was extinct, and even if he was challenged Lewis would say he was a scion of the Hanbury-Tracys.

Over the coming days they worked feverishly to transform Pryce Lewis from a Chicago detective into an English aristocrat. Pinkerton assigned another operative to the mission, Virginia-born Sam Bridgeman, the forty-year-old former soldier, to act as Lewis's coachman, and then he procured a carriage "and a pair of strong gray horses, which were both substantial-looking and good roadsters [and] . . . stocked the vehicle with such articles of necessity and luxury as would enable them to subsist themselves if necessary, and at the same time give the appearance of truth to such professions as the sight-seeing Englishman might feel authorized to make."

Lewis approved of what he was given. There was a silk top hat, a frock coat, a collection of white dress shirts, all tailored in London, and a dandy pair of red leather shoes. Into his coat pockets he slipped a small fortune in gold sovereigns, some forged documents all bearing the name Lord Tracy, and "a handsome segar [sic] case with the British lion in ivory conspicuously embossed on it." Someone, somehow, had managed to get his hands on "a genuine English army chest made in the reign of George III," and this was ostentatiously strapped to the back of the carriage. Inside the chest were "several boxes of segars [sic], a case of champagne and one of port." To finish the disguise, Pinkerton removed his own gold watch and diamond ring and handed them to Lewis. "Lord Tracy" was ready to depart.

In the early evening of Thursday, June 27, the carriage with the British army chest prominent at the rear arrived at the Cincinnati wharf. Several Union army officers milling about on the covered deck of the *Cricket* watched as the driver of the carriage jumped down and opened the door. Out stepped an immaculately attired young man with a marvelous set of whiskers. As he began to walk imperiously toward the steamer the gentleman suddenly turned and remonstrated with his coachman. Out of earshot of the steamer's passengers, "Lord Tracy" quietly but forcefully reminded his coachman that, no, he couldn't help unload a bale of hay from the trunk of the carriage; English aristocrats weren't in the habit of dirtying their hands.

The two-decked *Cricket* was soon heading east along the Ohio River. The vessel was a combined passenger and cargo steamer, its funnels in the stern and the paddle in the bow, in front of a small covered deck that led to the restaurant and cabins. Underneath was the cargo hold, where wagons, carriages and valises were stored. Most on board were either Union soldiers or Virginians loyal to the Lincoln government. The soldiers talked among themselves, but one or two civilians sidled up to his lordship as he stood on deck in the warm night air, one hand perched elegantly on the handrail, the other holding an expensive cigar. Why was he going to Virginia, they wanted to know, didn't he know there was a war on? Lord Tracy snorted and told them that this was no real war. He had served in the Crimea; now *that* was a war. Anyway, he continued, he was on vacation and intended to visit the White Sulphur Springs come what may. After Lord Tracy had discussed the restorative qualities of the fabled springs with his fellow passengers, he asked their advice on other attractions that might interest an intrepid Englishman such as himself. Before he had retired for the night, Tracy had promised his new friends that he would indeed take their advice and visit the Natural Bridge and the Hawk's Nest.

The next day, as the *Cricket* passed through Ironton and Huntingdon, Lord Tracy jocularly broached the subject of Virginia, teasing from his passengers tidbits of information about the rupture of the state. They all professed to be Union men, and expressed their regrets about the war, but regarded their separation from Eastern Virginia with fierce pride.

Such sentiments ceased to be voiced the farther they traveled down the Ohio River, and by the time the *Cricket* reached the village of Guyandotte late on the evening of Friday, June 28, people kept their opinions to themselves. Although there was a small Union army outpost at Guyandotte— at the confluence of the Guyandotte and Ohio rivers—it was an open secret that some of the villagers were secessionists who noted unusual activity, be it on the river or along the James River and Kanawha Turnpike, and passed it on to rebel authorities.

Lord Tracy and his coachman disembarked and drove to Guyandotte's solitary hotel. While Sam Bridgeman unloaded his master's chest, his lordship wafted into the reception area. The manager asked him to register, and the Englishman obliged, hesitating for a moment before writing "Pryce Lewis, Esq., London." Before they went to their separate rooms, Lewis told Bridgeman of his decision, explaining that from his experience on the *Cricket*, it was easier and safer to simply play the part of a well-heeled English gentleman; pretending to be an aristocrat only complicated matters. Bridgeman had no objection, so once in his room Lewis dispensed with all outward signs of Lord Tracy and "carefully destroyed the papers bearing out that character."

If Bridgeman woke the next morning in the expectation that he was now less Lewis's servant and more his companion, he was rapidly disabused of the notion. The moment he appeared for breakfast, Bridgeman was told to fetch the horses—and be quick about it. It was more of an act than usual, put on for the "number of country-looking fellows sitting about," whom Lewis sensed were rebels. The Englishman clicked his fingers and asked the landlord what he owed him. Two dollars. Lewis muttered about the bothersome foreign currency, then "threw down a couple of sovereigns and would not take any change." Bridgeman brought the carriage to the front of the hotel and, doffing his hat, held the door open as Lewis climbed inside onto the leather seat. As Bridgeman cracked the whip, Lewis stroked his whiskers, hiding the smirk that spread across his face as he observed "the looks of wonder and admiration in the faces of the bystanders."

Charleston was nearly fifty miles to the east, across the ageless green beauty of Kanawha County, and they made good progress throughout the morning. As they traveled deeper, the hills became steeper and more densely forested.

Verbal communication between the pair was impossible unless Lewis leaned out of the window, and through the dust spun up by the wheels of the carriage, shouted to Bridgeman in the driver's seat. Instead each man was left alone with his thoughts, rehearsing his role and keeping an eye open for rebel troops. The carriage reminded Lewis of a "Clarence," the four-wheeled vehicle named in honor of the Duke of Clarence, and the preferred mode of transport for the more successful of Newtown's woolen manufacturers.

Toward midday they saw a house up ahead and an old man sitting in a garden enjoying the sunshine. Lewis banged on the roof of the carriage with his cane—the signal for Bridgeman to stop—and the carriage halted outside the farmhouse. The old man came to his gate, and Bridgeman requested dinner, and provisions for the horses. Of course, he replied, and invited them inside, whereupon he fed both humans and animals royally. Lewis explained his story, that he was a vacationing Englishman who'd heard a stay in the White Sulphur Springs resort was just the ticket for a chap who felt run-down. That it was, replied the Virginian, who told his visitor that people came from all around to take the sulphuric waters and cure themselves of ulcers, sores, swelling stiffness and ailments of a more delicate nature, if the gentleman knew what he meant, which Lewis did.

Lewis gave the old man a sovereign for his trouble, then asked him the quickest way to the White Sulphur Springs. He had a long way to go, the man said, well over one hundred miles, on through Charleston, Gauley

Bridge, and then keep following the road to Lewisburg. The springs were east of Lewisburg, in a beautiful valley at the base of the Allegheny Mountains.

Once they were on their way east again along the James River and Kanawha Turnpike, Lewis put up his feet and slept off his lunch. Not long after he had woken from his nap he saw a group of horsemen emerge from a copse to his left and ride hard toward the carriage. Ahead, in the curve of the road, more uniformed men appeared with their weapons raised. The carriage slowed, and the sergeant of the troop approached Bridgeman and demanded to see a permit to travel.

Bridgeman indicated with his head that the soldier should speak to the occupant of the carriage. The man rapped on the side, and Lewis's aggrieved face appeared at the window. The sergeant, "a gentlemanly fellow," asked to see Lewis's pass. A pass, snapped Lewis, whatever did he mean? The soldier explained that anyone traveling this way needed authorization. Lewis looked disdainfully at his inquisitor and said he was unaware that in this day and age one needed a pass to travel on a public domain. The soldier apologized but insisted that that was the case. So what am I to do? asked Lewis. The sergeant offered to accompany the Englishman to his regimental headquarters from where he could obtain a pass from Colonel George Patton. It wouldn't take long, and his carriage and driver would still be here when he returned.

Lewis smoothed down his whiskers and with a heavy sigh stepped from the carriage. Wait here, he instructed Bridgeman, and set off across the field with the sergeant. As he stepped delicately across the field, taking care not to dirty his shoes of red leather, Lewis considered his predicament. His orders were to report on the readiness of Confederate forces in Charleston, while keeping a discreet distance, yet here he was walking toward a rebel encampment. Lewis was "considerably taken aback" by the turn of events, but he steeled himself "to make the best of the situation and adopt a new programme if necessary."

He was escorted through the trees, and past a mountain range of white canvas tents, to the broad veranda of a stately farmhouse. As the sergeant disappeared inside, Lewis lounged nonchalantly against the white railings, conscious that many of the rebel soldiers had stopped what they were doing and were now sitting in the late afternoon sun, discussing the arrival of the strange-looking man.

At length the sergeant reappeared and informed Lewis the colonel was ready to receive him. Lewis entered the farmhouse and came face-to-face with Colonel George Patton (the grandfather of General George Smith Patton III of World War II fame). The spy's first impression, as Patton rose from his seat and extended his arm, was that he was "a pleasant-featured, rather young officer in neat uniform."

Patton was twenty-eight years old, a Virginian, who had graduated from the state's military institute in 1852 before studying law. In 1856 he moved his young family to Charleston and established a legal firm with Thomas Buroun. As the firm had grown, so had Patton's standing in Kanawha County. He served as commissioner in chancery to the county court and, even before war erupted, had raised a local militia unit called the Kanawha Riflemen. On the outbreak of hostilities with the North, the Kanawha Riflemen had become Company I of the Twenty-second Virginia Regiment, better known locally as the First Kanawha Infantry Regiment.

As he emerged from behind his desk to welcome his visitor, Patton's sophistication was immediately evident to Lewis. Here was a Southern gentleman, he thought, in all probability an Anglophile, so instead of acting outraged Lewis addressed Patton as his equal, two men of cultivation thrown together by extraordinary events. He explained who he was, where he was from, and that having traveled extensively through the delightful Southern states he was rather hoping to see some of the natural curiosities of Virginia such as the White Sulphur Springs, Gauley Bridge and Hawk's Nest before his return. In his memoirs Lewis recalled Patton's gracious response: "My good sir!" he exclaimed, "we have no intention to stop Englishmen travelling in our country." Turning to his adjutant, Patton ordered a pass to be made out to Mr. Pryce Lewis, then he put a gentle hand on Lewis's back and guided him out onto the veranda. "Once in Charleston," added Patton, "go and see General Wise and he will give you a pass to go further on." The name sent a chill through Lewis's body, and he "felt the hair on his head standing straight." He knew all about Henry Wise's reputation, not just for his role in Virginia's secession but more particularly for the relish with which he'd hanged John Brown. Wise was not a merciful man.

While they waited for the pass, the pair sat on the veranda and engaged in some lively conversation. Patton asked innocent questions about his tour, and Lewis replied with a mix of truths, half truths and lies. He talked of Tennessee and fabricated stories of other places he knew from his days as a traveling book salesman. Then Patton turned toward the camp and pointed out his soldiers' uniform: aren't they smart? he commented with a proud smile and explained that he himself had designed the uniforms, the dark green trousers with a black stripe down the leg—a gold stripe for officers—the frock coat of a similar color, the cuffs and collar trimmed with black lace, and the slouch hat adorned with ostrich feathers and on the front the letters *KR*. Lewis agreed that the uniforms were splendid, a match for any regiment in the British army. The more Patton talked, the more Lewis found him "bright and affable." As the adjutant appeared with the pass, Lewis took his cigar case from his pocket and offered the colonel a little something in return. Then he "proposed that we should take a glass of wine."

Patton threw back his head and laughed, informing Lewis that wine was a scarce commodity thanks to the war. Lewis flashed a conspiratorial smile at Patton and said, "If you will allow your orderly to go to the road and order my carriage up, we will have some that is good."

Patton dispatched one of his men to fetch the carriage, and a few minutes later it rumbled along the track that led to the farmhouse. The setting sun reflecting off the silver-mounted harness added to the luster of the moment. Lewis "saw the colonel was surprised for he first looked at the carriage and then at me." Lewis ordered Bridgeman to fetch a bottle of champagne from the chest.

"A what, sir?" said Bridgeman, who thought at first that they were under arrest.

"Damn it, man!" cried Lewis, "bring me a bottle of champagne." He turned to the colonel and apologized for his servant's "stupidity." Good servants were hard to find in these troubled times. Patton raised an understanding hand, and soon the pair were enjoying the "good fellowship developed by sips of champagne."

As they sat on the veranda watching the sun dip to the west, it was hard to believe there was a war on. Warmed by a second glass of champagne, Patton explained that the camp was called Tompkins, after Colonel Christopher Tompkins, commanding officer of the Twenty-second Virginia Regiment. As to its exact location, it was ten miles outside Charleston, just east of the Kanawha River, which lay on the other side of the James River and Kanawha Turnpike. The Coal River, one of the Kanawha River's tributaries, was close by, and Patton's principal responsibility was to defend the forty miles of turnpike that ran between Guyandotte and Charleston.

Lewis listened, taking his eyes off Patton only when he signaled Bridgeman to refill their glasses. The garrulous colonel drained the last drops from the bottle as Lewis looked on, encouraging his companion to slake his thirst. After all, he had plenty more where that one came from. Patton thanked him and Lewis smiled, satisfied that he "had evidently won his entire confidence."

Next the colonel asked if he had encountered any Federal soldiers on his travels. Lewis said he had, unfortunately, and they had left nothing but a "rather unfavorable impression." Patton wasn't surprised. "I have fortifications here," he said, with a sweep of his arm, "that with 900 Confederate soldiers I can defend against 10,000 Yankees for ten years." Lewis said he didn't doubt it, that he hadn't seen such impressive fortifications since he'd served on Lord Raglan's [the British commander] staff in the Crimean War.

What! cried Patton. Not only was Lewis a gentleman, he was also a fellow soldier. Patton demanded that Lewis stay the night as a guest of the Kanawha Riflemen. The Englishman was humbled at such an invitation, but really he must be on his way. They faced each other on veranda, dueling with their wills, Sam Bridgeman and the adjutant hovering in the background like dutiful seconds. Finally, Patton suggested a compromise: if Lewis would not stay the night, he must at least have supper. Lewis agreed, but when supper arrived it was a disappointment, just "pork and crackers served on tin plates." Patton sensed his guest had expected more and apologized for the paucity of food but imagined he had eaten worse in the Crimea.

Lewis dabbed daintily at his mouth with his handkerchief and reassured Patton that during the Crimean he and Lord Raglan had often been glad to eat the thinnest strips of salted pork. Then he went on to regale Patton about the time in 1854 when "the transports [ships] went down in the Black Sea one night, fourteen of them, leaving us entirely out of provisions." How dreadful, commiserated Patton, who was eager to hear more of Lewis's war. He himself was untested as a fighting soldier, yet here was a battle-hardened veteran of the Crimea. In normal circumstances Patton would have been too discreet to pose the question, but now, emboldened by the champagne, he asked Lewis what it was like to fight a war.

It was a question that needed an accompaniment, so Lewis "called upon Sam for a bottle of port and damned him for the bungling way in which he opened the bottle." Then he drew two cigars from his case and in the still night air waxed lyrical about the glory of war.

He surprised even himself with what he remembered of Henry Tyrrell's *History of the War with Russia: Giving full details of the operations of the Allied Armies*. Dates and names rolled off Lewis's tongue as Patton sat engrossed, hardly able to credit that here was a man who had witnessed the Charge of the Light Brigade. Lewis steered the conversation away from Crimea to America, and for a while it was Patton's turn to hold forth, as he compared and contrasted the merits of General Winfield Scott of the Union army and General William Hardee of the Confederate army. The evening ended in merry uproar with the veranda transformed into a temporary parade ground and Patton teaching Bridgeman, a veteran of the Mexican War of 1846–48, how to drill like a Kanawha Rifleman. Eventually Lewis, wiping the tears from his eyes, insisted he really must be on his way. Patton urged him to stay the night—it was too late to leave for Charleston—but Lewis had drunk too much and "was afraid something might happen to show that I had not entirely learned my part."

He thanked his host for his first-class hospitality but made it clear he wouldn't be dissuaded a second time. Patton gave him directions to a country inn between the camp and Charleston, and then the pair bid each other a fond farewell. It had been a memorable evening, they both agreed. Perhaps one day they would meet again.

CHAPTER SEVEN

"Don't You Know There Is a War in This Country, Sir?"

CHARLESTON IS QUITE A PRETTY PLACE," commented one newspaper in the summer of 1861. "It is located on the beautiful bottom on the northeast bank of the river and is entirely surrounded by lofty hills. There are many pretty residences but they and the public buildings are built after the old style and have not much pretension to magnificence."

On the morning of Sunday, June 30, Charleston, Virginia, was quieter than normal. Most of the town's 1,500 inhabitants were in church, and regardless of whether they were Presbyterians, Methodists or Episcopalians, they prayed for the Lord to take care of their Southern soldiers.

Just east of McFarland Street, on which stood St. John's Episcopal Church, was the white-timbered "Elm Grove," home to Colonel George Patton and his family. Mrs. Patton and the children were worshipping, as were the storekeepers who on any other day would have been open for business in Charleston's commercial center.

Visitors approaching Charleston from the west along the James River and Kanawha Turnpike arrived on the southern side of the Kanawha River and crossed the water by means of an old bridge. Once on Lovell Street (present-day Washington Street) they continued east toward the heart of the town, traversing the Elk River, which flowed from the north to join the Kanawha River at Charleston, on an iron suspension bridge. Before them now were Charleston's biggest stores, finest hotels and the impressive Kanawha Courthouse.

A month earlier, on May 30, Colonel Christopher Tompkins had issued a rallying cry from the steps of the courthouse: "Men of Virginia! Men of Kanawha! To Arms! The enemy has invaded your soil and overrun your country under the pretext of protection. You cannot serve two masters. You have not the right to repudiate allegiance to your own State. Be not seduced by his sophistry or intimidated by his threats. Rise and strike for your firesides and altars. Repel the aggressors and preserve your honor and your rights."

Tompkins, forty-eight, a West Point graduate and veteran of the Mexican War, had struggled to recruit volunteers since his appointment as colonel of the Army of Kanawha on May 3. His predecessor, Lieutenant Colonel John McCausland, had raised five companies totaling 350 men in the three weeks since the bombardment of Fort Sumter, but Tompkins had found these men poorly equipped and badly trained. Unfortunately Tompkins labored to improve either the recruitment or the training; it had been fourteen years since he'd last shouldered arms, and in the interim he'd become a successful coal mine operator. Business, not soldiering, was now his occupation.

Tompkins's call to arms had been his last significant act as commander of the Kanawha forces. A few days later, in early June, General Wise was appointed to the position by Robert Lee, and Tompkins was demoted to commanding officer of the Twenty-second Virginia Regiment.

Wise had already gathered his own militiamen, known as "Wise's Legion," and he marched them northwest from Richmond into Kanawha County, arriving on June 26. Aided by appeals in the pages of the *Kanawha Valley Star* newspaper, the county's volunteers numbered nearly four thousand (including the "legion") by the time Wise commandeered the best room of the Kanawha House Hotel.

With the nine hundred men of Colonel Patton's command established at Camp Tompkins, Wise dispatched smaller forces of men in three westerly directions to guard against Union incursions across the Ohio River at Point Pleasant, Ripley and Barboursville. While a further one thousand troops were deployed at various points from Gauley Bridge (thirty-five

miles southeast of Charleston, the small town assumed strategic importance because of its location at the head of the Kanawha Valley) to as far
north as Suttonsville. The bulk of Wise's force, however, approximately
sixteen hundred men, remained close at hand, encamped at Kanawha Two
Mile, just north of Charleston. Wise had originally intended to install himself in the home of the Littlepage family, whose stone mansion lay on the
bank of Kanawha Two Mile Creek surrounded by one thousand acres of
their farmland, but that was before he encountered the lady of the house.

Mrs. Littlepage refused to give her house to General Wise. She didn't
care who he was, she told him, the Confederate army had taken her husband for its army, but it wouldn't take her house. Wise warned her that
the house would be "blown down over your head" if she didn't comply.
Mrs. Littlepage gathered her six young children around her and dared
Wise to do it. The general ordered his men to fire on the house, but they
refused. Many of them were friends of the family. Humiliated and infuriated, Wise cursed Mrs. Littlepage and let her be, though he instructed his
soldiers to set up camp on the family's one thousand acres. On the hill
overlooking the stone mansion, Wise's men constructed a one-hundred-
square-foot fort in which were mounted several small artillery pieces.
Fort Fife, named after a Confederate officer, commanded excellent views
of the James River and Kanawha Turnpike and its junction with the road
to Parkersburg, the town seventy miles northwest from where it was
suspected General McClellan's soldiers would come. In spite of Mrs.
Littlepage's impertinence, Wise was a satisfied man as he surveyed the
Kanawha countryside. Never mind the Yankees, he bragged, with the defenses he had built he could "whip the world."

Pryce Lewis was a little slow in rising on the morning of Sunday, June
30, though he presumed Colonel Patton's head was even sorer. After a
recuperative breakfast he ordered Bridgeman to fetch the horses, and
they were soon on their way east toward Charleston. Looking out of the
carriage window, Lewis rejoiced in the fact the "sky was clear, the air inspiriting and the scenery along our way delightful—meadows, upland
and faraway peaks of the Alleghenies." He reflected on the resounding
success of the previous day, and with the colonel's pass tucked inside his
frock coat he "anticipated little difficulty in making my way out of the

rebel lines." But a worry, small but persistent, like a Kanawha mosquito, wouldn't let Lewis alone. It burrowed its way into his mind, irritating his contentment. Its name was Henry Wise. Lewis had no wish to meet Wise, a man "whose reputation as a fierce Southern fire-eater and as the actual executioner [sic]* of old John Brown was well known the country over." But if he wanted a pass out of Virginia, Lewis would have to go begging to Wise.

They reached Charleston around midday, not long after the churches had scattered their flocks. Bridgeman asked for the best hotel in town and was directed to the four-story Kanawha House on the corner of Summers and Kanawha streets. As the carriage moved along Summers Street Lewis sat back and made subtle observations of soldiers he passed, all of whom were "rough-looking men, mountaineers in woolen shirts and overalls with little or no indication of uniforms, but all heavily armed, some with two revolvers at the belt, others with revolver and bowie knife."

As the carriage pulled up outside the Kanawha House Hotel two well-dressed officers emerged from the front door. Both wore slouch hats, and one, the older of the two, cradled a shotgun in the crook of his arm. The pair stood and watched with cool curiosity as Bridgeman helped his master out of the carriage. Lewis raised a finger to his silk top hat as he swanned past the soldiers and into the hotel. At the reception desk he asked for a room but was informed by the landlord, Mr. Wright, that the hotel was full on account of General Wise and his staff. The landlord gestured toward the general standing at the entrance, beside the man carrying the shotgun.

Then the landlord looked beyond General Wise to Lewis's gleaming carriage. Instantly his demeanor changed and he remembered that there was a room available, though he would have to expel one of the general's officers. Wright the landlord, a moon-faced man, said it with soft relish, and Lewis sensed they were on the same side. He wrote "Pryce Lewis and servant, London, England" in the register, and then, as if to emphasize his status, he turned and barked at Bridgeman to get a move on with his valise.

A Confederate officer was busy packing his trunk when Lewis

---

* Wise ordered Brown's execution, but was not his actual executioner.

entered the room in the company of the landlord. Lewis was most apologetic, but the officer didn't seem too bothered. Bridgeman deposited his master's valise and was shown to the servants' quarters on the top floor of the hotel. Lewis freshened up, brushed his whiskers and then went for a Sunday afternoon stroll through Charleston. Groups of soldiers were clustered on street corners chattering with excitement about the recent rebel victory at Big Bethel on the Virginia Peninsula. The news was patchy, no one seemed sure of the exact details, but Johnny Reb had won a famous victory* and now the soldiers joked about the "slaughtered Yankees" and wondered when it would be their turn to join the fun.

The more Lewis saw of Charleston, the more he realized the danger he was in. He was to all intents and purposes a prisoner, unable to go anywhere until he had a pass from General Wise. Lewis returned to the hotel, his head swarming with doubts and anxieties. He paced his room, telling himself that self-possession and nerve could carry him through, but he knew what happened to wartime spies. In Henry Tyrrell's book of the Crimean War Lewis had read about the fate of the Russian spy captured by the Allied forces: interrogated, beaten, executed.

By the time he heard the gong for supper Lewis had composed himself and was attired in his finest clothes with a mask of insouciance to match. He sauntered into the dining room and stopped. Arrayed in front of him must have been every officer on General Wise's staff. There wasn't a civilian to be seen, and worst of all, the only available chair in the room was opposite the man Lewis now knew to be General Wise.

Lewis was shown to his chair, but neither Wise nor the other officers acknowledged his presence. Throughout the meal Lewis stole glances at the general, short, careful glances, lest he incur the wrath of a man who during his younger days had dueled with his adversaries.

Lewis found Wise "thin and below the average size, not so old as I supposed, fifty-five perhaps, face smooth-shaven, mouth very stern, jaws somewhat cadaverous. His straggling iron gray hair was pushed behind his ears, his eyes were dark and restless."

---

* The village of Big Bethel was the scene of the first major land battle in Virginia on June 10, 1861. Though the Confederates won a resounding victory, casualties were light on both sides with eighteen Union soldiers killed and only one rebel fatality.

The dinner table conversation was similar to that of the enlisted men, the sketchy details of the action at Big Bethel and the number of Union casualties. Estimates were more temperate, and few of the officers reveled in the victory.

After dinner the officers retired to the parlor for a smoke, and Lewis followed in the hope of finding a convenient moment to ask the general for a pass. He was kept waiting for what seemed like an age as one officer after another occupied Wise's attention. Then he was alone, and Lewis, like a timorous boy steeling himself to ask a girl for a dance, took a deep breath and moved across the parlor floor.

"I would like to speak to your Excellency in private for a minute or two," said Lewis. Wise sized up the Englishman for a second or two, running his dark eyes from the Dundreary whiskers to the red leather shoes. All right, Wise said at length, and instructed Lewis to follow him to his office. The reply took Lewis by surprise, but he accompanied Wise to the office that had been installed inside his bedroom. Lewis was disconcerted to discover it was opposite his own room.

Wise sat down behind his desk and in a brusque tone asked what Lewis wanted. Lewis held Colonel Patton's pass in the sweaty palm of his hand as he explained who he was, where he was from and what he was doing in Virginia. Then he mentioned George Patton's name and repeated what the colonel had told him about obtaining a further pass from the general. Lewis went to show the pass, but Wise waved it away. Instead he sat back in his chair and eyed Lewis "in a suspicious manner" before refusing the request. Lewis asked why, and Wise, not used to being queried, snapped, "Don't you know there is a War in this country sir?"

Lewis tried to soften the general by excusing his oversight on the fact that when he'd left England there had been no war. But Wise didn't care. He began attending to some papers on his desk, a clear indication that the meeting was now over. Lewis stood staring at the lank iron gray hair for a few moments and then asked the general if he'd mind if he applied to the British consul at Richmond for a travel permit. Wise replied that he had no objection, appending an unequivocal "Good night, sir" to his answer.

Bridgeman was waiting for his master in the lobby of the hotel, desperate to know the upshot of the meeting. Lewis instructed him to ask the landlord for some writing materials and bring them to his room.

Bridgeman appeared a few minutes later, and Lewis, his heart still rac-
ing, explained what had been said. The coachman was appalled. There
was only one thing to do, advised Bridgeman, "Let's leave everything
behind us, let carriage and horses go to hell and take to the woods. We
can find our way to the Ohio River."

Lewis said it was an absurd idea, that the rebels would hunt them down
and exact a terrible revenge. But if we stay in Charleston, said Bridgeman, "then they will hang us both." He reminded Lewis he had a wife and
children back in Chicago; spying for the Union cause was one thing, dying
for it was another matter.

Lewis sympathized with Bridgeman's predicament but insisted they
stay put. As for the letter, if Bridgeman wouldn't mail it to the British
consul, Lewis would do it himself.

Bridgeman fell into a sullen silence as Lewis wrote his letter in which he
explained that he "was traveling as an inoffensive tourist, etc., and had
been arbitrarily stopped by General Wise, who appeared to enjoy a display
of petty authority by treating me very discourteously." He asked Consul
George Moore to make out a pass forthwith so that one of Her Majesty's
subjects could continue on his journey without further impediment.

Lewis sealed the letter inside the envelope. The rebels are sure to
open it, said Bridgeman sulkily. Lewis knew that, but what would it matter? There was nothing incriminating in its contents, everything was as
he had explained to Colonel Patton and General Wise. Lewis held out
the letter, but Bridgeman made no move. Take it, urged Lewis, assuring
Bridgeman that "if the consul should be suspicious and write for further
evidence of my identity . . . then there would be time enough to take to
the woods." Bridgeman accepted the letter but wanted to know what
they would do while they waited for a response from the British consul.
Collect information that might aid their escape, replied Lewis, as well as
any details that might be of value to General McClellan.

Bridgeman might not have taken the letter if he had known the true
state of affairs of the British consulate in Richmond at that time. Chaos
reigned, as the English governess Sarah Jones discovered when she arrived at the beginning of July seeking a pass out of Virginia. Jones had
entered the state nine months earlier, just days before Abraham Lincoln
was voted into office, and though the first few months had passed agreeably enough she was now desperate to leave the bellicose city.

Unfortunately for Jones, and the dozens of other British citizens stranded in Richmond, Consul George Moore had left for England two months earlier on account of his twenty-three-year-old daughter's "incipient insanity." The physician told Moore that the only cure for such a case was "a more bracing climate," hence his request to the British Foreign Office for an immediate transfer home. While the condition of his daughter was regrettable, the prescribed treatment was agreeably convenient for George Moore. He was a fey individual, fragile in both mind and body. For the first twenty-two years of his diplomatic career, Moore had been posted in Italy, a country whose rich culture he adored. Virginia had come as a rude shock when he arrived in 1858 to take up the post of state consul. The climate and the people were too much for his weak character, as they evidently were for his daughter, so there were smiles all around when the physician pronounced his novel remedy for "incipient insanity."

The man appointed to replace Moore couldn't have been more different. Frederick Cridland—he preferred Fred—was thirty-six years old and altogether more robust than his predecessor. Cridland liked America from the moment he arrived in 1845 to start work as a clerk in the consulate at Norfolk, Virginia. The food, the landscape, the weather, the women, everything appealed to him.

Cridland was already well acquainted with Richmond, having acted as an unpaid vice-consul in the city during the 1850s, but that now seemed a lifetime ago. He had spent 1860 working as the secretary to the consul general in Venice, Italy, while gleaning what information he could from the European newspapers about the calamitous events in America. But nothing could have prepared Cridland for the shambolic state of affairs he found in Richmond in May 1861.

When Sarah Jones arrived at the consulate in the first week of July "Mr. Cridland begged me to be seated and requested my patience while he dispatched the business of those already waiting . . . there were British subjects, and subjects of all nations in all sorts of emergencies, all seeking the aid of the consul." Frightened men and women shouted over one another in their desperation to attract Cridland's attention. "I have waited so long for an opportunity of getting across [into the North], that I have resolved to foot it," yelled one British subject. "I shall try and fight my way through," said another, "but what can I do with my luggage?" "I was arrested as a spy as I came through Washington," cried a third. "My trunks were seized and searched for contraband articles, and were retained after I was released. How can I obtain them?" "When shall we receive our English letters?" "When can we send our English despatches?" "How am I to be redressed for the loss of my property?" Cridland was pounded by questions from every side.

When it was Jones's turn she was informed by a ruffled but still courteous Cridland that unless her journey was necessary, he would strongly advise her not to attempt it as it was too perilous. Jones persisted, and Cridland promised to see what he could do. Day after day she returned to the consulate, on each occasion battling her way past a motley crowd of people all shouting at Cridland "expecting him to do some impossible thing."

His resourcefulness was being tested in other ways, too, as he explained to Jones during one of her many visits to his office. "Look at the paper I am obliged to use!" he exclaimed, dangling a miserable-looking sheet between thumb and finger. "Even a tailor would not send a message to his cobbler on such a piece at home. And as for envelopes and seals, why, I cannot even find a piece of colored paper in the city for my official stamp."

Jones got her pass eventually and took possession of it with a promise to Cridland that she'd never forget his kindness. For Pryce Lewis, however, trapped 230 miles northwest of Richmond, the name Cridland meant nothing; he was pinning his hopes on George Moore and the letter Sam Bridgeman had mailed on the evening of Sunday, June 30.

CHAPTER EIGHT

"Grossly Insulting to Some of the Officers"

EVEN AS HIS SOLDIERS dug themselves in on Kanawha Two Mile General Wise reported to his superiors that "the grass of the soil we are defending is full of the copperhead traitors; they invite the enemy, feed him and he arms and drills them." Worse, Wise was convinced that "a spy is on every hill top, at every cabin, and from Charleston to Point Pleasant they swarm."

A consequence of Wise's belief was that dozens of Virginians were arrested and imprisoned on suspicion of being in some way involved in the Federal cause. On Monday, July 1, as Lewis went for his morning constitutional through the streets of Charleston, he learned that the town's small jail was full of Union men. Suddenly he saw the general approaching on horseback, flanked on either side by a coterie of Confederate officers. Lewis stepped to one side as Wise rode by without a second glance at the troublesome Englishman.

For the next couple of days Lewis spent little time out and about; it was left to Bridgeman to frequent the town's saloons and stand a soldier a drink or two as he mocked the Yankees. Lewis divided his time between his room, where he read or looked discreetly out of the window, and the landlord's office. Mr. Wright rarely talked of war, much less the military might of the South, preferring to hear tales of England and the empire.

The longer Lewis remained at liberty in Charleston, the more his confidence grew. And if he became too reclusive, might not that arouse curiosity? He decided to visit the barroom of the Wilson House Hotel and enjoy a game of billiards. A game was in progress when he walked in, so Lewis ordered a whiskey and stood at the bar. Two Confederate officers entered, and Lewis, in the process of paying for his drink, invited the pair to join him. They accepted and asked for whiskeys, then one of the men said he'd also take a cigar. No, please, said Lewis, allow me, and he took out his cigar case with the ivory British lion.

The rebel officer saw the lion and smiled, saying England was the right protector to have because "she always protects her subjects."

The three fell into conversation, and Lewis soon made it plain "how natural it was for Englishmen of good birth to sympathize with the South and how likely it was that England's guns would soon be heard if the North didn't keep her hands off the South." That was what the officers wanted to hear! More whiskey, they demanded from the bartender.

They talked and laughed, united in whiskey kinship, and when the moment was right Lewis mentioned that he had seen service in the Crimea. My God! interjected one of the men, who had introduced himself a major and the son-in-law of Mr. Wright, the landlord of Lewis's hotel, in that case "we should like you to come down to camp with us, and show you our troops. Of course, you have seen finer in the British army, but I think you will be surprised at the precision of our drill."

Lewis was grateful for the offer but explained he couldn't accept. Why ever not? they asked. Lewis looked about him and then, lowering his voice, explained about his encounter with the ornery General Wise. He rather feared the general suspected he was a Union spy, and if he turned up at their camp the general might have him arrested. The officers looked at each other, then at Lewis, and burst out laughing. Lewis was confused. What was so funny?

The soldiers grinned as they told Lewis that they were already aware of his background. Apparently Wise had summoned Colonel Patton to Charleston for "a consultation" about the mysterious visitor. Patton's glowing endorsement of Lewis had reassured Wise that he was indeed just a harmless Englishman with a strange choice in vacation destinations. But anyway, one of the men added, take no notice of Wise, "he's a fussy old fellow," and what's more he'd left Charleston for a few days to oversee the construction of defensive fortifications at Ripley, forty miles northwest. Cheered by the news, Lewis ordered another round of drinks, and they parted with a promise that the following afternoon he would visit the camp.

The officers arrived at the hotel at four o'clock the next day, and Lewis was waiting with a bottle of champagne and three cigars. The soldiers were young and inexperienced, "more impressed by the exalted position I had held in the British army than by anything else." He fed them further stories of the Crimea as they attacked the champagne, and later they "started off to camp in a merry mood, as if going to a picnic."

The camp was about two miles away, and in the carriage they discussed such topics as drills and dress parades. As well as the anecdotes gleaned from the history books, Lewis had a collection of polished military terms, an amusing nickname here, a peculiar expression there, that every now and again he dropped into the conversation. He was "always careful to avoid details [but] danger, I discovered, made my faculties wonderfully accurate."

Once they arrived at the camp Lewis was treated to a drill and then a dress parade. Most of the enlisted men wore their own clothes, the overalls of farmers and laborers, but despite the lack of uniform, there was a sharpness to their bearing that impressed the Englishman. Later he had drinks with a group of officers, and a vigorous debate ensued about how an army should feed its men. Lewis left the camp with a detailed knowledge of the rebels' rationing system. Back in the hotel he and Bridgeman "compared notes and planned modes of escapes."

Lewis had learned that the mail service between Charleston and Richmond "was so irregular that it might take from ten to fourteen days before an answer to my letter could reach me." Bridgeman had more encouraging news: he had discovered a possible way out. About ten miles east of Charleston on the road to Richmond was the village of Browntown (present-day Marmet). It lay on the south side of the Kanawha River at the mouth of Lens Creek, and Bridgeman had been told that there was a track that led up the creek from Browntown to Boone County, on to Logan County and then across the state line into the safety of Kentucky's Pike County. The trail was rough and steep, but there were few rebels in the vicinity. They decided to remain in Charleston for another week or so; then if they had heard nothing from Consul Moore in Richmond, they'd try and escape.

There was an alternative to fleeing Charleston by road, however, which came to Lewis as he strolled by the green and glassy water of the Kanawha River. The opportunity to examine the feasibility of escaping by boat arose through another of Lewis's newfound friends. He had made the acquaintance of a veterinary surgeon in the parlor of the Kanawha House Hotel, and the man suggested they hire a boat and have an outing on the river. Apparently there was much wildlife to be seen.

The Kanawha River, or Great Kanawha River (the Little Kanawha River is farther north), originates thirty-five miles southeast of Charleston, at Gauley Bridge. A confluence of the Gauley River and the New River, which rises in the mountains of North Carolina, the Kanawha meanders ninety-seven miles from Gauley Bridge until it meets the Ohio River at Point Pleasant. A steamboat first tried to navigate the river in 1819 but came to grief at the Red House Shoals, approximately thirty miles west of Charleston. That prompted the Virginia legislature to approve a bill for "cutting chutes through the river's shoals, building wing dams and removing snags," and so began the era of the Kanawha steamboat service, as tourists and traders proceeded serenely down the river agog at the beauty of the scenery.

When war broke out the rebels acted swiftly to guard against a Union attack. Allan Pinkerton had reported to General McClellan in early summer that "the rebels have sunk two boats laden with stone . . . near the Red House shoals, twenty or thirty miles from Charleston, and they are now erecting a battery of two six pounders concealed by bushes." Colonel Patton established Camp Tompkins farther east along the river, and smaller outposts were scattered the length of the Kanawha.

Lewis had been briefed by Pinkerton about the defenses at the Red House Shoals, but he hoped it might be possible to steal a small, flat-bottomed boat and row the fifty or so miles west to Point Pleasant. He and his veterinary friend set off on a beautiful summer's day, the latter at the oars. They were soon challenged by a sentry on the bank. The soldier recognized the vet and with a cheery wave let him pass, but a little farther on they encountered a second guard, who ordered them to turn around.

Lewis discarded the idea of a waterborne escape as he returned to the hotel. It would be impossible, even at night, to avoid detection. At the reception desk Lewis asked a bellboy to summon Sam Bridgeman, but he was informed the servant had gone out for a drink. There was still no sign of him after supper, nor while Lewis sat in the parlor with a port and a newspaper. Finally he retired to bed, not unduly concerned at his companion's absence.

The next morning Lewis was intercepted on his way to breakfast by a flustered landlord, who ushered the Englishman into his office and described in graphic detail the return the previous evening of Sam Bridgeman. He'd crashed through the front door reeling drunk and was then "grossly insulting to some of the officers here [and] talking recklessly about the war."

Lewis blanched. Even if the information confirmed his suspicion that Mr. Wright was a Union man, it also bore out his concern that Bridgeman's nerves were fraying. He thanked the landlord for the warning, assured him that it wouldn't happen again, and set off to give Bridgeman a piece of his mind. He found him in his room, still half drunk and utterly disheveled. Lewis damned him as a fool and reminded him their lives were at stake. They were staying in the same hotel as General Wise, who had just returned from Ripley, and if Bridgeman didn't get himself in order he would surely be hanged. Bridgeman mumbled an apology and promised it wouldn't happen again, but three days later it did.

This time a furious Lewis forbade Bridgeman from entering any saloon and billiard room, and to reinforce his order he discontinued his accomplice's daily allowance. A contrite Bridgeman blamed it on their situation, pleading with Lewis to take to the woods. No, replied Lewis, they must remain for another few days. Privately, however, Lewis was becoming ever more disturbed. It was now Wednesday, July 10, and they had been in Charleston for a week and a half. In that time they had collected important information on the rebel forces, but there was still no word from the British consulate in Richmond and Lewis began to wonder if perhaps Consul Moore was making inquiries about the mysterious English visitor. Lewis "passed a miserable day reviewing every plan of escape . . . [and] went to bed at night fully determined to take some action the next day—no matter how desperate. Further anxiety was insupportable."

Lewis lay awake until long after midnight, his head too full of thoughts for sleep. Outside his window Charleston dozed without a sound. But then a noise, a far-off sound, too faint, at first, to be distinguishable. Lewis listened, then sat up with a start. It was a horse, and its rider was in a hurry. The clatter of hooves came nearer and nearer, right up to the hotel entrance. Lewis heard the horseman descend, heard him bound up the front steps, heard him banging on the hotel door and then he "heard some one ascending the stairs with clanking saber and coming toward my room. Then a rap."

The only sound now was Lewis's heart, pounding, it seemed, with more force than any galloping horse. Suddenly he realized the rap wasn't at his door but the one opposite: General Wise's. He slid out of bed and listened at the keyhole. He heard Wise open the door to the horseman but couldn't catch the words being spoken. All he made out was the final sentence, "Call Colonel Tompkins." Lewis remained where he was for several minutes, a spectral vision in a white nightdress crouched by the door. He heard Wise emerge from his room and stride purposefully along the corridor and down the stairs. Now all the activity was beneath Lewis's window as horsemen came and went.

Eventually Lewis tiptoed back to bed and fell into a broken sleep. He rose at five o'clock and stole downstairs, the soft groaning of the floorboards underfoot emphasizing the "unusual quiet [that] seemed to pervade the place." Mr. Wright emerged from his office and asked Lewis if he'd heard the news. No, he hadn't. Wright explained that Union forces were advancing south from Parkersburg and "Wise has gone to meet them." Lewis pressed the landlord for more details, but Wright knew only that Wise had taken the bulk of his force, leaving a couple of hundred men to guard Charleston under the command of Colonel Tompkins.

Lewis sat down stupefied, trying to work out what this meant for him and Bridgeman.

Wright went to fetch a coffee for the Englishman, but before he left his office he turned to Lewis and with a smile as wide as the Ohio River declared, "The Yankees will give him hell!"

General McClellan had arrived at Parkersburg on June 21 and, as was his way, dithered. Two days after his appearance on the Ohio River, while Wise was still bringing his men to Charleston, McClellan promised

Washington an attack would soon be launched. But for the next few days the general, who encouraged comparisons between himself and Napoleon Bonaparte, sat on his hands. He continued to augment his army, so that by the end of June, as Wise's men threw up their earthworks at Kanawha Two Mile, nearly twenty thousand Union soldiers assembled in the north of Virginia: six companies were at Parkersburg, eleven companies on the railroad at the Cheat River bridge; there were regiments at Clarksburg, Weston and Grafton, and a force of fifty-one companies and one battery under Brigadier General Thomas Morris was at Philippi. In the meantime McClellan intended that a combined force of some three thousand men—composed of soldiers from Kentucky and Ohio—under the command of General Jacob Cox should advance up the Kanawha River as far as possible and hem in Wise at Charleston.

On Friday, July 5, McClellan was asked by Washington when he was going to attack. Soon, he said, pledging to "repeat the movement of Cerro Gordo" (a comprehensive victory for American troops in 1847 during the war with Mexico). The following day a brigade under Alexander McCook overran a Confederate picket between Buckhannon and Rich Mountain, nearly one hundred miles northeast of Charleston, and on Tuesday, July 9, and Wednesday, the tenth, soldiers from McClellan's army probed the enemy's strength on the lower slopes of Rich Mountain and brought back favorable reports.

Finally, late on the day of July 10, McClellan had the confidence to order the invasion to begin. As General William Rosecrans marched his men toward Rich Mountain to the north of Charleston early on the eleventh, Cox was ordered into action.

Since the initial order from McClellan, Cox's instructions had changed. He was no longer to "remain on the defensive" in Kanawha County containing General Wise, but instead his five regiments were ordered to push deep into western Virginia in a three-pronged attack. The sharpest prong comprised the Eleventh, Twelfth and Twenty-first Ohio, which were instructed to thrust east from Point Pleasant toward Charleston. To the north and south of this force was the First and Second Kentucky regiments. The First, under the command of Colonel James Guthrie, was tasked with taking Ripley, forty miles northwest of Charleston; the Second was to follow the route taken by Lewis and Bridgeman from Guyandotte toward Charleston, clearing pockets of resistance they encountered on the James

River and Kanawha Turnpike. McClellan had told Cox to "punish" the Confederate forces and "drive Wise out and catch him if you can. If you do catch him, send him to Columbus penitentiary."

The Confederate commander of the Virginian forces, General Lee, had responded to the increased activity in the north of the state by ordering the Forty-fourth Virginia Regiment, under Colonel William C. Scott, to reinforce the rebel troops on Rich Mountain, and two more regiments were also on their way north from Richmond. In addition, Lee ordered Wise to move from Charleston upon Parkersburg in a divisionary attack that would relieve the pressure on the men on Rich Mountain.

Wise's orders from Lee were the ones Pryce Lewis had strained to hear through the keyhole of the Kanawha House Hotel in the early hours of July 11. Lewis ruminated on the disclosure over breakfast. On the one hand, with a bit of luck, Union troops might soon be marching through Charleston, but then again, the town might soon be rejoicing to the news of rebel triumph. Either way, Kanawha County was now at war, and the countryside would be crawling with soldiers of gray and blue, most of whom would be frightened and inexperienced, more likely to shoot first and question later.

CHAPTER NINE

"I See You Are a Stranger in These Parts"

OVER BREAKFAST ON JULY 11, 1861, Lewis decided that the time had come to implement Bridgeman's plan: they would leave Charleston and ride east along the road to Richmond until they reached Browntown; there they would take the rough trail south through Boone County and on to Kentucky. All he needed was a pass that would allow him to travel east to Browntown. After breakfast Lewis knocked on landlord Wright's door and asked if he would be so good as to introduce him to the colonel. Presently Lewis was shaking hands with Tompkins, whom he found to be "a fine-looking, middle-aged man—a free and easy Virginian."

The pair chatted for a while, and then Lewis, having established that Wise had told Tompkins nothing about his story, explained that he was eager to press on to Richmond, but alas, General Wise had refused to issue him a pass. Might the colonel see his way to authorizing a pass? wondered Lewis with a most ingratiating smile.

Tompkins looked surprised. A pass isn't required for Richmond, he said, explaining that the roads in that direction were open. General Wise must have misunderstood. Lewis feigned bafflement and blustered that indeed the general must have thought he wanted a pass north through Confederate lines. Tompkins agreed. Lewis searched the colonel's face for suspicion, but there was none. It appeared Tompkins believed his story. Nevertheless, said Lewis, couldn't he have a pass to be on the safe side?

Tompkins shook his head and said he wasn't authorized to issue passes, but told Lewis not to fret. There were hardly any Confederate troops east of Charleston, and those that were there were at Gauley Bridge. If they should accost Lewis (and there was no reason why they should), he should simply mention the colonel's name—and he would be free to continue.

Not wishing to appear in too much of a rush to leave Charleston, Lewis thanked the colonel and told him he would set off in a day or two, whenever he felt inclined. Having instructed Bridgeman to prepare the horses for an early start the following morning, Lewis spent the day in his room, praying that General Wise wouldn't return to discover his convoluted story. The sound of every gallop brought him running to the window, and the day dragged interminably. Supper came eventually, and afterward Lewis knocked on Mr. Wright's door and explained he would be off early the next day. Wright told him he'd have some breakfast ready. They settled the bill there and then: twelve nights' stay for Mr. Lewis, his servant and two horses—a total of $35.75.

Lewis rose at dawn, and after a breakfast heavy with nerves, he and Bridgeman bade good-bye to the Kanawha House Hotel and set off east in the direction of Browntown.

There wasn't much to Browntown except a couple of salt furnaces, an old tavern and a few other ramshackle buildings at the intersection of the road to Richmond and the turning south toward Kentucky. The carriage slowed, and Bridgeman looked around him, checking for signs of human life. Lewis, too, glanced surreptitiously from side to side, aware that the moment they turned off the Richmond road their cover was in danger of being blown. If they encountered any rebel soldiers who recognized them from Charleston, they would have some explaining to do.

For the next hour or two the carriage jarred and jolted, tossing Lewis from side to side as they negotiated "a rough road through a hilly country . . . there were long stretches crossed with deep gullies and ruts filled with stones." Toward noon they stopped alongside a farmhouse, one of the few inhabited dwellings they'd encountered on the track, where they were warmly welcomed by the farmer and his wife. After an abundant lunch they continued north toward the village of Logan Courthouse.

There was a fort at the entrance to Logan Courthouse, so they pulled in and the blacksmith shod the tired horses. Word of the strange arrival at the smithy filtered back to the villagers, and by the time they stopped in front of Logan's solitary hotel a curious crowd had assembled, "most of whom were rough-looking soldiers . . . [with] looks of suspicion or hostility in their faces." Bridgeman helped Lewis out of the carriage as a man in black broadcloth pushed his way to the front of the mob. He asked where he'd come from.

Charleston, replied Lewis. The man had more questions, but the Englishman wasn't in the mood. He wished him a curt good day and walked into the hotel. As he signed the resister he felt a hand upon his arm. Turning he saw an old gentleman, more refined and not so rough as the men outside.

"I see you are a stranger in these parts," he said, with a polite smile. Lewis nodded.

The man wondered what a cultivated gentleman was doing in the backwoods of Virginia, so far from the civilization to which he was accustomed. Lewis already had an explanation, a new story to fit their changed circumstances.

Lewis explained that his family owned several cotton mills in the north of England and it was his job to investigate the feasibility of shipping Southern cotton across the Atlantic. His first destination was Louisville, where he had an appointment with the British consul, and from there he intended to visit Washington.

The man gave a perfunctory nod of his head, but he wasn't much interested in Lewis's background. He was the Logan meddler, a man who had an opinion on everything. With the conviction of the know-it-all he told Lewis his carriage wouldn't stand the journey. Lewis thanked him but said he would give it a go. The man sighed at the Englishman's obstinacy. In that case, he advised, Lewis should meet Major Browning, the commander of the local militia. He knew the region like the back of his hand, and if anyone could plot a course through the mountains the major could.

Lewis accompanied the man across the street and into a saloon. A group of soldiers was propped against the bar and "among them was a little old man in blue jean overalls and checked shirt, with an old-fashioned, very narrow brim stovepipe hat." He removed his hat and introduced himself as Major Rees Browning, the officer commanding the Logan militia.

He was sixty years old, a wealthy farmer and former sheriff of the county, whose family was one of the most prominent in the region. Browning had little hard military experience, but he had influence, which was why he was in charge.

He listened to Lewis's story and then waved a hand dismissively and said it would be no problem to reach Kentucky. What was more, he would be happy to take Lewis to his office and sketch a map of the best route through the mountains. Lewis was delighted. Excellent news, he exclaimed, tapping the floor with the tip of his walking cane. He bought the major a whiskey for his trouble, and the village busybody, too, and then threw a handful of coins on the counter and told the bartender to buy a round for everyone in uniform.

Lewis accompanied Major Browning to his office a short walk from the saloon. A short while later he had a detailed map of the route into Kentucky and a letter of introduction from the major to a friend whose farm lay on the trail. As Lewis tucked the letter into the pocket of his frock coat, the major "sat back in his chair, stretched out his legs, looked at me attentively and said 'what do you think of the war?' "

Like all educated Southerners in the summer of 1861, Browning hoped one morning to hear the news that Great Britain had recognized the independence of the Confederate States. In May a delegation of rebel commissioners, headed by William Lowndes Yancey, had arrived in London for an audience with the British foreign secretary, Lord John Russell. The rebels took great heart from what was said. Russell had discussed the constitutional rights of secession, and Yancey had pledged the South's desire for free trade, reminding the British minister of the importance to his people of Southern cotton. Russell's principal concern, however, was the issue of the African slave trade. He had heard that the Confederate government was keen to restore this abomination. Was this true? Yancey reassured Russell that the South "had prohibited the slave-trade, and did not mean to revive it."

Lord Russell was in a tricky position, as were all the members of the British government. Though they opposed slavery, there wasn't a true democrat among them, not in the mold of Abraham Lincoln. A "rail-splitter" like him could never have risen to become a British minister; to be that, one had to have been born into privilege, with wealth and property the only prerequisites. The members of the British government believed in "aristocratic government," and anyone who challenged them was crushed mercilessly, as the Chartists had discovered a generation earlier. By temperament and political philosophy, therefore, ministers such as Lord Russell and the prime minister, seventy-seven-year-old Lord Palmerston, had more in common with the Confederate government than they did with the Federal. Lincoln's administration believed in equal rights and espoused the cause of the workingman, themes that were anathema to the British government. Lord Russell's nickname was "Finality John," a moniker bestowed in 1832 when he proclaimed the Reform Act of that year would be Britain's final concession to democracy.

The mouthpiece of the British establishment was the *Times* of London. Its views were followed by men of power and privilege on both sides of the Atlantic. In the months between Lincoln's election victory in 1860 and his inauguration on March 4, the *Times* had been his supporter, praising his commitment to the antislavery cause and condemning the people of the Southern states as a "poor, proud, lazy, excitable and violent class, ever ready with knife and revolver." But when Lincoln used his inauguration address to reassure Americans he had "no purpose, directly or indirectly to interfere with the institution of slavery in the States where it exists," the *Times* began to revise its opinion. If it wasn't a dispute about slavery, it asked, then what was it about? The outbreak of war, and Lincoln's order on April 19 for Federal ships to patrol the 3,500 miles of Confederacy coastline and seize all vessels entering and leaving, confirmed the *Times'* view that the North was going to war not out of any righteous cause but to seize control of the South's cotton fields (whence came 75 percent of the world's cotton supplies and as much as 84 percent of Britain's), thereby posing a serious threat to Britain's economic stability.

The South was sure that cotton would win British support for its cause, if not militarily, at least diplomatically. As early as March 1858, Senator James Henry Hammond of South Carolina had asked, in an address (that became known as the "Cotton Is King" speech) to the U.S. Senate, about the consequences if the Southern states ceased to produce cotton for any length of time. "I will not stop to depict what everyone can imagine," he said, "but this is certain: England would topple headlong and carry the whole civilized world with her, save the South. No, you dare not make war on cotton. No power on earth dares to make war upon it. Cotton is king. Until lately the Bank of England was king; but she tried to put her screws as usual, the fall before last, upon the cotton crop, and was utterly vanquished. The last power has been conquered. Who can doubt, that has looked at recent events, that cotton is supreme?" Two years later Hammond's belief in the influence of cotton had grown still further, and he pompously declared that "the slave-holding South is now the controlling power of the world."

Taking its lead from Senator Hammond, South Carolina's *Charleston Mercury* predicted that "cotton would bring England to her knees," and there was much evidence to back up such dramatic claims. In 1861 the London *Times* estimated that one fifth of the British population was dependent, directly or indirectly, on the success of the cotton districts. As the overwhelming bulk of the cotton was imported from the Southern United States, they were thereby reliant on this region for their existence. The situation was especially acute in the north of England, Britain's industrial heartland, where all but 500 of the country's 2,650 cotton factories were located. Half a million men and women were employed in these factories, and the consequences of widespread redundancy terrified the British government, which envisioned social unrest leading to revolution.

But by a quirk of fate, the 1860 cotton crop in America had been the largest ever—four million bales—and of the three and a half million shipped abroad, most went to Britain, which carefully husbanded the surplus bales, mindful of the economic depression of 1857 that had affected supplies. When war began the British government was naturally concerned about the impact on the cotton trade, but not as much as the South thought, certainly not enough to forcibly remove the Federal blockade as *De Bow's Review* had foreseen in January 1861. This Southern journal, with its emphasis on agricultural and industrial progress, wrote that "the first demonstration of blockade of the Southern ports would be swept away by the English fleets of observation hovering on the Southern coasts, to protect English commerce, and especially the free flow of cotton." The British government had no choice, concluded *De Bow's*, for a disruption to the cotton trade "would produce the most disastrous political results—if not a revolution in England."

.   .   .

Following his interview with Yancey in May 1861, Lord Russell reported to the prime minister, Lord Palmerston, and the rest of the cabinet. Though there were aristocratic murmurings of sympathy for the Southern states, and splutterings of indignation at their uncouth Federal counterparts, it was agreed that Britain would refuse, for the time being, to recognize Southern sovereignty. As the *Times* wrote in its editorial of May 9, while the war appeared to be "a conflict where there were in fact no such ideals involved as had been earlier attributed to it . . . Southern rights are now more clearly understood, and in any case since war, though greatly to be regretted, was now at hand, it was England's business to keep strictly out of it and to maintain neutrality." Five days later, on Tuesday, May 14, Queen Victoria, on the advice of her prime minister, issued Britain's "Proclamation of Neutrality." The proclamation was avidly reported in the American press, with *Harper's Weekly* summarizing it in its edition of June 8. "The proclamation of the Queen has been issued by the Privy Council at Whitehall, warning all British subjects from interfering, at their peril, with either party in the American conflict, or giving aid and comfort in any way, by personal service and supplying munitions of war, to either party. The proclamation announces it as the intention of the British Government to preserve the strictest neutrality in the contest between the Government of the United States and the Government of those States calling themselves the Confederate States of America."

In its editorial of the same issue, the Union-supporting *Harper's* criticized Britain for its proclamation, for it recognized the 750,000 square miles of the Confederacy as a belligerent power, which allowed Davis's government under international law to do business with other nations; business such as the purchase of armaments and ships. *Harper's* was piqued that the British government had given succor to the rebels when it prided itself on the ruthless alacrity with which it crushed its own rebellions, such as the one in India four years earlier.*

Nonetheless, *Harper's Weekly* crowed that Britain's Proclamation of Neutrality was a devastating blow for the Confederacy because "the whole

---

* The Indian Mutiny began in May 1857 when Indian soldiers rebelled against British rule. The unrest spread throughout India, involving atrocities on both sides, before the British reestablished control the following year.

rebellion has rested upon two points: first, that the North was cowardly
and divided, and then that England, which must have cotton, would open
the Southern Ports. But the traitors forgot how much the one depended
upon the other. If England had seen the Slave States united in the movement, and the Free States hesitating and divided, she would doubtless
have taken some more decided action. But she has seen just in time, in the
Free States, an enthusiastic unanimity unparalleled in history—all the vast
resources of a great, intelligent, skillful, industrious, and wealthy people,
she has seen heaped and lavished in the measures of defense against this
conspiracy."

Lewis knew the words Major Browning wanted to hear and so told him
that "England is bound to have the cotton in the south. Millions of English
operatives depend on it. Without it there will be famine and revolution
[and] England will risk ten foreign wars to prevent a civil one. She must
and will open the Northern blockade with her immense fleet." To heighten
the dramatic effect of his words, Lewis banged his fist on the major's desk
and cursed the Yankees. Browning jumped to his feet, and the pair shook
hands on behalf of their respective nations. Lewis suggested they retire
to his hotel and seal their fidelity in champagne.

The champagne led to supper and the subsequent revelation from the
major that early the next day he and his men were moving northeast to reinforce General Wise. He thought Lewis such an accomplished "speechi-
fier" that he requested the Englishman say a few words to his boys; most
had never been in action, and it would do their morale a power of good to
know that England would soon be their ally in war.

Lewis shook his head regretfully and told the major he couldn't
possibly accept the invitation because Queen Victoria had issued a
proclamation against any of her subjects interfering in the American
dispute. Lewis explained to Browning that if word reached Washington
that he had give a speech in support of the Confederacy "it might prevent my getting a permit to move the cotton, and compromise all our
interests."

The major appreciated the delicacy of Lewis's position but might he
not talk informally to the men perhaps? Lewis relented, and after supper
he was introduced to the militia over a whiskey. Then the major sprang
his trap. Calling for quiet, he told his men that Lewis wished to address

them. Standing in the parlor of the major's house, surrounded by a large number of rebel soldiers, Lewis "went over England's history and spoke for half an hour using most of the arguments of my former speech, spinning the cotton plea down fine." When he'd finished, Lewis had practically convinced himself that Britain must wage war against the North. He broke into a rousing rendition of "God Save the Queen!" and its finale was greeted with three tremendous cheers.

Later the major apologized for the ambush, but Lewis laughed it off. He liked Browning and considered him "an excellent old fellow, one of the rarest and best characters I ever met." He was also a diligent host, and when three of the militia began playing their fiddles he insisted Lewis watch some Southern-style dancing. There were no women present, just rough mountain men letting off steam on the eve of battle. Lewis politely clapped his hands to the beat of the music, and "it was past two o'clock before I could get away."

Three hours later Lewis was roused by Bridgeman. He dressed with his eyelids still half closed, then made his way downstairs. Waiting in the lobby was Major Browning and several members of the militia. Lewis sensed something was up. The major took his arm and whispered, "Let's go upstairs." Lewis was led back to his room, conscious that there was a quiet firmness about the major. Browning stepped aside and motioned for Lewis to enter first.

The Englishman watched as the major shut the door and then reached inside his tunic pocket. It was a telegram, he was sure of it, ordering his arrest, "but, no, it was a bottle!" The major wanted Lewis to share a final toast and thrust a bottle of homemade wine toward Lewis. The Englishman took a swig. It was revolting, but he swallowed, for queen and country.

Eventually they set off amid more detonating cheers with one of Browning's mounted soldiers as a guide. For twelve miles he escorted them toward the mountain, and then, wishing them the best of luck, he turned for Logan. For the rest of the day, Saturday, July 13, they headed southwest. Frequently Lewis stuck his head out of the window and looked back along the rough trail, each time dreading the distant sight of galloping horsemen—Browning and his men alerted to the deception. But nothing marred the beautiful landscape. Late in the afternoon they reached the farm of the major's friend, and Lewis handed him the letter of introduction. They ate, washed and slept, and were on the move early next morning as dawn mottled the night sky.

Not until they had crossed the Big Sandy River and were traveling through Pike County did their stomachs begin to unknot. After spending Sunday night in a guesthouse they pushed on north to Catlettsburg, at the confluence of the Big Sandy and Ohio rivers, and then covered the six miles to Ironton. They were "quite fagged out" as they fell into bed on Monday, but they knew they had to relay their information without delay. On Tuesday morning they took the steamer west to Cincinnati. Lewis and Bridgeman sat on deck, smoking and talking, and agreeing that though "we had been gone only nineteen days . . . it seemed like an age." For Lewis there was no respite once he reached Cincinnati. Pinkerton cabled news of Lewis's remarkable mission to McClellan's headquarters, and the Englishman was ordered to report his findings to General Cox without delay. To his consternation, Lewis learned that Cox had established his command at Poca, a village at the confluence of the Kanawha and Pocatalico rivers, half a dozen miles upstream from Camp Tompkins and the generous hospitality of Colonel Patton.

CHAPTER TEN

"Do You Mean to Say That You Have Been in Wise's Camp?"

A CONTEMPORARY OF GENERAL JACOB DOLSON COX described him as "six feet in height, very erect and slender, his weight about one hundred and forty-five pounds. His hair was fine, dark brown, worn rather long, and always brushed with scrupulous care. His beard was full and, when allowed to grow long, became wavy . . . his prominent brow betokened deep thought. The searching deep-set eyes were those of a man who saw everything, and saw clearly."

He had been born thirty-two years earlier in Montreal, where his father, a New York architect, was designing the suspended ceiling of the city's Notre Dame Cathedral. Cox had no wish to emulate his father; law was his vocation, and he was admitted to the bar in 1852. Seven years later Cox was elected to the Ohio State Senate, but ill health dogged his term, and attacks of quinsy and diphtheria laid him low for much of 1860. Nevertheless, when war broke out, Governor William Dennison of Ohio appointed Cox his chief of staff and placed him under McClellan's command.

Cox lacked McClellan's flamboyance, but he was his equal in ambition. The order to invade the Kanawha Valley on July 11 was therefore an opportunity to be exploited, a chance to further his political ambitions. Cox commandeered the fleet of river steamboats and loaded them with soldiers from the three Ohio regiments. As they set off east along the Kanawha, two companies of infantrymen marched in front along each riverbank. Cox was at the head of the convoy, standing in the prow of the steamer so "he might see over the banks of the stream and across the bottom land to the hills which bounded the valley." He ordered his band to strike up the national anthem, and as they winded their way upstream they passed the houses of Union supporters who cheered them on their way. It was a glorious scene, said Cox, who felt liberated from the drudgery of office life. He perceived that "the landscape seemed more beautiful, the sunshine more bright and the exhilaration of outdoors life more joyous" than it had in his previous existence.

At the Red House Shoals the invasion force removed the sunken barges from the river and then continued east. Rebel sharpshooters on the overlooking hills fired intermittently, but Cox pressed on until he pitched his camp at Poca. Cox's three regiments of Ohio troops were joined by half the First Kentucky Regiment, whose objective had been the town of Ripley. The Kentuckians explained to Cox that General Wise had avoided a fight and appeared to be running scared of the Union army.*

On Tuesday, July 16, the day Lewis and Bridgeman arrived back in Cincinnati, Cox's three forces were reunited when the Second Kentucky Regiment appeared from the south bringing with them wonderful news. Two days earlier they'd defeated the Confederates at Barbourville and planted the American flag on top of the courthouse.

Cox was encouraged by the news and the next day dispatched reconnaissance patrols east to probe the rebels' strength. Under hot sunshine in a cornfield near Little Scary Creek two sentries spotted bluecoats moving toward them. They turned tail and fled, not stopping till they reached the rickety wooden bridge across the creek. There they breathlessly told their comrades what they'd seen. A messenger was sent to Camp Tompkins with the news that the Yankees were coming.

There were two hundred rebels at Scary Creek, and they now prepared

---

* Wise judged that his force was too small and too poorly equipped to attack the Federal troops. He sent a request that General Robert Garnett, in charge of rebel troops at Rich Mountain, reinforce him, but it was too late—the Union troops had seized Rich Mountain and routed Garnett's troops. Wise withdrew to Tyler Mountain, five miles north of Charleston and approximately three miles east of Colonel Patton's camp.

for battle. Their position was on the southern bank of the creek, close to where its stream met the Kanawha River. Though the banks of the creek were steep, its name was undeserved; there was nothing scary about it. Hills to the north and the south overlooked it, and a church and a few log cabins lay on the north side. An Englishman passing through on a sight-seeing tour of Virginia might have paused on the bridge and reflected on the beauty of the countryside.

As Cox was listening to the information brought back by his scouts, some of the two hundred rebels at Scary Creek were moving across the bridge and taking up positions on the northern bank. At the same time more rebel troops were arriving from the south, dressed in the smart dark green of Colonel Patton's Kanawha Riflemen. A Kanawha artillery unit arrived pulling two six-pounders, and three companies of cavalry were soon on the scene. At two o'clock the rebels were ready. Under a burning sun, the rebel soldiers lay in wait, wiping the sweat from their eyes as they watched the hill to their north.

On the other side of the hill, Colonel John Lowe was assembling his force of 1,500 Federal troops. As well as his own Twelfth Ohio Regiment, there was a cavalry company, an artillery battery led by Captain Charles Cotter and two companies of the Twenty-first Ohio Regiment under the command of Jesse Norton. In a subsequent letter to the *Perrysburg Journal* one of Norton's infantrymen described what happened: "At this juncture Col. Norton ordered the left wing, consisting of five companies, including two from the 21st regiment, to fall in line in a ravine. He then ordered them forward to the brow of the hill, and gave them the order to open fire. Col. Norton then designated Capt. Cotter his position upon the brow of the hill, in full view of the enemy's battery, which position he took, and immediately prepared his battery for action, and opened fire with astonishing effect."

Union troops cheered as a shell from Captain Cotter's battery landed on one of the rebels' two cannons, "taking off a wheel from the gun carriage and the head of the First Lieutenant in the artillery." Now the farm boys and water men of Kanawha knew what war was. While the Union cannons continued to bombard the rebel positions, Confederate sharpshooters in the log cabins on the northern side of the creek fired into the thick ranks of Federal troops on the crest of the hill. The letter writer to the *Perrysburg Journal* recounted how the Confederates, armed with their

Sharps rifles, "had no difficulty in reaching us, and were wounding and killing our men with impunity." The Union troops dropped to the grass and returned fire, but their muskets were old and their bullets fell short.

Colonel Lowe was nowhere to be found, so Colonel Norton assumed command. He formed up three companies of the Twelfth Ohio and two companies of the Twenty-first, and led them down the hill. It was ordered, disciplined, like they'd rehearsed on the training ground. Norton halted his men at the foot of the hill, where a fence ran parallel to the creek. As rebel sharpshooters continued to pick off his men, he calmly moved the two companies of the Twenty-first left, toward the Kanawha River, and lined up three companies of the Twelfth Ohio behind the fence. They were less than one hundred yards from the log cabins. Inside the rebel marksmen heard the chilling chorus of steel as the enemy fixed its bayonets. They watched as the Union troops began to move toward them on the double quick. Fifty yards from the log cabins the "front rank were ordered to fire and charge . . . this they did gallantly and with effect, taking several prisoners and pricking them out of their various hiding places." The rebels that broke from cover and made for the creek were cut down by fire from the Twenty-first Ohio. But a few made it across, and when the last one was safely over, the rebels torched the bridge.

Scary Creek now lived up to its name as Norton and the two companies of the Twenty-first Ohio charged toward the burning bridge with Union sharpshooters in the log cabins providing covering fire. The creek became a killing ground as Virginian and Ohioan fought hand to hand in the knee-deep water. Men were shot and stabbed and clubbed. Captain Thomas Allen, a lawyer from Cincinnati, the officer commanding D Company of the Twenty-first Ohio, was struck down by a rebel bullet. Lieutenant Pomeroy assumed command but dropped dead a few minutes later. Colonel Norton "took off his cap and turning partly around . . . was shot directly through the hips. The ball passed in at the right hip, just missing the end of the spine and out on the opposite hip."

Norton was carried into one of the log cabins, screaming in anger as much as pain. Where the hell is Colonel Lowe? he shouted. Get a message to the colonel, he ordered his messenger, tell him to launch the Twelfth Ohio against the enemy's left. The day is nearly ours. Then Norton passed out.

On the other side of the creek the rebels were falling back, the once proud men of Kanawha reduced to a bloody rabble. Colonel Patton had been ordered by General Wise to withdraw his regiment to Camp Tompkins so they could fight another day. Patton set off east as instructed but then changed his mind. His duty was at Scary Creek. He returned to find the Twenty-first Ohio advancing slowly but remorselessly toward the southern side of the creek. For fifteen minutes Patton rode among his men, exhorting them on. Then a Union sharpshooter put a bullet through his shoulder.

With Norton unconscious, Colonel Lowe finally ordered his three companies of Ohio infantry to ford the stream and attack the rebels' left. One company got lost in the woods; another company hunkered down behind a corncrib listening to their terrified captain sob and wail. A third company did as instructed but was driven back by Patton's men.

When the sun set, the Southern army was in charge of Scary Creek. Seventy-five men in blue or gray lay dead or wounded. The next morning the rebels dug a pit at the bottom of the hill down which the Yankees had charged, and buried their enemy's dead.

A messenger brought Cox word of the defeat, not long after an earlier harbinger had arrived with news of victory. The general was phlegmatic, noting later that "as was common with new troops, they pass from confidence to discouragement as soon as they were checked and they retreated." The Union soldiers who stumbled into camp were less tempered in their views. Colonel Lowe was to blame, they muttered among one another, and the letter writer to the *Perrysburg Journal* agreed: "From the time the enemy opened fire upon us he gave no command. He did nothing to inspire his men with confidence. He kept well in the rear, out of range of fire, and on but one occasion did he approach the line . . . and took good care to keep a log building between himself and the shots of the enemy."

On the morning of Sunday, July 21, General Cox's mood had darkened. Defeated by the enemy, he had been humiliated by five of his officers—three colonels (including William Woodruff, commanding officer of the Second Kentucky Regiment) and two captains—who had ridden off to see the scene of the battle and got themselves captured by the enemy. Cox had also been excoriated by General McClellan for his failure at Scary Creek. "Cox checked on the Kanawha. Has fought something between a victory and a defeat," McClellan wrote on July 19 in his official report of the action, adding irascibly: "In Heaven's name, give me some general officers who understand their profession. I give orders, and find some who cannot execute them unless I stand by them. Unless I command every picket and lead every column I cannot be sure of success."

Cox was in disgrace, instructed by McClellan to remain at Poca and wait for General Wise to make the next move. He was still brooding when one of his officers told him there was a gentleman to see him, an Englishman by the name of Pryce Lewis.

From Cincinnati, Lewis had traveled east to Parkersburg and boarded a military vessel going to Poca. He was the sole civilian on board; everyone else was a Union soldier, en route to reinforce Cox's army. The ferry captain spotted Lewis loitering on deck and "in a bullying manner" wanted to know who he was and where he was headed. Lewis said he couldn't answer either question, so the captain "ordered me off the boat, employing an oath or two to ornament his display of authority." Lewis refused to move, and as Union soldiers ringed the two protagonists, the Englishman turned to one and asked for his commander. A Captain Russell appeared and "wanted to know the cause of the fuss." Lewis asked to see him in private. They went below deck, and Lewis explained who he was and showed the captain a letter addressed to General Cox. It was sealed, but Lewis told the captain he was free to read its contents; it would verify his story. Russell said it wasn't necessary and he was only sorry "that every bunk on the boat was full." Nevertheless, the captain ordered his men to fetch some blankets, and Lewis slept on deck next to the ferry's funnel.

They reached Cox's army early in the afternoon of Sunday, July 21. Lewis asked to be taken to the general's headquarters, and he was led toward a steamer moored at the wharf. Inside he found Cox alone in the saloon. Allan Pinkerton had told Lewis "that Cox was not a soldier, but a lawyer," and the scholarly-looking gentleman sitting at his desk validated Pinkerton's description. Lewis introduced himself and handed Cox the letter. The general motioned for his guest to sit and began to read the letter. When he'd finished he looked up and searched the face of Lewis. "Do you mean to say that you have been in Wise's camp?" Lewis nodded and at the behest of the general began "relating my conversation with Colonel Patton, my interview with Wise and my visit to the camp at Charleston . . . I gave the number of troops in Wise's command as 5,500, including those under Patton and Browning, told the number of rations issued at Charleston, and the number of pieces of artillery there." Lewis added that in his opinion if Cox moved on Charleston "he would have two fights, one at the junction of Coal Mouth and the Kanawha [Patton's camp] and the other at Elk River Suspension bridge."

When Lewis had finished his account "the general appeared astonished." For a few seconds he could say nothing, but then he summoned an orderly and told him to fetch Major Charles Whittlesey, the assistant quartermaster general.

While they waited Cox admired the red leather shoes that Lewis had on his feet. The Englishman thanked the general for his compliment and entertained him with tales of champagne, cigars and Major Browning's native wine. When Whittlesey appeared, Lewis repeated his story with similar results.

Cox called for a council of war and told Lewis to tour his camp. He wanted to know how it compared with those he had seen farther east. When Lewis returned he estimated that Wise had more men but that the Union army had more artillery pieces and of a better quality.

Later Lewis took a nap in Major Whittlesey's bed, and at supper he was a guest at the general's table. Cox told him of the battle with the rebels "at a place called Scary near the Coal Mouth and that our men had been driven back."

The next day, Monday, July 22, Lewis enjoyed the freedom of the camp and made several acquaintances among the officers. At one moment he doffed his cap and stood in silence as "the remains of Captain Allen of Cincinnati, who had been killed in the skirmish at Scary on the 17th were brought into camp to be forwarded to his family." Throughout the day Lewis was summoned from time to time to Cox's headquarters to answer a question or clarify a point relating to his mission. As the general pondered his next move, aware that his orders from McClellan were to remain where he was, a steady stream of vessels arrived from the west bringing men, munitions and wagons.

Lewis learned on Tuesday that Cox had decided to act on his information. A large patrol had already departed to reconnoiter east toward

Scary Creek, and a second patrol was about to set off by boat. Lewis asked permission to accompany the troops. Cox acceded to the request, and Lewis squeezed onto the vessel among the Union soldiers.

For several miles they ascended the river without incident. Then up ahead they saw smoke rising from the trees. The vessel stopped and soldiers disembarked, moving cautiously toward the smoke. Lewis remained on board, smoking, and passing the time of day with two army surgeons. Presently, a detail of Union soldiers appeared prodding a captured rebel at the end of their bayonets. Lewis recognized the prisoner's dark green uniform as that of Colonel Patton's regiment. The man refused to speak, but his guards explained that the Confederates were in retreat and were burning bridges as they went. A short while later a messenger arrived from the foot patrol. He requested a surgeon because "the commander of the rebel forces had been captured and was at his headquarters badly wounded."

Both surgeons stepped ashore and asked Lewis if he wished to accompany them. He accepted, and they set off with the messenger and a military escort toward the wounded rebel officer. They reached a road that Lewis recognized as the James River and Kanawha Turnpike. It seemed an eternity since he and Bridgeman had come this way in a carriage. They passed some Union soldiers sheltering from the sun under a tree, and soon the messenger was explaining that the captured rebel officer was around the next bend. Lewis turned the corner but he already knew what he would find: the farmhouse in which he had been entertained by Colonel Patton.

On the grass in front of the farmhouse scores of Union soldiers were warming themselves in the sun while two sentries stood on the veranda. Lewis knew it was Patton lying wounded inside; his intuition told him so, but he had no wish to meet a man "whose gentlemanly confidence I had so completely won." He excused himself from going inside the house, explaining to the surgeons that the sight of blood made him queasy.

When Lewis met the surgeons back on the boat they confirmed that the wounded officer had indeed been Patton. Shot in the shoulder during the Scary Creek fight, he was recovering at his headquarters when the Union troops attacked. Whether the colonel had been abandoned by his fleeing men, or whether he was too ill to be moved, the surgeons didn't say. But he was now a prisoner of the Union army.

Later that evening Lewis was summoned to Cox's headquarters. He "found him on the upper deck pacing up and down, apparently in deep study." Cox told Lewis he was confronted by a dilemma: the good news was that the patrols had returned triumphant, not only with a captured Confederate colonel but with reports indicating the rebels were not the formidable force he had been led to believe. Lewis agreed that the enemy was there for the taking, so why the delay?

The bad news was contained on a slip of paper Cox handed Lewis. It was a message he'd just received from Colonel Guthrie (commanding officer of the First Kentucky Regiment) that gave Wise's troop strength as somewhere in the region of sixty thousand men. Lewis gave a laugh of disbelief and dismissed it as a falsehood, spread either by Wise's spies or by genuine Unionists who had been duped by the rebels. Lewis told Cox that such wild claims were not unusual in Kanawha County and that "ten miles from Charleston I heard that Wise had 20,000 men, and as I got further away in the mountains, his force was estimated at 50 and 60,000." Cox went to the deck rail and stared at the dark water below. After a few seconds he turned and asked Lewis if he'd eaten. No, replied Lewis, he hadn't. Cox told him to do so and return at eight o'clock. The spy did as instructed, and when he arrived at the general's headquarters he found him "at a large round table with eight or ten officers." Cox ordered Lewis to repeat his account of his trip through the Kanawha Valley, "the whole story, omit nothing."

While Cox agonized over his next move, his rebel counterpart was in a similar state of flux. For the past week General Wise had been sending begging dispatches south. On July 17 he had implored Richmond to "re-enforce us with men, arms and ammunition"; on July 18 he pleaded for four twelve-pound howitzers so he could follow up the success at Scary Creek by attacking Cox's main camp; on July 19, with no response to his earlier requests, a desperate Wise demanded the following: "double the number of officers we have . . . pay, forage for horses . . . two sixed rifles, two 12-pound howitzers, and allow us four small 4-pounders . . . by all means, then, hasten on re-enforcements, arms and ammunition."

Wise knew the Northern net was tightening, and he wanted to make sure Richmond knew it too. He entrusted his dispatch of July 19 to Major C. B. Duffield, a doughty soldier who could be relied upon to deliver what Wise feared might be his epitaph. Wise closed the report by stating his predicament, explaining that Cox was at Pocotaligo Mouth. "He is now there, about three thousand, three hundred strong, awaiting re-enforcements. We are threatened by that number in the valley, by about one thousand five hundred from Ripley to Sissonville, and by forces from Weston, Glenville, and Sutton, via Summersville. If I go toward Point Pleasant they rush on Coal, on Two Mile, and the Elk and Gauley, and if I move out of the [Kanawha] valley in any direction with anything like an effective force, they rush in and rake the valley, and if I stand still they move from all sides and shut me in."

When Wise turned in for the night at his headquarters on Tyler Mountain on Tuesday, July 23, he had received neither arms nor men. He hadn't even taken delivery of more forage for his horses. Abandoned by the Confederate High Command, surrounded by Federal forces, Wise was certain an attack was imminent, but he had no clear idea from which direction it would come.

Having listened to Pryce Lewis, Cox and his officers decided to attack the next day, Wednesday, July 24. They burned the midnight oil, discussing what strategy to adopt. Wise's position was five miles north of Charleston and approximately ten miles east of the Union camp. Cox knew that the Confederates had an accurate estimate of his army, but he was confident the rebels assumed he would launch his assault from the west, along the same route his two patrols had taken earlier that day. Cox studied the map of the Kanawha Valley and concluded that the best chance of surprising Wise was to march his men north, then wheel and strike his rear.

At dawn on July 24, as Lewis waited to catch a ride on the first steamer heading back up the Kanawha toward Cincinnati, the bulk of Cox's army went to war. Leaving one regiment to guard the camp and steamboats, Cox marched his men north and then swung east. Just before sundown, as the smell of sizzling meat wafted through the wooded mountainside, Cox's men attacked. It was a rout, reported the general, with Wise's army reduced to "a panic-stricken force running off, leaving their camp in confusion, and their supper which they were cooking."

The remnants of the rebel army fled south, through the former camp at Kanawha Two Mile, from where Wise had earlier predicted he could "whip the world," and over the iron suspension bridge that spanned the

Elk River. The fleeing men vandalized the bridge the best they could, severing cables and removing flooring, and then continued their pell-mell dash to Charleston.

Cox's men pursued the rebels all the way, though the damaged suspension bridge cost them precious time. While Wise and his men piled into steamboats and headed east along the Kanawha toward Gauley Bridge, the Federal troops constructed a pontoon from the empty coal barges moored on the Elk, and crossed the river into Charleston. There to greet the invaders was Mayor Jacob Goshorn, dignified but terrified, mindful that Wise had warned him the "murdering Yankees" were close on his heels.

The Union general set up his headquarters in Charleston and on Friday, July 26, took off after Wise. For three days he marched his men southeast toward Gauley Bridge, expecting at any moment to be ambushed. But they reached the town without incident. Cox learned that the rebels had paused in Gauley Bridge just long enough to burn the 190-yard wooden covered bridge that carried the James River and Kanawha Turnpike across the Gauley River, and then pushed on to Lewisburg.

Cox gave up the chase at Gauley Bridge. The farther east he headed, the more he stretched his supply line, and why risk running into the rebels when he already had what he wanted: Charleston, Gauley Bridge and control of the Kanawha River. General McClellan was jubilant when he heard of Cox's success; he ignored the fact that by pushing on to Gauley Bridge, Cox had disobeyed his order not to advance east beyond Charleston. That didn't matter; what did was the defeat of Wise, coming as it did just three days after the Confederate victory at Bull Run.* But now he, General George McClellan, had restored the reputation of the Northern army.

Wise's force reached Lewisburg on August 1. Not a man among them believed any more in the glory of war. The sixty-four miles from Gauley Bridge had been a living hell. Sickened by measles, weakened by hunger, drenched by thunderstorms, the survivors who staggered into Lewisburg were no longer soldiers; they were scarecrows bereft of equipment and respect. Wise overheard one of his men describing to a civilian what

---

* Bull Run was the Union name for the battle; to the Confederates it was Manassas, so called after the town that served as their camp.

they had endured on the "retreat." He came running over screaming: "Retreat! Never dare call it a 'retreat' again, sir. It was only a 'retrograde' movement." The soldier no longer cared for military protocol; he was too exhausted. Looking up at his commanding officer with a wry smile, he replied, "I don't know nothing about your retrogrades, general, but I do know we did some damn tall walking."

Two days later Wisconsin's *Prescott Transcript* reported that a dispatch had been received from General Cox in which he described how the "rapid pursuit of Wise's forces resulted in the capture of 1,000 stand of arms and a large amount of gunpowder left behind by the enemy . . . there was no chance for a fight, for the rebels retreated faster than retreat could be made." As for the number of Confederate troops encountered by the Union troops, the *Prescott Transcript* gave the figure as around "5000 or 6000," just as Lewis had forecast.*

---

* Wise learned in Lewisburg that the reinforcements for which he had begged were being assembled in Monterey, on the eastern side of the Allegheny Mountains. While he was recalled to Richmond, General Lee went north to take charge of the twenty-thousand-strong rebel army, and throughout late August and September there were sporadic clashes in the Allegheny passes. But the rebels were unable to make the decisive breakthrough, and in October Lee left Virginia for South Carolina. In the same month the people of western Virginia voted to establish a separate state, and in May 1862 the creation of West Virginia was officially sanctioned.

CHAPTER ELEVEN

"That Is Tim Webster"

I T WAS LATE AUGUST 1861, and Pryce Lewis and Sam Bridgeman were reunited, though this time there was no need for disguises. The pair were at Baltimore's Miller's Hotel, on the corner of German and Pacer streets, awaiting instructions from Allan Pinkerton. After the success of their mission to Charleston, the pair were Pinkerton's new golden boys. Or, at least, Lewis was. When he'd returned to Cincinnati from his trip to General Cox's camp, Lewis learned that Bridgeman was no longer an employee of the Pinkerton detective agency. He'd been "discharged for celebrating our safe return too hilariously." Lewis went to see Pinkerton and told him that, yes, Sam liked a drink now and again, but he'd done a good job as his coachman and he deserved a second chance. Pinkerton acquiesced but emphasized Bridgeman was on his final warning.

Although Baltimore belonged to the Union in August 1861, it still seethed with discontent. The plot to assassinate President Lincoln might have been nothing more than a Pinkerton concoction, but what had happened on April 19 was anything but. On that day the Sixth Massachusetts Regiment had marched through the city, the first Northern troops to do so, and their presence wasn't appreciated. A furious mob attacked the soldiers as they headed to the train station, and in the ensuing chaos four troops and twelve civilians were killed. The following month the situation remained tense, as the correspondent of the *New York Herald* discovered when he arrived at Baltimore's Camden Station: "Half-drunken loafers swarmed therein," he reported. "They carried costly daggers, revolvers of the latest fashion, and knives of glittering polish, while as they swaggered through the long passage, they d-d the Union, gave maudlin cheers for Maryland, and boasted of their future prowess . . . at every corner [of the city], in the middle of the streets, and around the hotel doorways, stood and shouted always the same brutal swarm. No life is safe there unless its possessor will say their says, no person is sacred there unless its possessor will say their says, no person is sacred there unless its spirit is against the Federal Union, and no property will long be inviolate whose holder does not loud and long proclaim his devotions to Southern interests and his seal for the Southern cause."

Secessionists burned bridges and felled telegraph poles, while the city's legislature censured the Federal government but quailed at open rebellion. Governor Thomas Hicks described Baltimore's position as one of neutrality, so more Union troops came to the city to ensure it stayed that way. Nevertheless the secessionists continued to foment sedition, particularly after the victory at Bull Run, a triumph that emboldened the city's Confederate-leaning politicians to the extent that they publicly condemned Lincoln as a tyrant.

Pinkerton was asked to find out what he could about the secessionists in Baltimore, so he sent Lewis and Bridgeman there. They had no precise objectives; they were to observe and report. Lewis's favorite observation post was the veranda of Miller's Hotel. There they ordered drinks from a bartender named John Earl, a known secessionist. Lewis was taking in the view from the veranda one afternoon when "Bridgeman directed my attention to a gentlemanly-looking, stalwart passer-by, who was accompanied by a lady."

"That," said Bridgeman, leaning across to whisper in Lewis's ear, "is Tim Webster."

Allan Pinkerton described Tim Webster in 1861 as "a tall, broad-shouldered, good-looking man of about forty years of age. In height he was about five feet ten inches; his brown hair, which was brushed carelessly back from a broad, high forehead, surmounted a face of a character to at once attract attention."

There was a beard as well, precise and modest, a reflection of his personality. Nothing about Timothy Webster was ostentatious; after all, he was descended from that most stolid of stock, the English yeoman.

Timothy Webster Senior had been one of the Duke of Wellington's men during the Napoleonic Wars of half a century earlier, and once France had been crushed he returned to being a tinsmith, the occupation of his father and the trade to which he himself had been apprenticed before he'd left to be a soldier. Then he married his childhood sweetheart, Frances, and they moved from Leicester, in central England, to the county of Sussex on the southern coast in order to find work.

Timothy and Frances settled in the village of Newhaven and started a family: two healthy daughters named Mary and Maria, and at the end of 1819 their first son, Samuel, was born. Three years later, on March 12, 1822, Frances Webster gave birth to another boy. This one they named after his father.

When Timothy was two, Reverend T. W. Horsfield visited Newhaven on a research trip for a book he was writing about the region. When the book was published the literate among Newhaven's 929 inhabitants appreciated Horsfield's description of their town: "The residents of Newhaven are chiefly engaged in maritime pursuits," he explained. "There are, however, two extensive breweries and the place is noted for the excellence of its beer. There are four comfortable inns, and within the last twenty years the number of houses built is estimated at forty. The town is extremely neat and clean. Over the [river] Ouse is a handsome drawbridge, which was erected some years ago by an act of parliament in lieu of an ancient ferry."

The reverend neglected to describe Newhaven's centuries-old harbor (the reason why such a small town required a quartet of inns) from which a ferry sailed twice a week to France. Trading vessels also made frequent calls to Newhaven, and several ships a week arrived to transport boulders to the pottery districts of England. The boulders were collected from the Sussex countryside by the county's poor and heaved down to the harbor. In 1823 the townsfolk of Newhaven amassed five and a half thousand tons of boulders.

For young boys too weak to help harvest boulders, Newhaven was a rural idyll in the 1820s. They might have scrambled up the hill behind the church of St. Michael (where Tim Webster had been baptized) to look out over the English Channel for the arrival of the ferry from France. And while they waited for the sails to appear, the young boys might have dug into the hillside searching for relics from the region's previous inhabitants: a Stone Age flint, an Iron Age arrowhead or a Roman vase.

In the harbor they might have helped the fishermen unload the day's catch: brill and sole and plaice. They might have pranced behind the hawkers who came to sell their wares, imitating their cries of "Taters O!" and "Damsons O!" and in the summer they might have dived from the wooden drawbridge into the river Ouse or swum in the cold waters of the Channel.

In 1827 Frances gave birth to her sixth child (a daughter, Esther, had been born in 1824), a boy who was christened Godfrey but lived just fifty-nine days. The following year Mrs. Webster produced twins, James and Jonathan, increasing her brood to seven.

Her husband probably made up his mind to emigrate at the start of 1830. Perhaps it was his New Year's resolution. Struggling to support his large family, Webster would have suffered along with everyone else because of the poor harvest of 1829. It was the second consecutive bad harvest, and now "men were found dead behind hedges with nothing but sour sorrel in their famished bellies."

He wasn't alone in casting his eyes west toward America. Other men in Sussex, particularly those who worked the land, feared what the invention of the threshing machine meant for them. While some farmworkers resisted the Industrial Revolution, destroying threshing machines and torching the barns of farmers who owned the hated contraptions, others chose to escape the upheaval. In February 1830 Robert Peel, the home secretary, received a letter from an anxious Sussex magistrate complaining "about the number of Sussex laborers emigrating to America . . . leaving their families dependent on the parish."

But Timothy Webster had no intention of abandoning his family. When he applied to the overseers of Newhaven Parish for assistance in emigrating, he explained that he wished to take with him his pregnant wife and their seven children: Mary, fifteen, Maria, thirteen, Samuel, ten, Tim, eight, Esther, six, and the two-year-old twins, Jonathan and James.

The committee of Newhaven Parish would have been willing to help Webster, as they were in assisting most paupers. For years they had been doling out money to the family, keeping them in food and clothes; now with one final sum they would be released from all further obligations. In 1830 it cost parishes such as Newhaven six pounds and five shillings (there were twenty shillings to the pound, and a shilling was subdivided into twelve pennies) to send one adult pauper to North America and three pounds and two shillings for each child under the age of fourteen. On arrival, the adults were given two pounds each and one additional pound for each of their children. With this pittance they entered their new world.

England had not been kind to Timothy Webster. If one was born into poverty, that was how one remained, no matter how hard one worked, or how valiantly one fought. When he and his family reached America in 1830, with eleven pounds between them, he looked to the future. From now on the Websters would consider themselves Americans.

The Tim Webster that Pryce Lewis watched stroll along a Baltimore sidewalk in August 1861 looked, and sounded, every bit the American. The man himself might have retained a vague memory of swimming in the river Ouse or playing in the streets of Newhaven, but Webster was now an American citizen, married to an American, with three American children. His accent was New Jersey—Princeton, to be precise—where his father had built the family home thirty-one years earlier. Though his mother, Frances, had been in the ground for years, worn out by all the children she had brought into the world, Timothy Webster Senior had died in 1860 at the age of sixty-nine.

After he married at nineteen and became a dad at twenty-one, Tim Webster's life had appeared to be set for the same unremitting grind as his own father's, the same constant struggle to put food on the family table. He'd been handed down the paternal profession, that of tinsmith, and in the early 1840s scraped a living in Princeton. But at some point in the latter half of the decade Webster took a different path.

When the Federal Census was compiled in 1850, Tim Webster and his wife, Charlotte, were living in New York City. It was a big household, with their four children, one of Tim's brothers (and his wife) and one of his sisters. But Webster could afford it; he was a police officer earning far more than he had as a tinsmith.

By 1853 Webster was a sergeant, and that summer he was one of the officers responsible for policing the huge crowds that descended on the Crystal Palace exhibition in the city's Reservoir Park. When Horace Greeley visited the palace in his capacity as editor of the *New York Tribune* he described how "the thickly-studded drinking shops were flaunting in their intemperate seductions, the various shows of monsters, mountebanks and animals, numerous as on the jubilee days of the Champs Elysees, opened wide their attractions to simple folk [and] little speculators in meats, fruits and drinks had their tables and stalls al fresco. A rush and a whirl of omnibuses, coaches and pedestrians encircled the palace, but amid all this were plainly discernible the excellent provisions of the police to maintain order. The entrances to the palace were kept clear and no disturbance manifested itself through the day."

One of the visitors elbowing his way through the crowds at the Crystal Palace was Allan Pinkerton, there not so much to admire the exhibitions as to recruit detectives to his agency. He noted Webster's calm but firm authority, and asked his friend James Leonard, a captain in the New York Police, for his name along with those of five other policemen whom he judged to be detective material. Most accepted Pinkerton's offer but not Webster, who didn't wish to uproot his family to Chicago. Three years later, however, Webster changed his mind and joined the Pinkerton agency. His family remained in New York until 1858, by which time he'd saved enough money to have a house built for them in Onarga, a community ninety-five miles south of Chicago.

By 1861 Webster was the undisputed star of the agency. When he wasn't on duty, "he was of a quiet, reserved disposition, seldom speaking unless spoken to, and never betraying emotion or excitement under any pressure of circumstances." Pinkerton, with his belief that a man's face was the window to his soul, remarked that Webster "always wore that calm, imperturbable expression denoting a well-balanced mind and a thorough self-control, while the immobile countenance and close-set lips showed that he was naturally as inscrutable as the Sphinx."

But Webster was transformed the moment he went undercover. He was no longer the silent, stoic son of the tinsmith turned soldier; instead he changed into what Pinkerton described as "a genial, jovial, convivial spirit, with an inexhaustible fund of anecdotes and amusing reminiscences, and a wonderful faculty for making everybody like him." The Scot said Webster's ability to play a part amounted "to positive genius, and it was this that forced me to admire the man as sincerely as I prized his services."

Pinkerton believed that the secret to being an effective detective was the operative's talent for acting, and Webster was a natural. Clearly he'd inherited some genes from his paternal grandfather, Samuel, a tinsmith by training but an actor by calling, who had appeared in numerous amateur stage productions throughout the county of Leicester.

Webster's first wartime assignment had been to travel from Cincinnati to Memphis, acting the part of a wealthy Baltimorean, a hater of the Union and a loyal secessionist. In the latter half of May 1861 Webster booked into the Worsham House Hotel on the corner of Front and Jefferson streets, and wove himself into the city's tapestry. Using his real name, he made a particular friend of an overbearing army doctor named Burton, all gold braid and no brain, who showed off his standing in the city by taking Webster on a tour of his camp.

Webster had returned to Cincinnati toward the end of June, around the time Pryce Lewis and Sam Bridgeman set out for Charleston, but on July 23 he departed once more for Tennessee. Riding the train to Memphis the following day, Webster "got in conversation with men from Louisville going to Camp Boone, Tenn., under Col. Tillman. Near the State line in Tennessee there is a camp of 200 men but few of them are armed. At Camp Boone near Clarksville under Col. Tillman there is 1800 men [sic], all Kentuckians not armed. At Clarksville an officer from Fort Dover near the Cumberland River near the Ohio said there was 500 men well armed and 4-32 pounders (iron) to guard the river."

The next day Webster's train was detained at Humboldt so he alighted and "drank and talked with officers from Union City. They said they had 6,000 men nearly all armed and 2-32 pounders (iron)."

In Memphis Webster looked up his old friends. They were delighted to see him. Join us for a night's carousing, they proposed, so that evening Webster went from bar to bar with Colonel Robert Seeley and the military engineer "Bob" Rowley, and "the whole conversation was about how they, the Southern Army, had cleaned out the 'Yankees' at Bulls Run [sic]."

On July 29 Webster was still warming the bar stools of Memphis, along with the faithful Colonel Seeley. They hailed a Confederate captain, stood him a couple of whiskeys, and the officer whispered loudly to Webster "that there was 3,000 men at Randolph [Tennessee,] there was 1,000 men at Fort Clearborn and 35 heavy guns and . . . that the officers that were there were talking about the Manassas battle. They all wanted to rush to Washington and St. Louis."

Webster left Memphis on July 31 with warm demands to hurry back, as well as a pocketful of introductions to trusted men in Richmond, Virginia, where Webster said he intended to stay during the winter; to Charles Stebbins, the proprietor of a china, glass and crockery store; to Colonel William Ritchie; to Colonel J. S. Calvert, state treasurer; and to George Bagby, the editor of the *Southern Literary Messenger* and the associate editor of the *Richmond Whig*.

Webster had also on his person several other letters of a more sensitive nature, letters that were to be delivered to trusted secessionists in Baltimore and that were on no account to fall into Federal hands. The information concerned the Confederate effort, not just the overt activities in the Southern states, but also the covert work being carried out in Maryland.

Webster was now a double agent, embarking upon missions for two sides but betraying only the South. He returned north using the Confederate pass signed by Secretary of War Judah Benjamin, and delivered his hoard to Pinkerton's headquarters in Cincinnati. The letters were painstakingly steamed open with every scrap of information noted, and then they were resealed with equal thoroughness. Webster tucked the letters into his satchel and continued east to Baltimore, where he handed them to their rebel recipients.

Webster was still in Baltimore when Lewis and Bridgeman arrived in early August. Webster was portraying himself as a wealthy gentleman of leisure and to that end Pinkerton had supplied him with the carriage used by Lewis. It had needed a spot of repair work after its flight through the mountains of Kentucky, and a new driver was recruited, but it complemented Webster's role as an affluent Baltimorean. With him was Hattie Lawton, the young female detective who had worked with Webster during the febrile days of February.

She was his "wife," the devoted Mrs. Webster, a woman of few words but great beauty. Webster's rebel friends were impressed; a man with a wife so toothsome should be admired as well as envied.

Before Lewis had the opportunity to discreetly introduce himself to Webster, he and Bridgeman were summoned to Washington, where Pinkerton had recently relocated. As the pair took a train south, Webster remained in Baltimore fortifying the persona of a trusted confidant of the Confederate cause. By the end of August he'd been invited to join the Order of the Sons of Liberty, Baltimore's branch of a secretive organization first founded by American patriots during the Revolutionary War, and whose enemy now was the North.

On August 23 he had a long discussion with a man named Merrill, a gun store owner and a rebel to the core. Webster told him he wanted to buy his stock of three hundred rifles. Not a problem, said Merrill, who added that he could also supply some Bowie knives. From the gun store Webster went to William Allen's Eating Saloon, where Alexander Slayden told him "there was 5 to 6,000 stand of arms in Baltimore . . . and all of our boys had been getting muskets, rifles and pistols since wherever they could buy them." Later Webster, Slayden and a thirty-year-old lumber merchant named Sam Sloan went to the Baltimore racetrack, where they met ten other rebels, and in between gambling and drinking, they discussed in low tones how to seize control. Who would lead an uprising now that George Kane, the chief of police, had been imprisoned for disloyalty to the Union? asked Webster. Slayden told him not to worry; "we have leaders enough. There is Colonel Street, just as good a man as we want and he is ready at any time."

When Webster returned to his hotel he wrote a detailed report of everything he had learned. In the report was a name, that of Daniel Stiltz, a twenty-five-year-old photographic artist. Webster explained that Stiltz was a dedicated secessionist about to visit Federal camps in the Washington area "and take likenesses." He'd even duped a prominent Unionist into writing him a letter of introduction. Webster asked Pinkerton to rush an operative to Baltimore so he could put him on the tail of Stiltz. Webster suggested sending John Scully, a young Irish detective whose energy compensated for his inexperience. The next morning, August 24, Hattie Lawton left Baltimore early to deliver the information to Pinkerton's Washington headquarters. Webster spent the day moping about town, pining for his "wife" who'd been suddenly called away on a family matter.

CHAPTER TWELVE

"The Most Persuasive Woman That Was Ever Known in Washington"

O N WHAT WAS CALLED "BLACK MONDAY," the North woke to learn that the day before, Sunday, July 21, its troops had been smashed at Bull Run. "We are utterly and disgracefully routed, beaten, whipped," asserted Horace Greeley, editor of the *New York Tribune*. A few days later he wrote to Abraham Lincoln, inquiring if perhaps "it is best for the country and for mankind that we make peace with the rebels." But by the time Greeley sent his letter the president had already implemented a new policy, one which was diametrically opposed to that suggested by the newspaper editor

Bull Run was a painful blow for the North, but Lincoln used it as a chance to administer some stringent medicine. It would no longer be a "Ninety-Day war," as the more martial of the Union newspapers had glibly prophesized. The rebels had proved themselves worthy opponents, so on Black Monday Lincoln authorized the recruitment of half a million men, not for three months, which had been the original terms of enlistment back in April, but for three years. On July 25 Lincoln agreed to a demand to draft a further half million men.

To command them, Lincoln ordered George McClellan to hand over the army in western Virginia to General Rosecrans and hurry to Washington. He arrived on July 26 and was told to turn the willing volunteers into the Army of the Potomac. McClellan soon demonstrated that his military skill was on the training ground, not the battleground, and that he was as punctilious in raising an army as he had been pusillanimous in fighting a battle.

The tens of thousands of recruits learning to become soldiers admired their leader and called him "Little Mac." Others were not so well disposed toward McClellan, notably the officers who were purged from the new army on account of their incompetence or inefficiency. There was also a crackdown on debauchery, led by the new provost marshal, Colonel Andrew Porter, who arrested scores of soldiers for drinking and fighting.

McClellan bolstered Washington's defenses against any rebel attempt to attack the city; then he turned his attention to the enemy within. Before his arrival in the capital McClellan had written to Pinkerton informing him that in future he was to report to General Rosecrans. However, McClellan added, Pinkerton should "be prepared to hear from me that I need your services elsewhere." Sure enough, once he was established in Washington McClellan summoned Pinkerton and instructed him to set about "procuring from all possible sources, information regarding the strength, positions and movements of the enemy. All spies, 'contrabands,' deserters, refugees and prisoners of war, coming into our lines from the front, were to be carefully examined."

Pinkerton accepted the challenge with brio, replying to McClellan's instruction with an overview of the strategy he planned to adopt. At the same time, he warned the general that there must be no political or military interference, regardless of what his investigations revealed. It was, he continued, his belief "that the rebels have spies who are in the employment of this government, or who possess facilities for acquiring information from the civil and military authorities . . . and that this information is imparted to others, and transmitted within a very short time to the rebel government. Many of the parties thus leagued with the enemy are said to be persons of wealth and position."

When Pinkerton warned McClellan that certain aspects of his work might be somewhat distasteful, he had someone particular in mind. Her name was Mrs. Rose O'Neale Greenhow.

Rose Greenhow was not an agreeable woman. Conceited, vain, petulant, manipulative, hypocritical, dishonest and a shameless bigot, Greenhow nevertheless had one quality that outshone all her myriad defects: intoxicating beauty. Her looks simply overpowered most men. Though she was scorned by her female rivals in Washington's antebellum society—they knew her for what she was, an unsophisticated country girl whose ruthless scheming had snared a rich and influential husband—Greenhow won male admirers with every artful tilt of her gorgeous head.

Greenhow's husband had been killed in an accident in 1854 while working in San Francisco, a tragedy that was attributed to ongoing street repairs. Greenhow received ten thousand dollars in compensation, and Congress saw fit to award her a further forty-two thousand dollars as her husband had been engaged in government business at the time of his death. Such largesse was unusual, but Rose Greenhow's links to Washington's political elite were unusual. Her niece was the wife of Illinois senator Stephen Douglas, and she had been a good friend of John Calhoun during his illustrious political career.

Greenhow used the money to buy a spacious, two-story house at 398 Sixteenth Street West, on the corner of K Street. With all but one of Greenhow's daughters grown-up and independent, she had time to cultivate her standing within Washington society. Such was "her love of notoriety and dread of sinking back into her early obscurity" that her dinner parties became legendary. Rarely was there a dance or a ball without the bewitching presence of the widowed Rose. Stephen Mallory, a Florida senator, marveled at the way "she hunted man with that resistless zeal and unfailing instinct." By the late 1850s it was widely rumored that her friendship with President Andrew Buchanan, a bachelor, had moved from the platonic to the carnal, and in 1860 tongues began to wag that Greenhow and Henry Wilson, a married Massachusetts senator, were engaged in an improper relationship.

Greenhow was now in her midforties, but she still possessed the power to turn men's heads. She had a voluptuous body, commented one man, with "black eyes, an olive complexion, firm teeth, and small hands and feet. Her carriage was graceful and dignified, her enunciation too distinct to be natural, and her manners bordering on the theatrical." Despite her pretentious mannerisms, Greenhow found few men strong enough to resist her charms, although one who did—barely—was Colonel Erasmus Darwin Keyes, military secretary to Major General Winfield Scott, chief of the Union army. At a dinner party shortly after the outbreak of war,

Keyes found himself sitting next to the shimmering Greenhow. Later he recalled how "after expiating on the injustice of the North, [she] tried to persuade me not to take part in the war." A flushed Keyes managed to extricate himself but confessed Greenhow was "the most persuasive woman that was ever known in Washington."

Greenhow never bothered to conceal her contempt for the North, nor her disdain for Abraham Lincoln, a man she disparaged as a "beanpole." At a dinner party in the autumn of 1860 she had told her guests, among them Senator William Seward and Congressman Charles Adams, that John Brown "was a traitor and met a traitor's doom." But she refused to follow many of her secessionist-supporting friends south when war broke out, preferring instead to remain in Washington and let the Confederacy come to her. It did, in the handsome guise of Captain Thomas Jordan, erstwhile quartermaster of the U.S. Army, who was on the brink of deserting to the rebel cause. Before he fled Washington, however, Jordan visited Rose and, in between alleged amorous encounters in Greenhow's boudoir, asked if she would be prepared to run a network of Confederate spies.

Greenhow readily agreed and began to learn the craftwork of a spy. Jordan taught her a cipher code and how to conceal messages; between them they recruited other rebels to the network, and on May 21 Jordan reckoned her to be ready. He left Washington and headed to the Confederate camp at Manassas Junction, thirty miles south of the capital.

Six weeks later, on July 9, Greenhow sent a coded message to the Confederates. It was concealed in the chignon hair of sixteen-year-old Bettie Duval, one of Greenhow's couriers, and when decoded it read: "McDowell has certainly been ordered to advance on the sixteenth. ROG." It was confirmation that Brigadier General Irvin McDowell planned to lead his Union troops south in one week's time to attack the rebels at Manassas, a decision that the general had made a fortnight earlier.

That at least was how Greenhow remembered it in her memoirs, published a couple of years later, but self-aggrandizement came as naturally to Greenhow as flirting. Without doubt Greenhow did send a message to General Pierre Beauregard at the headquarters of the Confederate Army of the Potomac warning him that the Union army was about to march south, but no evidence exists to validate her claim that she predicted the exact date. Indeed, Beauregard later said of Manassas that while he had been informed of the Federal army's main purpose, he knew nothing of their plans, confirmation that the Confederates knew an attack was imminent but they didn't know when.

Greenhow sent another message on July 16, this one giving the route McDowell's army would take, as well as its strength. Fifty-five thousand men were marching south, according to Greenhow, a wildly inaccurate overestimation. McDowell had thirty thousand men. When Beauregard received the message late on July 16, he didn't telegraph Richmond pleading for immediate reinforcements; instead he waited for the reports from his scouts who earlier in the day had tracked the progress of the Union vanguard. Only on the next day, July 17, did Beauregard cable Richmond to ask for more men, and that wasn't because of Greenhow's message; it was because General Milledge Bonham had begun to pull back from Fairfax as the Union army got ever closer.

Nonetheless a few days after the Battle of Manassas, Greenhow received a coded message from Captain Jordan: "Our President and our General direct me to thank you. We rely upon you for further information. The Confederacy owes you a debt. Jordan, Adjutant-General."

The praise was excessive, though Greenhow did deserve some of it for her message of July 9, warning of an impending attack, had galvanized Beauregard into action after weeks of frustrating inactivity. For that she merited gratitude.

Greenhow was euphoric at the presidential endorsement. She felt she was where she liked to be—the center of attention, a celebrity who had earned the thanks of the president. She became addicted to her new role, sending nearly a dozen messages in the next month and recruiting more informers to her spy ring. But Greenhow was becoming indiscreet—or perhaps she believed herself, with all her connections, untouchable. Hubris replaced caution, and by the second half of August the attention came not from her admirers but from her enemies.

Allan Pinkerton heard the name Rose Greenhow from Thomas A. Scott, assistant secretary of war, who had summoned the detective to his office. Pinkerton was told that her "movements had excited suspicion and . . . it was believed [she] was engaged in corresponding with the rebel authorities and furnishing them with much valuable information." Once Pinkerton had his orders he returned to his headquarters on E Street, near the post office, and informed three of his most discreet men that he had a mission for them. The men were William Scott, Pryce Lewis and Sam Bridgeman.

Lewis and Bridgeman had only been in Washington a few days, but in that short space of time Lewis had seen how Pinkerton's "natural shrewdness, experience and patriotic zeal made him wholly fitted" for his role of spy catcher. Lewis himself was more committed now to military espionage. There had been a time in Jackson when he'd considered quitting the agency and enlisting in the Northern army, a reaction provoked by the feeling he was loafing while others were fighting. But his mission to Charleston had "induced me to remain in a service which I now regarded not inferior to the military service in importance to the country."

Greenhow claimed later that she knew she had been under surveillance for several weeks, and "this was a subject of amusement to me." In fact she had no idea. Pinkerton moved swiftly to bring an end to a woman he viewed as a Southern succubus. A few hours after his meeting with Scott, Pinkerton and his three men were standing in the shadows opposite the Greenhow residence, their collars turned up against the driving rain as they observed a "two-storey and basement brick building, the parlors of which were elevated several feet above the ground, and [the] entrance was obtained by ascending a flight of stairs in the center."*

Pinkerton crept up to the house for a closer look while Lewis and his accomplices "remained a little distance across the street and watched his movements as best we could in the feeble light of the street lamps." For a few moments Pinkerton sheltered behind a large tree in front of the house, then he tiptoed forward and jumped noiselessly from the sidewalk to the outside of the basement. He skirted the house, ducking under the stoop upon which were the dozen or so steps that led to the front door, but found the windows were closed and there was no sign of life inside the house.

Pinkerton returned to his men and told them it appeared Mrs. Greenhow wasn't at home. Nevertheless they decided to hang around a while longer. They were now "drenched to the skin," but the storm had

---

* A sketch of the house published in *Frank Leslie's Illustrated Newspaper* on September 14, 1861, depicted Greenhow's house with a basement and three stories.

at least emptied the streets of passersby. Suddenly they saw one of the ground-floor windows at the side of the house edged in light. Pinkerton and Scott stole forward, while Lewis and Bridgeman were told to "stand under a tree and to watch and notify [Pinkerton] if any one left the house."

In a few minutes they heard the brisk click of footsteps approaching the house. Lewis and Bridgeman shrank behind the thick trunk of the tree and watched a man in military uniform bound up the steps and disappear inside the house. Lewis padded silently through the rain and told Pinkerton, who climbed onto the shoulders of Scott and peered through the shuttered window. He got a glimpse of the uniform, just a fleeting glimpse, but enough to identify its wearer as a Union captain.

Sheltering under the stoop of the house, Pinkerton whispered what they would do when the captain reemerged: he and Scott would tail him, while Lewis and Bridgeman resumed their position by the tree. They heard the front door open an hour later, followed by farewell words and "something that sounded very much like a kiss." The man descended the steps and walked off along the sidewalk. Pinkerton and Scott climbed up from their hiding place and set off in pursuit.

Lewis and Bridgeman remained behind the tree for the rest of the night, cursing the thick drops of rain that fell from the leaves onto their heads. When Lewis finally got to bed he slept until after lunch, arriving at Pinkerton's office in the early afternoon. The "Old Man," as they called the boss, beckoned him into his office and regaled Lewis with an account of what had unfolded after they'd set off after the officer.

Pinkerton and Scott had tracked him as far as Pennsylvania Avenue and Fifteenth Street. They'd seen him glance back once or twice, but thought nothing of it, until the moment the man disappeared into a doorway. They followed him but were suddenly confronted by four armed soldiers. It transpired that Greenhow's visitor was Captain John Elwood, the officer in charge of a provost marshal station. Pinkerton could see the funny side now, though he hadn't a few hours earlier when he and Scott sat shivering in a cell. Fortunately, said Pinkerton, he contrived to have a note sent to Assistant Secretary of War Scott, who authorized their release.

Pinkerton would like to have arrested Elwood, but first he needed ironclad proof of treachery. At the moment the officer had committed no crime, other than to visit the house of a known Southern sympathizer.

But if enjoying the charms of Rose Greenhow was an arrestable offense, the prisons of Washington would be full to bursting with officers and dignitaries. What Pinkerton did have, however, was suspicion enough to order a search of the Greenhow residence.

Two days later, on Friday, August 23, Greenhow was relaxing in her parlor after a promenade with a "distinguished member of the diplomatic corps" when the doorbell rang. A servant opened the door, and Pinkerton and William Scott barged in. Pryce Lewis followed a few seconds later and caught sight of "a beautiful woman . . . a brunette richly dressed." Greenhow demanded to see a warrant. Pinkerton shook his head and sneered that he had "verbal authority from the War and State Departments" and that was all he needed.

Other detectives now arrived, and Pinkerton ordered them to search every room of the house. Then he turned to Lewis and told him "to take charge of this lady, detain her in the parlor." Lewis motioned for Greenhow to resume her place in the parlor. She did as she was told "for I knew that the fate of some of the best and bravest belonging to our cause hung upon my own coolness and courage."

While Pinkerton and his detectives rummaged indelicately through Greenhow's possessions, Lewis and the lady of the house sat in the parlor and "conversed on impersonal subjects." He could see that she "was evidently taken by surprise though . . . she strove to hide any signs of excitement." In Greenhow's version of events, however, she bristled with defiance, even though there were "stern eyes fixed upon my face." At first Greenhow was "careless and sarcastic and, I know, tantalizing in the extreme" in her conversation with Lewis. Then she changed tack and "resolved to test the truth of the old saying that the devil is no match for a clever woman." Lewis had all but given up on trying to be civil to Greenhow when "she asked in such a winning way if she could go upstairs for a few minutes." Yes, replied Lewis, though he added, "it was my imperative duty to go with her." With a swish of her skirt, Greenhow flounced out of the parlor and climbed the stairs, with Lewis close behind. Once inside a "large, well-lighted room, she went directly to the mantelpiece [and] snatched a revolver from it." Greenhow wheeled around, the gun pointing at Lewis and her eyes flaming with contempt: "If I had known who you were when you came in," she snickered, "I would have shot you dead!"

Lewis stood before the barrel of the gun, silent and expressionless, his eyes fixed on Greenhow. Then he smiled and politely remarked that "the revolver had to be cocked before it would go off." One of Pinkerton's men, Paul Dennis, appeared in the room and disarmed Greenhow without a fuss. It was clear to Lewis that "she was not so desperate as she talked."

By the time the search was over, Pinkerton had unearthed a treasure trove of incriminating information, as well as letters of a more salacious hue. Among the evidence that damned Greenhow as a spy were reams of notes about the Union fortifications in and around Washington, copies of orders issued by the War Department and messages in cipher, some of which were in a stove waiting to be burned. There were names, too, lots of names, of men and women in thrall to Greenhow, either because they believed in the righteous cause of the Confederacy or because they believed her to be a paramour par excellence.

Among those implicated in the network of spies were Colonel Thompson, a lawyer; a society dentist named Dr. Van Camp; William T. Smithson, a banker; and a former clerk of the Department of the Interior named George Donellan.

Pinkerton left to report to the War Department, having instructed his men to remain inside the house and prevent anyone from leaving. In addition, they were to arrest all visitors to the residence. Lewis sat and listened as Greenhow "compared herself to Marie Antoinette." At other times she cast herself as Mary, Queen of Scots. For hours they were subjected to Greenhow's hauteur; she accused them of lacking personal hygiene; she upbraided them for sitting in shirtsleeves at her kitchen table; she accused them of being slaves of Lincoln, "the Abolition despot."

Lewis answered back, to the surprise of Greenhow, who wasn't used to male impertinence. Later she claimed that her guards had been all brutes—and drunken ones at that—but "two of the most insolent of these men [were] an Englishman named Lewis, and an Irishman named [John] Scully." Doubtless, Lewis and Greenhow did exchange strong words, but Greenhow had a habit of exaggeration, or sometimes plain mendacity. She described Allan Pinkerton, the dourest of dour Scots, as "a German Jew, and possessed [of] all the national instincts of his race."

In the days that followed, Pinkerton's men pulled in the people implicated in the spy network. The day after Greenhow's arrest, it was the turn of Eugenia Phillips, "a beautiful and clever Jewess," and her husband, Philip Phillips, a former Alabaman congressman, who lived on I Street between Seventeenth and Eighteenth. Six days later Mr. Phillips was released without charge, but his wife, his sister-in-law, Martha Levy, and his two grown-up daughters, Fannie and Caroline, were removed to the house on the corner of K Street and Sixteenth Street West.

The women were confined in various rooms throughout the house. Initially they amused themselves by singing rebel songs about the imminent arrival in Washington of General Beauregard and his men or by scrawling defiant messages on the wall. But soon their bravado waned in the monotony of captivity, and their spirits "sunk down into a quiet gloom." Eugenia Phillips tried to rally her daughters, urging them to be strong so they could "live to plague mankind a little more . . . in the hope of seeing a few of these detectives hung."

Downstairs Pryce Lewis was enduring his own gloom as a guard of Fort Greenhow. This was not the sort of war he had envisioned, particularly after the adventure of Charleston. He was daily in "a war of words" with the prisoners, and one evening "had been severely scolded for lighting and using the gas in the parlor to read by." There had been screams and stamps, but Lewis had "insisted upon our privileges" and continued his book.

On the evening of Saturday, September 7, Lewis was on guard when there was a knock at the front door. Two distinguished-looking gentlemen were outside, one of whom "presented a pass signed by Secretary of War [Simon] Cameron," while the other explained they had come to see Rose Greenhow and Eugenia Phillips. Without bothering to examine the pass, Lewis stepped aside and allowed the men upstairs.

The men were Colonel Thomas Key, an aide-de-camp to General McClellan, and Edwin Stanton, the attorney general during the Buchanan administration and now a legal adviser working for Simon Cameron. (Stanton replaced Simon Cameron as secretary of war on January 15, 1862.) Stanton knew Greenhow and Phillips, and had been asked to check on their condition by the latter's husband.

Stanton greeted Greenhow with a quip, wondering what she had done to "bring down the wrath of the abolitionists on your head?" Greenhow didn't find it funny. She urged him to help free them from this intolerable predicament, but Stanton gave only a vague promise to see what he could do. While the colonel continued to talk to the women, Stanton went downstairs and accused Lewis of mistreating his prisoners

Lewis lowered his book and eyed the "stout, long-whiskered man with an air of authority." Stanton pressed his point, saying he found it "very strange that the government employ such men to guard a lady's house."

Lewis's temper snapped at the "cool insolence" of the man before him, and he demanded to see again Stanton's pass. Stanton fished it from his pocket and handed it to Lewis, who examined the pass and exclaimed that it gave neither him nor his colleague authorization to see Greenhow. Lewis ordered Stanton and Colonel Key to leave the house, and as the former departed he promised vengeance. A few days later Lewis was told by Pinkerton that Stanton had "lodged a complaint against me in the war department." But don't worry, Pinkerton added, the charge had been dismissed.*

---

* Mrs. Phillips and her daughters were released on September 18, thanks to Stanton's intervention, but they were banished from Washington. A few months later Eugenia Phillips was arrested in New Orleans (then in Federal hands) for laughing as a Union army funeral procession passed by. As a result she spent several months in a prison ship in the Gulf of Mexico.

CHAPTER THIRTEEN

"You'll Have to Be Mighty Careful Now, or You'll Be Arrested"

OVER THE ENSUING WEEKS those newspapers loyal to the North poked fun at Rose Greenhow and her ilk. The *New York Times* christened her home "Hotel Greenhow" and *Harper's Weekly* ran several cartoons in its edition of October 12 titled "How to Deal with Female Traitors." One illustration depicted a row of hats arrayed in front of a forlorn woman trapped behind bars; the caption beneath ran: "Let them see but not touch all the latest novelties in hats." Another showed a jailor reading a newspaper in front of a prison door with the accompanying caption: "Have the fashionable intelligence read in their hearing to their intense aggravation."

Not all papers adopted the same mocking tone. The *Baltimore Exchange* thought the affair shameful and wondered what a founding father would have said if one day he had known that "virtuous, refined, pureminded women, would be arrested, searched, shipped, shut up as prisoners in the custody of men, attended as prisoners by armed men, precisely as if they were men themselves."

Allan Pinkerton was equally indignant, although for different reasons. Rose Greenhow had been using her fragrant influence around Washington in an attempt to win her freedom, and Pinkerton feared she might soon be released. In November he dispatched a report to his immediate superior, Brigadier General Andrew Porter, Washington's provost marshal, warning him against such a move. Not only had the "untiring energies of this very remarkable woman" already inflicted grievous damage on the Federal army, but there was nothing in her recent behavior to suggest she was reformed. Pinkerton was adamant that if released she would continue to pose a serious threat because she was an utterly "unscrupulous" woman. He concluded by reminding Porter that "nothing has been too sacred for her appropriation . . . she made use of whoever and whatever she could as mediums to carry into effect her unholy purposes. She has used her almost irresistible seductive powers to win to her aid persons who were holding responsible places of honor."

Pinkerton had been correct in his assessment of Rose Greenhow. She continued to slip messages to her handler, Thomas Jordan, throughout her confinement, usually bribing one of the soldiers who had replaced Pinkerton's men as her sentinels. Unbeknownst to Greenhow, however, the soldiers took the bribes but also took the messages to Pinkerton, who was keen to let Greenhow believe she was still a successful spy. Greenhow liked to boast that "the devil is no match for a clever woman" but nor was he a match for a canny Scot.

By the winter of 1861 Tim Webster was known as "Captain Webster," considered to be one of the Confederacy's most cherished spies, a man entrusted even with the letters of Judah Benjamin, the secretary of war. In Richmond Webster stayed at the Spottswood Hotel, one the city's treasures, and only after he'd been lavishly wined and dined was he allowed to return North with his satchel full of letters. Webster charged $1.50 a letter—the same in the other direction—and on a good run he might have three hundred to deliver to Baltimore. Usually he made two round-trips a month, sometimes going via Fredericksburg, at other times crossing Chesapeake Bay in a sailboat between Gloucester Point and Cape Charles on Virginia's eastern shore. When he wasn't carrying letters, Webster continued to scheme rebellion in Maryland with the Order of the Sons of Liberty. It was a secretive organization, one had to be invited to join, but its membership was exclusive: Webster got to know Frank Key Howard, one of the editors of the *Baltimore Exchange*, the paper that had so stridently denounced the treatment meted out to Rose Greenhow; Thomas Hall, editor of the *South*; and Thomas Parkin Scott, a lawyer and author of *The Crisis*, a tract on the U.S. Constitution, published the previous year.

The order met infrequently and always late at night, somewhere ordinary and unobtrusive. Pinkerton told Webster to attend each meeting and report back to him. He in turn liaised with Simon Cameron, the secretary of war. In the second week of September Cameron told Pinkerton he wanted the Order of the Sons of Liberty arraigned. Webster provided details of the next meeting, and shortly before midnight on Wednesday, September 11, Pinkerton and a team of his detectives, augmented by a squad of Fourth cavalry under the command of a Lieutenant Wilson, burst in on the Sons of Liberty. Howard was arrested, so too Hall, and Henry May and Teackle Wallis and half a dozen others. Webster managed to "escape."

He took off into Virginia, telling his secessionist friends that he was now a wanted man. In fact Webster used the time to make detailed notes of Confederate troop strengths, including those at Manassas and Centreville. He was as methodical as ever, observing such details as the make of rifles, the price of corn by the bushel and the prevalence of disease. He estimated that General Joseph Johnston's army in the Shenandoah Valley comprised 104 regiments; that the regimental strength of General John Magruder's Army of the Peninsula was twenty-nine, and that Richmond was defended by six regiments.*

It was a quick turnaround for Webster, who was instructed to return to Baltimore and mingle once more with his rebel friends. He booked into his old room at Miller's Hotel and reestablished contact with John Earl, the establishment's secessionist bartender. Earl was thrilled to see Webster again; so too was William Hart, another rebel who had evaded capture. Sam Sloan, a lumber merchant, met Webster for a drink at Miller's and warned him, "You'll have to be mighty careful now, or you'll be arrested yet."

Webster was soon headed back to Richmond via Fredericksburg. It

---

* Subsequent research showed that in fact Johnston had eighty-seven regiments at his disposal, Magruder twenty and Richmond could call upon four regiments. Webster's computations were among the more accurate of Pinkerton's spies. After the war both McClellan and Pinkerton were accused of wildly overestimating the enemy strength. Pinkerton received much of the opprobrium and was accused of rank incompetence, but others believed that McClellan was happy to use the inflated estimates as a means of avoiding a battle.

was probably in the bar of the Spottswood Hotel that he read in the November 21 edition of the *New York Times* that the previous morning detectives had descended on Miller's Hotel, "seizing the whole establishment and all its contents . . . a number of letters were seized but have not yet been examined. Two parties, Wm. Hart and John Earl, were arrested. The nature of the evidence against them is not known."

Papers such as the *Times* and *Chicago Tribune* were devoured by Richmond's citizens; not because they disbelieved what their own papers told them, but because the antirebel views propagated in their pages amused and angered in equal measure. There was another reason, however, to scan the Yankee papers, as the forty-one-year-old John Beauchamp Jones had noted in his diary of November 8. "The Northern press bears testimony of the fact that the spies in our midst are still at work."

Before the war Jones had edited the Philadelphia-based *Southern Monitor*, a pro-slavery newspaper whose offices had been ransacked following events at Fort Sumter. Jones fled to Richmond and secured a position as clerk to LeRoy Pope Walker, secretary of war for the Confederacy. When Walker was replaced by Judah Benjamin in September, Jones remained in his post, and ever since he had been complaining to his diary about his new master's generosity in issuing passports. "I have declared my purpose to sign no more for the Secretary without his official order," wrote Jones on November 8, the same day he alluded to the spies operating in Richmond. On November 17 Jones damned the letter carriers operating from the city, confiding to his diary that "it is my belief that they render as much service to the enemy as to us; and they certainly do obtain passports on the other side."

On December 11 Jones related an incident that had occurred in his office that day: "Several of Gen. [John] Winder's [the provost marshal general of Richmond] detectives came to me with a man named Webster, who, it appears, has been going between Richmond and Baltimore, conveying letters, money, etc. I refused him a passport. He said he could get it from the Secretary himself, but that it was sometimes difficult in gaining access to him. I told him to get it, then; I would give him none."

The unbending pedantry of a bureaucrat was no obstacle to Tim Webster. Sidestepping Jones, he obtained a passport from Benjamin and returned the 130 miles to Washington, where he handed to Pinkerton an important package that had come into his possession. He was back in

Richmond at the end of December, this time with Hattie Lawton posing as his "wife," the pair of them checking into the Spottswood Hotel on the southeast corner of Eighth and Main streets.

The five-story hotel was one of Richmond's most luxurious; room 83 was where Jefferson Davis and his wife, Varina, had stayed when the Confederate government relocated from Montgomery. In the early summer of 1861, before the Davises moved into the presidential mansion on Clay Street, the Spottswood became what one woman described as a "miniature world . . . the hum of conversation, the sound of careless, happy laughter, the music of a band playing outside." The fashionable ladies sat in the drawing room and talked of anything but the war, while beneath them, in the hotel basement, "brothers, husbands, sons, and sweethearts of most of them were learning the duties of artillerymen in the smart new corps, the Richmond Howitzers." Many of the regiment's officers based themselves in the hotel, relaxing with a large whiskey and a game of billiards whenever they were off-duty.

When Tim Webster walked into the hotel lobby he was warmly greeted by Theodore Hoenniger, who, in the opinion of the *Richmond Whig*, was "perhaps the youngest landlord of a large hotel in the world." Hoenniger was a New Yorker, still in his early twenties, but possessed of "unobtrusive manners and [a] genial disposition." He complimented Mrs. Webster on how well she looked and arranged for a porter to show the couple to their room.

Webster woke the next morning with a raging fever and an aching body. Hoenniger sent for a doctor, who diagnosed inflammatory rheumatism and told the patient to remain tucked up in bed. When the doctor had gone, Webster speculated to Hattie Lawton that the rheumatism was a consequence of what happened earlier in the month. He told her about his journey from Washington to Virginia, and of how, as usual, he had contacted John Moore, the rebel landlord of a small hotel in Leonardtown, Maryland. Webster stayed one night at the hotel, and the next day Moore had arranged for a boatman to ferry the spy across the Potomac. On this occasion, however, there were other passengers, the wives and children of two Confederate officers who were leaving Washington to join their husbands in Richmond.

It was a rough crossing, and by the time they reached the safehouse on the other side of the Potomac they were cold, wet and hungry. Their host fed them, and then the women and children bedded down in one room, while Webster spread his blanket upon the stone floor of the kitchen. As he was removing his boots Webster "noticed, lying upon the floor, a short distance from him, a small packet wrapped in oiled-cloth and tied with red tape." Webster removed the tape with a surgeon's precision and saw that "the contents of the bundle were complete maps of the country surrounding Washington, with a correct statement of the number and location of the Federal troops." He slipped the packet inside his coat until he returned to Washington a week later. How unfortunate, Webster told Lawton with a weak grin, that during his trip south he had picked up not only a vital packet but an attack of rheumatism. Such were the vagaries of war.

As Webster lay in his sickbed, the man responsible for the map, "James Howard, a native of the south and . . . a clerk in the Provost-Marshal's office," was arrested after his boss, Brigadier General Porter, recognized his handwriting on the maps. At first Howard denied Pinkerton's accusation that he was anything but a loyal Unionist, but soon he "confessed his treason and implicated several others in the conspiracy."

Webster was back on his feet by the second week of January. Though not fully recovered, he wished to fulfill a long-standing arrangement to travel to Nashville, Tennessee, with a government contractor, a good friend of his named William Campbell, who wished for some agreeable company on the trip. They were gone more than a week, and while Campbell returned having purchased a large quantity of leather, Webster brought back detailed observations of the Confederate army.

Stopping in Richmond just long enough to take delivery of another satchel of letters, Webster headed north and handed to Pinkerton his report of the trip to Tennessee. It was a masterpiece of espionage. Webster described the cavalry he had seen at Abingdon, Virginia, as "armed principally with breech-loading rifles, made in Baltimore, also each with Colt revolvers, Navy size, and several with heavy, large shot guns for buckshot, each having sabers. Artillery 2-6 pounders, iron, one smooth." Webster also related a conversation with a gloomy rebel officer in Knoxville, who "did not believe there were 10 good soldiers" in the town and predicted an easy victory should Union forces choose to attack. In Nashville itself, reported Webster, there are "2 regts. of Infantry, one stationed on Fair Ground, about one mile S.E. of Nashville; the other stationed across

Cumberland over from Nashville, at a short distance from the river; all comfortably but coarsely dressed; all armed with percussion muskets."

The final nugget of information had been mined in Bowling Green, Kentucky, from the mouth of Major George Harris, brother of Isham, the Tennessee governor. Harris told Webster that he couldn't wait until May, when his twelve-month term of enlistment expired. He was "getting tired of the war, especially of its inactivity," and he longed for the day he would be back in the arms of his wife. Harris then began to whine about the soldier's life, telling Webster to take a look at the men's shabby uniforms, their meager rations and their ancient muskets. Little wonder, he added, that the majority of soldiers in the First Arkansas Regiment "would refuse to serve beyond the termination of their enlistment."

Webster didn't linger in Washington; he stayed just long enough to purchase a few items that had been requested by his friends in the South, goods that were becoming scarce in Richmond. Pinkerton told him about the arrest of James Howard, and Webster in return mentioned his attack of rheumatism. He was fine now, he reassured Pinkerton, "impatient to be actively employed once more."

In Richmond Webster was reunited with Hattie Lawton, who had just returned from a mission to Leonardtown, where she "cultivated the acquaintance of the most important people in that locality." They arrived at the Spottswood Hotel at the end of January, but Theodore Hoenniger regretfully informed them that on this occasion it was full; he could, however, recommend the Monumental Hotel on the corner of Grace and Ninth streets.

The Websters checked into the less salubrious Monumental and soon encountered Samuel McCubbin, "a gentleman of about thirty-six, stout and squarely built . . . [of] dark complexion and open countenance." He knocked on the Websters' door, and before long they were catching up on news and exchanging gossip. McCubbin casually mentioned that he too was staying in the Monumental, lately transformed into the temporary office of the city's second auditor. Webster was puzzled. He knew McCubbin well and had come to like the former brush maker from Baltimore, but wondered why it was that the chief of the Confederate Military Police had booked a room adjacent to his own.

CHAPTER FOURTEEN

"It Would Be Folly for Me to Go to Richmond"

THE NEW YEAR BROUGHT NO RELIEF to the tedium felt by Pryce Lewis. It was more of the same repetitive, unexciting, rather unsavory work that he had been obliged to undertake in the autumn of 1861.

For several weeks he had tailed Captain John Elwood, the officer who had visited Rose Greenhow's house on that stormy August night. Lewis, more adroit at surveillance work than Pinkerton, had shadowed Elwood unchallenged and "discovered in his conduct several suspicious circumstances." Lewis didn't think there was enough evidence "to justify harsh measures [against Elwood], but Pinkerton was vindictive and ordered his arrest."*

Another task given to Lewis was to pay a visit to I Street and investigate the loyalties of Elizabeth Morton and her two sons and two daughters. Mrs. Morton was the well-to-do wife of Jackson, a former senator of Florida and one of the state's largest slaveholders.

It had been a long time since Elizabeth and her husband shared the

---

* Captain John Elwood was arrested and imprisoned in the Old Capitol Prison. Denied a trial and interrogated relentlessly, Elwood sank into depression and cut his throat with a penknife on December 3, 1862.

marital bed. Jackson preferred the intimacy of his female slaves, and his fathering of several children had prompted Mrs. Morton to leave the family estate ("Mortonia") in Santa Rosa County, Florida, and take up residence in Washington.

Lewis and three other Pinkerton operatives arrived at the house and told Mrs. Morton their "orders were to gather all letters within a certain date and transfer them to the provost marshal's office." One pair searched upstairs; the other scoured the ground floor. Lewis's partner was John Scully, the twenty-one-year-old Irishman who had recently returned from a brief trip with Tim Webster. For four days they sifted through the Mortons' correspondence, but there was nothing incriminating, just a few letters expressing solidarity with the Confederate cause.

Frustrated by the absence of treacherous material, the provost marshal told the detectives to turn the place upside down; he wanted proof. Lewis reluctantly informed the Mortons of his orders, which provoked "the great disgust of the ladies."

Lewis apologized, and Mrs. Morton accepted he was only following instructions. Unlike Rose Greenhow, Elizabeth Morton had innate polish. Forced to endure the indignity of strangers rifling through her house, she was nonetheless grace personified and "provided [Lewis] occasionally with refreshments." The sons were equally unflappable, and Lewis, once again, found himself enjoying the impeccable manners of the Southern gentlemen. The eldest son, Chase, liked to smoke, so he and Lewis often sat "passing the time of day" with a cigar or two.

The search turned up nothing, as the Mortons had known it would all along. From the start they had had nothing to hide, other than the shame visited on them by their father. Pryce Lewis had no idea of the family estrangement, but he must have found it odd that when the Mortons were eventually allowed to leave Washington, escorted to the station by John Scully, they announced their intention to head not to Florida but to Richmond.

By the beginning of February 1862 Lewis had just about reached the end of his tether. The previous month he had been reduced to a glorified chaperone, escorting an army doctor, Lieutenant Garradieu, to Baltimore, where he was to be exchanged for a Union prisoner. He'd felt emasculated in the soldiers' presence, a shirker among fighters, and decided it was time to confront Pinkerton and inform him that if he wasn't put to better use as a spy he would "take a musket, join the army and go to the front."

When Lewis arrived in the capital he found a message instructing him to attend a private interview with Pinkerton. The brevity of the order indicated it was something out of the ordinary. Upon entering Pinkerton's office, Lewis was told to take a seat and then asked if he had any objections to going to Richmond. Lewis replied that he did, so Pinkerton asked to hear them. "It would be folly for me to go to Richmond under any circumstances," Lewis told him and reminded his boss that with all the people he had arrested who had subsequently gone through the lines, "I believe I am better known in Richmond as a detective—though I have never been there—than I am in Washington."

Pinkerton disagreed, so Lewis listed some of the people now living in the South who knew his real identity; they included "Mrs. Phillips and Mrs. Levy . . . Mrs. Morton and her family, and Lieutenant Dr. Garradieu, who has only just gone through."

Don't worry about them, said Pinkerton, with a casual flick of his hand, explaining that "Mrs. Phillips and Mrs. Levy were in New Orleans, that Mrs. Morton and family had gone to Florida, and that Lieutenant Dr. Garradieu had gone to Charleston [South Carolina]."

Lewis wasn't convinced, but Pinkerton tetchily asked his operative to trust him for, after all, "it would be folly for me to ask you to go to Richmond if there were people there who would know you." Lewis asked what it was in Richmond that was of such pressing importance, and Pinkerton replied that he wanted to find out what had happened to Timothy Webster. He believed him to be lying sick in Richmond, but perhaps, just perhaps, he had been arrested.

The name Webster changed everything for Lewis. Not only did he know him to be "the most important spy in our service," but he was also, by all accounts, a decent fellow.

Lewis told Pinkerton he needed time to think. He was given until the following Sunday, February 16, to reach a decision.

When Lewis arrived on that date at the agency's headquarters on 288 I Street, he was shown into the parlor, where he found George Bangs, Pinkerton's deputy, and young John Scully sitting at a table on which "was a large map and a heap of gold coins." Pinkerton was pacing the room. He looked at Lewis and asked for his decision. Lewis told him he would go to Richmond. Pinkerton and Lewis joined the other two men at the table, and Lewis was handed a letter in an unsealed envelope.

Pinkerton told Lewis that it was to be delivered to Webster. Lewis opened the letter and read it while Pinkerton informed him that "the letter is a mere blind and purports to be written by a good rebel, a citizen of Baltimore [named Scott] warning Tim Webster that, if he ever comes North again, not to come by way of Leonardtown because the United States authorities have got wind of him and were on the lookout to catch him."

Lewis said nothing but gestured at a second letter now in Pinkerton's hand. The Scot said that it was an introduction to James A. Cowardin, editor of the *Richmond Dispatch*, written by a rebel friend in Washington. Pinkerton explained that Webster usually stayed at the Spottswood Hotel in Richmond, but if for any reason he wasn't there, Lewis should enlist the help of Cowardin to help find him. The letter was, of course, a forgery, said Pinkerton, but a very good forgery.

Lewis asked for a cover story; after all, he couldn't just waltz into Richmond in search of Timothy Webster. Pinkerton replied that he was to say he was an English businessman with Southern sympathies, on his way to Chattanooga to discuss a cotton transaction, but taking time to first perform a service to the Confederacy. All Lewis's doubts resurfaced. It was altogether too flimsy, too unfeasible. Pinkerton sensed Lewis's anxieties and implored him to go south, reminding his operative that General McClellan was on the brink of an offensive and that Webster might possess information crucial to any such military action.

Lewis was surprised that Pinkerton talked with such candor in front of John Scully. Then it suddenly dawned on him: Scully was going too. When Pinkerton confirmed the fact, Lewis refused to accept the mission; Sam Bridgeman's drunken exploits had nearly blown their cover in Charleston, and if that had taught Lewis one thing, it was that a mission deep inside enemy territory was best conducted independently and not as part of a team. "One man can tell a story and stick to it," said Lewis, "but two will be sure to differ."

Lewis turned to Scully, a tall, fair-headed Irishman, and assured him it was nothing personal, that in the previous occasions they had worked together he had struck him as an "honest and zealous" operative. But he preferred to go alone.

Pinkerton understood Lewis's concerns but insisted he would need an accomplice, explaining to the Englishman that Scully was "to come back at once with the information Webster will give you, while you go on further South, working your way to Chattanooga." Pinkerton added that Webster would give Scully directions how to get back promptly. And me, asked Lewis, how will I get back? That will be up to you, replied Pinkerton.

A sardonic smile spread across Lewis's face. Much of the mission appeared half-baked, but at least it promised adventure, of the kind he'd craved for the past six months. There was another reason, too, why he agreed to ignore his misgivings about taking Scully. If the truth be known, Lewis "felt rather proud" that he had been asked "to go in order to relieve McClellan's anxiety and permit a move forward."

Neither Pinkerton nor George Bangs could conceal their relief at Lewis's decision. In planning for the trip to Richmond, they had already suffered one setback when Charles Rosch, a skilled and experienced detective, "refused to undertake so dangerous a mission unless Pinkerton would first, by legal settlement, make provision for his family in case he was captured." Pinkerton had declined Rosch's request and selected in his place a man less assertive and more malleable: John Scully. The Irishman also had a family, but he was young and eager to impress, and accepted the assignment without a moment's hesitation.

Lewis and Scully spent Monday, February 17, preparing for their trip south. They "purchased a new suit of clothing apiece, ready made to travel in, we packed our best clothes in large valises [and] each of us carried a six-shooter in the outside pocket of our valises."

Pinkerton gave Lewis a third letter, this one addressed to General Joseph Hooker, in which he asked the Union commander to ensure his two operatives a safe passage through Maryland.

At noon on Tuesday Lewis and Scully rendezvoused at Pinkerton's headquarters. It was a cold, gray day, and the cheerless skies reflected Lewis's mood as he listened once more to Pinkerton's instructions. The waiting was the worst part; that was when he had time to think of all the "what ifs." Now he just wanted to get going.

At last they were on their way, accompanied by fellow Pinkerton man William Scott, whose rebel contacts in Maryland should prove useful on the initial leg of the journey. They trundled out of the capital in an old covered wagon driven by a taciturn man named Watts.

They stopped for the night in a small hotel at Port Tobacco, thirty miles south of Washington. Watts returned with the wagon, and Lewis and Scully discreetly disappeared upstairs to their room. Scott brought them their supper, and the next morning, just after dawn, he reappeared with breakfast. Before any other guests had risen they were en route to Newport, a small village six miles above the mouth of the Wicomico River.

Scott booked Lewis and Scully into an inn owned by a rebel sympathizer. He told the landlord the two men were Confederate spies and on no account was he to mention their presence to any of his guests or staff. Scott then went off "to negotiate with a man named Sherborne, who kept a store in the place, for a boat and guides." Sherborne was another of Scott's contacts, a secessionist who believed he was assisting two bold rebels reach Virginia. He told Scott he could get a boat and a guide, but it would take time. Why? asked Scott. Sherborne replied that the area was crawling with Union soldiers on the lookout for rebel spies and contraband traders; he wasn't going to take any unnecessary risks.

Lewis and Scully remained in their room, restless, fretful, irritable. Scott brought them food and books and newspapers, as if they were hospital patients, and in the evening they played cards and warmed themselves with a whiskey or two. Scott insisted that the pair spend part of each day rehearsing the story each should tell in case they fell into enemy hands.

On Saturday morning Sherborne came to the hotel and informed Scott that everything was arranged; they would set off down the Wicomico at first light on Sunday and then cross the Potomac that night. Two slaves belonging to a Maryland planter named Herbert would row them to Virginia. And the cost? asked Scott. One hundred dollars in gold, replied Sherborne. The two men shook hands, and Scott went upstairs to relay the good news.

On Saturday evening Lewis and Scully said good-bye to Scott and were taken by Sherborne to Herbert's plantation. Lewis found Herbert to be a planter of the old school, courteous and cultured, and an excellent host. He asked no questions but made it plain he held Tim Webster, a

man who had passed through this way on previous occasions, in high
regard.

There was another guest at the Herbert plantation, a young Confederate officer named James McChesney, who was on his way south having
paid a risky visit to his family in Maryland.

At dawn the next day, Sunday, February 23, the three men embarked
down the Wicomico in a small boat rowed by the two slaves. The pace was
leisurely, and it wasn't until "about an hour before sunset, at a place
called Cobb Neck, [that] we were in sight of the Potomac." They drew
into the bank and concealed themselves among some trees as the night
drew in. Union gunboats passed close by, whistling as they went, and Lewis
whispered to McChesney that only the Yankees would be so stupid to
patrol during the day and lay up at night, when "an army might have
crossed without discovery."

Soon the gunboats were gone, and for a time "everything was still as
death." Then the wind began to rise, and they heard the drum of rain.
Lewis dug out a stone from the bank and with it weighed down the letter
addressed to General Hooker. As they pushed off toward Virginia Lewis
dropped the stone in the water, destroying the last piece of material evidence that linked him and Scully to the Union.

It was a cold, wet, moonless night, but the men felt secure wrapped
in the blanket of darkness. They landed at the foot of a bluff, and while
McChesney and Scully scrambled up its steep sides, Lewis gave the two
slaves five dollars apiece and told them to hurry home before the storm
broke. The three men endured a miserable night in the woods. The wind
increased, and when the storm broke, the rain cascaded through the trees.

February 24 dawned bright and clear, and they emerged from the
woods to find a muddy track scarred by a recent set of wagon wheels.
They followed the tracks, which led to a rough, stony lane on the border
of a plantation. The men stopped and scanned the land around; there
wasn't a soul to be seen. McChesney found it disquieting and wondered
out loud if they weren't still in Virginia. Perhaps the slaves had become
disorientated in the darkness.

The planter's house was visible in the weak winter sunshine, so they
moved toward it. As they approached, the door opened and "suddenly
a pack of hounds came baying toward us." An old man appeared and
shouted at the dogs to quit their racket. Then he glared at the men,

"noticed McChesney's faded gray uniform, and began to denounce the Yankees in passionate terms." Over breakfast the man and his wife explained that they were in Westmoreland County, Virginia, and the plantation belonged to Richard Beale, a former Democratic congressman who was now an officer in the Confederate army based at nearby Hague. Lewis told the man they "wanted to go to Richmond by the most direct route and he amiably volunteered to show us in person the way to the nearest crossroads a mile or so away." At the crossroads they would be able to hire a conveyance from the postmaster to take them to Leedstown, from where they would take a boat west to Fredericksburg and then a train for the remaining sixty miles south to Richmond.

At the postmaster's house they encountered their first obstacle. The postmaster explained that he was willing to take them to Leedstown, but the first boat didn't depart until the next day, Tuesday, 25 February. He suggested they stay the night at the post office, which was also a guesthouse; then he would drive them to Leedstown the following morning. The three agreed and went upstairs to rest. Later they had some lunch, and the postmaster suggested that they might like "to see the spot where Washington was born, about a mile and a half away."

A few minutes later, as they were preparing to leave on their excursion, they heard the approach of horsemen. Lewis looked out of the window and saw a dozen Confederate soldiers "in dingy, ill-fitting uniforms . . . nearly all of them were middle-aged or oldish men."

Three of the soldiers dismounted and entered the post office, nodding at the postmaster and scrutinizing the strangers before them. When their leader spoke it was to confirm that they knew the trio had crossed the Potomac the previous evening. That's correct, replied McChesney. In that case, said the soldier, they would be escorted to a military camp at Westmoreland Courthouse and interrogated.

They rode the ten miles to the courthouse in the postmaster's buggy, the cavalrymen forming in front and rear of their conveyance. It was midafternoon when they arrived in Westmoreland, and the court had just adjourned for the day. A small crowd of people watched as the buggy passed, and Lewis heard a man ask one of the soldiers, "Where did you capture the Yankees?"

At the camp they were ordered out of the buggy and into a barracks full of Confederate soldiers. A hush fell on the room as the three men entered. Suddenly there were cries of "McChesney," and several soldiers sprang forward. As McChesney shook the hands of old comrades, he turned and "introduced [the] two gentlemen who had helped him to escape out of the Yankee lines." One of the soldiers started to sing "Maryland! My Maryland!" and soon the room reverberated to the sound of happy brothers.

The soldiers' commanding officer was Captain Saunders, "a small man with pleasant manners," who wanted to know where McChesney's friends were headed. Lewis opened his valise, explaining as he did that his duty was to deliver a letter to Timothy Webster in Richmond. He handed the sealed letter to the captain and invited him to open it. Saunders shook his head and replied that he was well acquainted with "Captain Webster" and knew him to be a loyal Confederate.

It wasn't until the evening of Tuesday, February 25, that Lewis and Scully finally boarded a boat at Leedstown for Fredericksburg. The vessel was full of rebel soldiers still raging at the news that Fort Donelson was now in Yankee hands. At six thirty on Wednesday morning they headed south from Fredericksburg on a train belonging to the Richmond, Fredericksburg and Potomac Railroad company. There were few soldiers on the train, and Lewis and Scully congratulated each other on their success so far. Lewis confessed to his companion that his "anxiety to reach Richmond had been very great." Now all they had to do was locate Webster and then get the hell out of the city.

CHAPTER FIFTEEN

"He Is a Noble Fellow, a Most Valuable Man to Us"

TO PROVINCIAL OFFICERS such as Captain Saunders, Timothy Webster was still the brave rebel mail carrier who relayed letters between Richmond and the North. Saunders's acquaintance with Webster was fleeting, and he had no reason to doubt he wasn't who he said he was. Yet in Richmond, General John Winder and his military police had started to harbor doubts about Webster.

So many of Webster's fellow secessionists in Baltimore had been arrested and imprisoned, yet he continued to move freely without molestation. Despite Webster's claims to be a gentleman of leisure, a few discreet inquiries had failed to unearth anyone who knew him prior to 1861.

Then the unmasking in Washington of James Howard, the clerk in Provost Marshal Porter's office, seemed to lead inextricably back to Captain Tim Webster. The woman who had smuggled the map of the capital's Federal defenses arrived in Richmond distraught at its loss, and her misery deepened when she learned it had fallen into Union hands. The Confederates retraced her movements to discover the likely mole.

She and her children had departed in a wagon from Washington with the map carefully concealed about her person. At Leonardtown she had spent the night in the hotel before continuing on to Cobb Neck and then the voyage across the Potomac when Webster had been a passenger. She recounted how she and her children had arrived cold and wet on the other side, and they and the other passengers had gone to the Virginian safehouse, where she'd removed her damp clothes and helped the children out of theirs. She must have lost the packet then, and someone else must have picked it up soon after. Webster was the most likely suspect.

If Webster was a double agent the damage he'd inflicted on the Confederacy was immense. He'd sat in the bar of the Spottswood Hotel drinking whiskey with the city's military police; he'd been shown around military camps; he'd even delivered letters on behalf of Judah Benjamin, the secretary of war.

But the Confederates needed proof, not speculation, if they were to bring Webster to justice. The problem was how to get the proof. He'd outfoxed them for a year, and he'd do so again if given the chance. Then Webster fell ill, and an idea came to the rebels. If Webster really was a Union agent, the longer he and his wife—for that's who they believed Hattie Lawton to be—remained incommunicado in Richmond, the more anxious his handlers would become.

Before long they would try to make contact with him; so all the Confederate military police had to do was keep a constant watch on Mr. and Mrs. Webster. Discretion didn't matter; in fact, the more Webster felt the net closing, the more likely he was to break cover.

Though sick with fever, Webster remained lucid. It wasn't delirium causing him to imagine the worst; he sensed it in Samuel McCubbin's demeanor. Webster told Hattie Lawton not to try to leave Richmond with a message for Pinkerton as it was too dangerous. She was to act as his devoted wife, to nurse him back to health, and the moment he was well enough they would flee. One week passed, then two, then three, and Webster was still too frail to stand. The weather that winter was singularly disagreeable, a succession of cold, wet days, with Saturday, February 22, particularly grim. From first light "a cold rain fell in sheets, turning the streets into seas of mud, the gutters into rushing torrents." Webster lay in bed listening to the rain drumming at his window, but the buzz of excited chatter soon drowned out the rain as people from across the Southern states filed past the Monumental Hotel toward Capitol Square to witness the inauguration of President Jefferson Davis. The square was "black with spectators . . . [and] the parade, the soggy footpaths and saturated grassplots, even the streets far back beyond the great iron gates of the entrance, were packed with people." Rain dripped from the bronze statue of George Washington upon his horse as nearby Davis mounted the covered podium to address his people who were huddled under oil clothes and umbrellas. Webster heard the crowd fall silent, and a short while later a the cry went up: "God Save Our President!"

Four days later, on Wednesday, February 26, Webster had been bedridden for almost a month, yet still Samuel McCubbin prowled the hotel, waiting, waiting, waiting for his perseverance to be rewarded.

For the first-time visitor Richmond was best viewed from the south. A passenger entering the city across the railroad bridge in the spring of 1861 wrote how "Richmond burst beautifully into view, spreading panorama-like over her swelling hills, with the evening sun gilding simple houses and towering spires alike into a glory. The city follows the curve of the [James] river, seated on amphitheatric hills retreating from its banks; fringes of dense woods shading their slopes, or making blue background against the sky. No city of the South has a grander or more picturesque approach."

The railroad from Fredericksburg entered Richmond from the north, a route less pleasing to the eye. As the train passed through the city line, just south of Shockoe Creek, the first buildings the passengers saw were the ramshackle houses of Richmond's poor. Most of these men and women—many of whom were German or Irish immigrants—worked in either the iron industry or in one of the city's dozens of flour mills or tobacco factories.

The average wage for these employees was approximately $1.25 a day, a pittance for their productivity. Each year Richmond's tobacco factories processed around fifteen million pounds of the weed, while the twelve flour mills brought in over three million dollars annually. The biggest industry was iron, the employer of 1,550 workers, 900 of whom worked at the Tredegar Iron Works. Among other things, they manufactured the tracks for the five railroads that serviced Richmond.

The train headed south for a mile, toward the heart of the city, before a ninety-degree turn at Sixteenth Street took it west along Broad Street. Now passengers sitting on the left-hand side of the train had a wonderful view of the capitol building, the centerpiece of the eight acres of Capitol Square, that sprang from Shockoe Hill. In 1862 the *New York Herald* described how Richmond consisted of "twelve parallel streets, nearly three miles in length, extending northwest and southeast [they] were originally distinguished by the letters of the alphabet, 'A' street being next to the river; but other names, however, are now generally used. The principal thoroughfare of business and fashion is Main, formerly 'E' Street. The cross streets, or those which intersect the streets, just mentioned, are designated by numbers such as First, Second and so on."

The train carrying Pryce Lewis and John Scully pulled into the Fredericksburg railroad depot, on the north side of Broad Street near Eighth, at one o'clock on the afternoon of Wednesday, February 26. They walked out of the depot to see "the long, gaily-painted buses from the hotels stood hub to hub" waiting to ferry passengers to their destination. The buses, like the cabs and hacks, threw up a fine spray of filth from the unpaved streets. All up Broad Street gangs of laborers worked to repair the damage caused by a recent storm; the roof of the Methodist Church needed three hundred slates replaced, and scaffolding was being erected outside Trinity Church. Colonel Biggar, meanwhile, was barking instructions at the workmen rebuilding the fence outside his home.

Lewis and Scully had no need of a bus or cab. They headed south with the brisk stride of men who knew where they were going, toward the Spottswood Hotel on the corner of Main and Eighth streets, a route they had rehearsed over and over in their minds. Beneath the confident exterior the men's senses worked furiously to absorb everything around: the sights, the sounds and, above all, the smells that were generated in a city of thirty-eight thousand inhabitants.*

One odor in particular unsettled all first-time visitors, as it had Sarah Jones, the English governess, who upon her arrival fifteen months earlier wrote in her diary that "the atmosphere of Richmond is redolent of tobacco. The tints of the pavements are those of tobacco. One seems to breathe tobacco, and smell tobacco at every turn, the town is filthy with it; not so much because it abounds in warehouses, and tobacco cases stand in every corner, but because it abounds in people's mouths."

The two spies passed the United Presbyterian Church, one of

---

* This was the figure recorded in the 1860 census, making it the country's twenty-fifth-largest city, but with the outbreak of war and the influx of soldiers, and civilians from other parts of Virginia, the population increased by several thousand.

thirty-three places of worship in the city, and approached the Spotts-wood Hotel. Leave the talking to me, Lewis told Scully under his breath. The lobby was full of Confederate army officers, none of whom took any notice of the newcomers. Lewis asked for two rooms. The clerk consulted the guest book, then apologized: there was nothing available. He suggested they try either the American or the Monumental. Which was closer? asked Lewis. The American, replied the clerk, it was two blocks farther up Main Street. As an afterthought, Lewis asked if there was a Mr. Webster staying in the hotel. The clerk searched the register but found no Webster. They walked up Main Street past Archer & Daly, the steel engravers, past the Farmer's Bank and the next-door bank of Virginia, past the store of George Bidgood, who sold books and stationery, and past Pizzini's, the confectioners, where the ice cream was legendary. They stepped to one side when "gay ladies and grande dames, bedecked in their silks or cashmere," approached, and they avoided eye contact with military men who might have wondered why two such strapping speci-mens were not in uniform.

The American Hotel was full. The clerk was most contrite, but the in-auguration had brought so many visitors to town and most were making a week of it. Lewis and Scully were directed to the Exchange and Ballard Hotel on Franklin Street at the corner of Fourteenth Street. Lewis gave a heavy sigh. How far? Four blocks east, the clerk replied.

The hotel was Richmond's most prestigious, despite what Theodore Hoenniger of the Spottswood might have said to the contrary. Certainly no other hotel boasted such an illustrious guest book; among the names were those of Charles Dickens, who had sat in his room at the Exchange in 1842, perspiring, longing to return to the North and cooler climes; William Makepeace Thackeray rated Richmond "the merriest little place and the most picturesque I have seen in America!" during his visit in 1856, and wrote to a friend from the Exchange with a gold fountain pen he had bought in the city for four dollars, "which is really very ingenious and not much more inconvenient than a common pen."

It was in the parlor of the Exchange that Edgar Allan Poe had lec-tured on "The Poetic Principle" on his final visit to Richmond in 1849, and the following year P. T. Barnum and his circus troupe checked in during their tour. Ten years later, in 1860, the establishment had hosted its most distinguished guest, Edward, Prince of Wales, an occasion that, as the *Richmond Dispatch* reported, was marred by the crowd who let excitement get the better of them. "During all the night of the arrival, every room and stairway in the Ballard Hotel was crammed with a low, wretched mob, each striving and hurtling to get some look into the apartments where his Royal Highness was staying. There were cat-calls, shouts and whooping, with cries for him to show himself—invitations with which I need scarcely say, his Royal Highness did not comply, for the rough, howling, brutal mob that had swarmed round his carriage on arriving at the hotel, had given him a pretty good insight into the general tendencies of a Richmond crowd."

As Lewis and Scully walked toward the Exchange and Ballard Hotel, they could see that it was two separate buildings linked by a raised and covered walkway above Fourteenth Street. From the outside the Exchange was the grander of the two with a colonnaded façade and turreted corners. Inside it was equally imposing. Brass gas lamps hung from the ceiling of the lobby illuminating the polished black-and-white marble floor beneath.

A bellboy took the pair's valises the moment they entered, and guided them to the reception desk. There were rooms available. Only the very wealthiest could afford the Exchange and Ballard Hotel, such as messieurs Lander, Gaither, Bonham, Arrington, Batson, Royston and the ten other senators who had taken up residence since the Confederate government relocated to Richmond from Montgomery.

Lewis and Scully registered in their own names and were relieved to learn they weren't too late for a spot of lunch. In the splendid dining room they studied the menu with mounting excitement; the rest of Richmond might have been suffering a shortage of food, but not the Exchange and Ballard Hotel. Senators needed nourishment if they were to lead their people to victory. Guests could choose from "rounds of beef, saddles of mutton, venison, whole shoats, hams, sausage of country make, rich with sage and redolent with pepper, turkies [*sic*], geese, ducks, chickens, with vegetables, such as potatoes, turnips, large as cannon balls, and beets like oblong shells."

In between courses Lewis and Scully spoke softly to each other, preparing for their visit to the offices of the *Richmond Dispatch*. They had passed the building on their way to the Exchange and Ballard Hotel. It was on the corner of Main and Thirteenth streets, a four-story block known as the "Dispatch Building."

When they arrived at the offices of the *Richmond Dispatch*, they were shown straight to the office of the editor, James Cowardin, a portly man in his early fifties who had founded the newspaper twelve years earlier. Like the editors of the city's other three daily newspapers,* Cowardin had been forced to downsize because of the shortage of paper. And what paper remained was of an inferior quality to that of the prewar days; it was coarse, vaguely brown, the sort of paper that a year earlier wouldn't have been deemed good enough to wrap presents.

Nevertheless, Cowardin's *Dispatch* still outsold its rivals: the *Whig*, *Examiner* and *Enquirer*. Its circulation figure of eighteen thousand was sustained "by the accuracy of its reporting and the moderation of its editorial policy," not something that could be said of the *Whig* or the *Examiner*. This pair were virulent in their denunciation of the Yankees, particularly the *Examiner*, which was edited by John Moncure Daniel, a man with "the qualities of the scimitar of Saladin and the battle-ax of Couer de Lion." In his eyes Abraham Lincoln was a "ferocious old Orang-Outang from the wilds of Illinois," while Jefferson Davis was too timid for a wartime leader. The Confederacy required "a dictator," wrote Daniel, someone who would do whatever necessary to win the war.

The interview with Cowardin was cordial but brief. It was the middle of the afternoon, and he was rushing to finish the next day's issue. Lewis handed him the letter, and Cowardin read it, then told him matter-of-factly he "would find Captain Webster at the Monumental Hotel laid up with rheumatism."

Lewis and Scully walked out of the Dispatch Building, crossed Main Street and approached the southern corner of Capitol Square. They passed the state courthouse and found themselves in the middle of the square, with the capitol building in front of them. Up close they realized that the beauty of the building was best beheld from afar. The nearer one was to the capitol, the more one saw that "the rough brick walls had been covered with stucco in a way that gave them a look of cheapness."

---

* Richmond also had the *Täglicher Anzeiger*, a German-language newspaper, popular with the city's Jewish population, and in 1863 a fifth English-language daily, the *Sentinel*, was published.

Richmonders in fine clothes promenaded under the linden trees and around the fountains, and they sat on the steps at the foot of George Washington's statue, gossiping about the war, about the weather and about the cost of food. Imagine, bacon at twenty-five cents a pound and butter twice as much! Beef was up from thirteen to thirty cents a pound, but the quality of the meat was down. The price of fish, even a pair of shad or a rockfish, was exorbitant, and coffee was $1.50 a pound. Ladies swapped tips on coffee substitute—roasted rye or roasted corn were favorites— while others extolled the virtues of dried willow leaves as a tolerable replacement for tea. "Dutch treats" were arranged, dinner parties where guests contributed to the meal with rare luxuries such as sardines, brandied peaches and French prunes. At least the women could be thankful that rich silks and laces not only were affordable but had actually dropped in price thanks to the number of merchants who had moved to the city from other parts of Virginia.

As Lewis and Scully walked north, they saw to their left the tall thin steeple of St. Paul's Episcopal Church, the place of worship for Jefferson Davis and General Robert Lee, and to their right, partially obscured by some linden trees, the Monumental Hotel.

It was four o'clock when Lewis and Scully strolled up to the desk and inquired after Mr. Timothy Webster. Yes, replied the clerk, Mr. and Mrs. Webster were guests of the Monumental. As a bellboy was summoned, Lewis glanced around and wondered what Webster was doing in "a second-rate house."

The bellboy led the pair upstairs to Webster's room, and Lewis entered "a long, narrow room [and] near the entrance on the right side of the door was a bed upon which Webster lay." Hattie Lawton sat in a chair close to Webster, and a man Lewis didn't recognize was also in the room. Lewis advanced and shook the clammy hand of Webster, who propped himself up and welcomed "old friends of his from Baltimore." Gesturing toward the man, Webster introduced Lewis and Scully to P. B. Price, a staunch member of Richmond's Young Men's Christian Association.

They exchanged pleasantries and swapped banalities, and then Lewis said he'd like a word with Webster in private. Lawton and Price invited Scully to observe Richmond through the window, and while they did so Lewis gave the letter to Webster, who read it with a look of "utter astonishment." Soon Lawton, Scully and Price returned to Webster's bedside, and some coffee was ordered as Lewis and Scully "remained for an hour or more," chatting to Mr. and Mrs. Webster, and hoping that Mr. Price might leave and allow old friends to catch up in private. But he didn't, and when Lewis declared it was time for Webster to get some rest, Price insisted the two visitors accompany him to the theater that evening.

Lewis and Scully departed with a promise to return the following morning. Look forward to it, replied Webster, who sank back into his pillow when he was alone with Lawton. He was scared, he told her, scared that the "unheralded appearance of his companions might lead to their being suspected."

Lewis and Scully had an early supper at the Exchange and Ballard Hotel and met Mr. Price in the lobby. There was no need to take a cab to the theater, he explained, as it was just across the street. It was a chill night, but the Metropolitan Hall was warm and snug. Price refused to let his guests pay for their fifty-cent tickets. On me, he told them, adding that they were in for a treat tonight. It was Harry Macarthy, not only the most celebrated entertainer in the Southern states but an Englishman turned Confederate. Like themselves.

The theater was busy when the curtain went up, and a "small, handsome man . . . brimful of humor" strolled onto the stage. The London-born Macarthy was a comic, a mimic, a musician and a songwriter. The *Richmond Enquirer* reckoned that "all who wish to enjoy a hearty laugh and hear a good song should not fail to see Macarthy." The song the audience wanted to hear, particularly those in uniform, was the "Bonnie Blue Flag," a battle anthem written by Macarthy after he'd witnessed delegates at the Tennessee Secession Convention waving a blue flag.

Macarthy knew how to work his audience, making them roar with laughter as he began with a few jokes about the Yankees. Then a song, another joke, some impressions—a Negro, a German, an Irishman—and more songs, with Macarthy joined on stage by his pianist (and wife), Lottie Estelle: "Missouri," "O the Sweet South," and "Let the Bugle Blow." Lewis tapped his feet to the music as all around "soldiers, free and easy in their ways . . . applauded the rebel songs of the actors vigorously." The climax would be a lusty rendition of "The Bonnie Blue Flag," but before that was another song guaranteed to get the crowd on their feet, "The Stars and Bars." Soldiers whooped and hollered and punched the air with their fists as they joined Macarthy in the song.

> Come, hucksters, from your markets,
> Come, bandits, from your caves,
> Come, venal spies; with brazen lies
> Bewildering your deluded eyes,
> That we may dig your graves;
> Come, creatures of a sordid clown
> And driveling traitor's breath,
> A single blast shall blow you down
> Upon the fields of Death.

Lewis and Scully allowed themselves the luxury of sleeping late the following morning, Thursday, February 27, enjoying the soft splendor of the hotel linen and their hair mattresses.

They met for breakfast and afterward retired to the large barroom with its French-plate mirrors and gas chandeliers, where they read the day's papers and listened to their fellow guests lament the fall of Nashville.

After an hour Scully got to his feet and told his companion he was going for a stroll. Lewis nodded and continued reading the paper, aware that Scully was heading to the Monumental and a rendezvous with Webster. Lewis would visit later in the day, and then first thing the next morning he and Scully would check out of the hotel and head their separate ways.

Lewis heard the brazen lunch gong and went to enjoy another extravagant meal. Afterward he climbed the stairs to the hotel's observatory and gasped at the view. He counted the hills, seven in total, and observed the capitol from a different angle. Over in the southwest he could make out the melancholic walls of the giant Hollywood Cemetery, and to the east was the Confederate navy yard. But the vista to the south was most stunning, beyond the flour mills, tobacco factories, cotton mills and ironworks that lined the banks of the James River. There, far away, Lewis watched "the river winding along and losing itself amongst undulating hills." For a moment he could have been back in Newtown.

By three o'clock Scully still hadn't returned, and Lewis was becoming concerned. He left the hotel and started to walk in the direction of the Monumental. Up ahead he saw Scully coming the other way. Lewis let him know he had been gone too long, but Scully assured his colleague that "there was no occasion for uneasiness." He then explained that Webster had asked him to carry some letters from his Richmond friends to their contacts in Maryland, and he would return in the evening to collect the letters. Lewis told his accomplice to return to his room and wait there; he wouldn't be long. He was going to call on Webster and check that all information had been communicated.

Lewis entered the Monumental and went directly to Webster's room. Hattie Lawton opened the door, and Lewis saw the unease in her eyes. Her "husband" was propped up in bed, talking to a squarely built gentleman with a dark complexion. The man looked up at the visitor and then turned to Webster in anticipation of an introduction. Webster explained that Lewis was "an old friend, an Englishman from Manchester." Pleased to meet you, said Lewis, extending a hand. The man got to his feet as Webster presented Captain Samuel McCubbin, head of the city's secret police. McCubbin smiled and informed Lewis "that he occupied the room adjoining that of Webster."

For a while the three men "had a pleasant chat upon indifferent subjects." Then Lewis pulled his watch from his pocket and declared it was time he was on his way. Suddenly McCubbin asked the Englishman if he had "reported to the military governor." Was that necessary? asked Lewis, with an innocent smile. He had been led to believe by the soldiers at Westmoreland that such protocol was superfluous.

Unfortunately not, said McCubbin, who explained that all persons who crossed the Potomac must report to General Winder's headquarters. But it's not a problem, he quickly added, flashing a grin at Lewis. If he and Mr. Scully would be good enough to visit General Winder's headquarters at four o'clock, the matter could be quickly dealt with. Most kind, replied Lewis, who said that as it was already nearly four o'clock he'd best go and fetch Scully right away.

McCubbin was waiting patiently when Lewis and Scully arrived a little after four at the general's headquarters on the corner of Ninth and Broad streets. McCubbin led his guests into Winder's office and introduced them to Richmond's provost marshal general. John H. Winder was sixty-two years old, a veteran of the Florida and Mexican wars and an instructor of Jefferson Davis when he had been a callow West Point cadet. Winder was "short and compact in frame and curt in act and speech," and despite his correct appearance he reeked of menace the way Richmond stank of tobacco. Among the Union soldiers languishing in Richmond's prisons, a visit by Winder was "a feared and fearful thing . . . leading to an inevitable roughening of our confinement." Winder's punishments were cruelly creative. There was the old favorite, the lash, whereby a prisoner would receive upwards of fifteen strokes on his bare back, sometimes as many as fifty, at which point the miscreant would be either unconscious or crying for his mother. If Winder ordered a man to be "trysted up," the prisoner was "tied up by the thumbs to a cross-piece overhead" and suspended with his feet above the floor for however long Winder thought fit. To be "bucked" and "gagged" entailed a long period lying on the damp stone floor with a wooden gag in the mouth and the elbows tied, or "bucked," to the knees. Then there was the ingenious "barrel shirt," reputed to be a trick Winder picked up from an old naval friend. The shirt was "made by sawing a common flour barrel in twin and cutting armholes in the sides and an aperture in the barrel head for the insertion of the wearer's head." A couple of days wearing the "barrel shirt" was enough to reform the most recalcitrant of men.

Even among his own people, the name Winder made men tremble. A careless remark about the government, a thoughtless joke about a general, and a man was liable to find himself festering in the cells, a plaything of Winder and his military police. John Beauchamp Jones, the diary-keeping clerk to the secretary of war, was aghast at the antics of Winder and his "Plug-Ugly Gang," his name for men such as Samuel McCubbin, the worst of the lot in Jones's caustic opinion. Not only was McCubbin "wholly illiterate," wrote Jones, but he was also "a Scotch-Irishman though reared in the mobs of Baltimore."

Jones considered them all to be unfit for the job, just "petty larceny detectives, dwelling in barrooms, ten-pin alleys, and such places. How can they detect political offenders, when they are too ignorant to comprehend what constitutes a political offense? They are illiterate men, of low instincts and desperate characters." They even seemed incapable of catching Richmond's pro-Unionists who crept out in the dead of night to daub the walls of buildings with slogans such GOD BLESS THE STARS AND STRIPES and UNION MEN TO THE RESCUE.

Unfortunately for Jones, life was about to become a great deal more unpleasant under Winder and his Plug-Uglies. On the day Lewis and Scully arrived in Richmond—February 26—Congress had sat in a secret session at the capitol and "authorized the declaration of martial law in this city and at some few other places."

President Davis was still putting the finishing touches to the proclamation that would come into effect on March 5, but Winder had been told its main points: the suspension of habeas corpus; the prohibition of liquor and the closure of all distilleries; the surrender of all private sidearms; a curfew from ten o'clock at night until dawn and the requirement of a passport for all journeys outside the city line.

This last order brought an ironic smile to the face of Jones, the man who two months earlier had refused to issue a passport to Tim Webster. Webster had still obtained a passport, and Jones suspected it had come from Winder and his Plug-Uglies. He had told his diary that they "seem to be on peculiar terms of intimacy with some of these [letter carriers], for they tell me they convey letters for them to Maryland, and deliver them to their families."

Winder was a Marylander; so too McCubbin and a couple of his colleagues. They had given private letters to Webster to carry north, including correspondence between Winder and his son, William, a Union artillery officer, who was in Washington waiting to be posted. Winder Junior had just returned from duty in California and was reluctant to become a combatant but realized nonetheless where his duty lay. The letters revealed that General Winder was urging his son "to resign his commission if he could not find the means of certain escape by desertion and come south." In the end the young Winder neither deserted nor fought; McClellan posted him back to California. The thought that Webster had read this intimate exchange was painful enough for General Winder, but the realization that he had been fooled was too much to bear. The desire to nail Webster was personal as well as professional.

Winder shook hands with Lewis and Scully, telling them with a broad smile that he was "very glad to meet any friends of Captain Webster's as he is a noble fellow, a most valuable man to us."

Lewis agreed, adding that that was why he was in Richmond, to pass a letter to Webster "warning him if he ever came north again, not to go by Leonardtown for, if he did, he would be captured [as] United States detectives were watching for him."

Winder nodded gravely and thanked the pair for undertaking such a perilous task. The three men talked for a while longer. Winder was eager to hear their impressions of the North. What was their opinion of the government? Would Great Britain come to the Confederacy's aid? For his part Winder made it plain "he regarded Lincoln as a mere figurehead" and instead charged William Seward "as most to blame for . . . the 'war on the South.' "

When Lewis asked Winder "for something from you to show that we have reported here and are all right, so to avoid interference from the guards," he was told that no pass or permit was required, not for two such stalwart friends of the Confederacy. In fact, said the general, as he escorted Lewis and Scully to the door, "call and see me whenever you feel like it." He was determined to make their brief sojourn in Richmond as pleasant as possible.

Lewis and Scully breathed a sigh of relief as they left General Winder's headquarters. The Monumental Hotel was only one block away, but they agreed to make their final call on Webster in the evening. First, now that they were "perfectly secure from any mishap," they would return to their hotel, freshen up and then enjoy a generous supper.

It was dark when Lewis and Scully walked out of the Exchange and Ballard Hotel. The banks and stores were closed, but Richmond's nocturnal business was about to begin. Behind the pair's hotel was a row of houses "occupied by parties of a dubious and uncertain character," with the "sinful abode of Ella Johnson" particularly notorious. Meanwhile in among the linden trees in Capitol Square the two men were subjected to what James Cowardin's *Dispatch* described as the "smirks and smiles, winks, and, when occasion served, remarks not of a choice kind . . . of the prostitutes of both sexes."

Lewis and Scully politely declined all services on offer and strode across the square and up to Webster's room. There was no Captain McCubbin, but there was the irritatingly solicitous Mr. Price, insisting once more on a trip to the theater. Mary Partington was playing in *The Hunchback* at the Franklin Hall. It would be a crime to miss it. Price suggested supper first, but Lewis told him they'd just eaten. In that case, said Price, he would nip out for a quick bite and return in half an hour.

Alone with Webster, Hattie Lawton and Scully, Lewis explained that he intended "to leave the following day and carry out my instructions to go to Chattanooga." Webster agreed and "said Scully, too, ought to be off as soon as possible." Unfortunately the letters from his friends had yet to arrive, but he expected them to be ready for Scully to collect in the morning.

They had been "conversing in low tones for perhaps fifteen minutes when there was a knock at the door. Webster called 'come in' and a gentleman, a stranger to Scully and [Lewis] entered, followed by a young gentleman about nineteen years of age." The light by the door was gloomy, and it wasn't until the second man had stepped forward that the gaslight revealed his face. It was Chase Morton.

Scully got to his feet, mumbled something incoherent and rushed out of the room leaving behind his overcoat. Lewis made a weak joke at his friend's expense and "betrayed no sign of recognition" as Webster introduced him to George Clackner, another one of General Winder's men.

Clackner shook Lewis's hand but didn't turn to introduce his companion. Instead he and Webster "began a commonplace talk, like old acquaintances," with Lewis chipping in the odd comment from time to time. Morton contributed nothing to the conversation. He stood and watched.

Lewis had an urge to ask Morton how the family was, just to see his reaction, perhaps surprise him with his nerve. Now that he "knew the game was up," Lewis felt strangely relieved, unshackled of suspense. His only concern "was to avoid being arrested in the room with Webster, for in his feeble state it would be a great shock."

After a few minutes Lewis got to his feet, put on his soft felt hat, collected Scully's overcoat and wished everyone a good evening. At the top of the stairs he found a fretful Scully. "The dog is dead," said Lewis, handing him his coat. He heard a door open, then a voice say "excuse me." Lewis turned. Clackner asked him and Scully to confirm their names. Then Clackner said their presence was required in General Winder's office. But we saw the general in the afternoon, replied Lewis. Too bad. Clackner's orders were to escort the pair to his chief's headquarters.

Lewis and Scully were led downstairs and into the hotel bar, where Samuel McCubbin and four other policemen were leaning against the counter drinking whiskey. Lewis asked McCubbin what was going on. The detective shrugged and said that all would soon be revealed.

CHAPTER SIXTEEN

"I Suspected You All Along"

I<small>T WAS A SHORT WALK</small> from the Monumental to General Winder's office. As Lewis and Scully were escorted up Ninth Street George Clackner asked if they had ever been to New York City. Lewis said they had. So then you know Mayor Fernando Wood? No, said Lewis. But he's the mayor of New York, replied Clackner.

Lewis gave a small puff of laughter and asked "if I ought to know the Lord Mayor because I had lived in London?" Clackner motioned for someone to come forward and the next instant Lewis was face-to-face with Chase Morton. He asked the Englishman if he recognized him, a touch of sarcasm in his voice. Lewis shook his head. Why, should he? Chase couldn't believe it and exclaimed, "Good heavens, don't you remember examining my father's papers in Washington?"

Lewis looked dumbfounded. Washington! He had only once been in the city, and that was a fleeting visit. Lewis gave a condescending smile and suggested Morton had him confused with someone else. Morton glanced nervously at the detectives. He wasn't wrong, he assured them, honestly. "It is impossible that I can be mistaken!" he cried. Morton pointed at Scully and said he too had searched the family home.

McCubbin intervened and ushered them all toward General Winder's office, where they found the provost marshal general waiting. He got to his feet and with a beaming smile asked Lewis if Secretary Seward was in good health.

Lewis continued to feign bemusement. He had never met Secretary Seward and implored the general to explain what was going on. Winder sat back in his chair and regarded Lewis, the silence as interrogative as the questions. "Mr. Lewis," he said, finally, "you are a smart man. If you were not, they would not send you on this mission. But we are smart enough for you this time. I suspected you all along." Lewis protested his innocence. It was all some frightful error, a ghastly case of mistaken identity. Winder heard him out and told Lewis he would be given an opportunity to state his case when his trial began.

Soon other detectives arrived with Lewis's and Scully's valises from the Exchange and Ballard Hotel. Lewis was outraged. Such behavior was preposterous, but Winder's men ignored his cries and began "spreading out our clothing, ripping out the lining of the trousers and feeling along all the seams." They removed and admired the men's revolvers and then turned their attention to Lewis and Scully themselves, who were ordered to shed their coats and shirts. And the pants? McCubbin inquired. Winder told him not to bother, saying the pair were too smart to have any incriminating papers about their persons. He instructed his detectives to hand back the pair's money and valuables but not their revolvers. Then he called McCubbin and another man into an adjoining room. As Lewis dressed he overheard them talking. They mentioned the names Dennis and Brandt, both fellow Northern detectives, and from the cadence of the conversation it sounded like they were going through a list of known Pinkerton men. Winder came back into the room and informed Lewis that he and Scully would remain in the custody of the military police overnight. In the morning they would be taken to the Henrico County Jail to await trial on charges of espionage.

There were no cells in Winder's offices, so the two prisoners were told they would spend the night in a local barracks. But first, said McCubbin, as he led them out into the street, let's have a drink. They headed to a nearby saloon. The bartender's back was to the party when they entered the saloon, but as he turned Lewis "recognized one of Pinkerton's men named E. H. Stein, whom I knew well enough though I had never been engaged with him on any cases." Pinkerton had not disclosed to Lewis that one of his operatives was working undercover in Richmond as a bartender, and the Englishman struggled momentarily to "repress feelings of astonishment." Clackner told Stein that as their guests were "two Englishmen [sic]" it was only natural that they should drink a bottle of Old Tom, a sweet gin popularized in London during the eighteenth century.

It was no coincidence that Lewis and Scully had been brought to the workplace of E. H. Stein. Winder and his men suspected Stein of being a Northern spy. Since his arrival the previous August he had made two trips North, something to do with ill relatives, or so he'd claimed. In fact on both occasions Stein reported to Pinkerton what little information he had gleaned in Richmond. In recent weeks he had curtailed any suspicious behavior for fear of being arrested. Stein knew he was being watched night and day, and as he poured a gin for Lewis and Scully he felt Clackner's eyes boring into him. Lewis, too, knew "that this meeting was brought about purposely . . . to see if we knew each other, but he [Clackner] could determine nothing from the manner of our meeting."

When they'd finished their drinks the two prisoners were escorted to the bunk room of a nearby barracks. McCubbin and Clackner made sure they were comfortable, procured some food from somewhere and then bade the pair a friendly good night.

The next morning, Friday, February 28, Lewis and Scully took breakfast with the soldiers. There was no hostility; one of the men even entertained them with his banjo over a pot of hot coffee. At ten o'clock the pair were collected by George Clackner.

Clackner was far more relaxed than he had been the previous night. As he escorted the prisoners to Henrico County Jail he talked freely with Lewis, reassuring him that they would be well treated in the jail. Lewis asked if they could obtain books there. Yes, replied Clackner, who added that most things could be got, for a small price. Clackner was in his midthirties, a tall man, just under six feet, with a dark complexion and a long face with a high forehead. He told Lewis he was from Baltimore, where once he'd worked as a clerk, but in the years leading up to the war he'd been a policeman in New York. Clackner didn't reveal why he'd joined the Confederacy, but the more he talked the more Lewis sensed he was ambivalent about the Southern cause

Henrico County Jail, also known as the City Jail, was on the corner of Marshall and Fifteenth streets. The Richmond, Fredericksburg and

Potomac Railroad passed a couple of hundred feet to the south. The jail was the smallest of Richmond's many prisons* It was enclosed by a twelve-foot-high stone wall with a thick wooden gate the only entrance. Clackner banged on the gate. It was opened by an elderly man named George Thomas, one of Henrico's five turnkeys. Thomas took in hand the prisoners, marching them across an outer courtyard toward an iron door that led to an inner yard. Once inside this yard Lewis and Scully were led into a rectangular two-story building made of granite and iron.

On the first floor were two cells, one occupied by Negroes, the other by three white men.

Thomas ordered Lewis and Scully to climb a heavy stepladder to the second floor. Here were two more occupied cells, and the pair were directed to the one above the Negroes' cell. It measured about ten by sixteen feet. There were two windows, each one foot by two, latticed with four iron bars. A bench lay against one wall, and a number of collapsible cots were stacked in a corner, on which was a pile of neatly folded blankets. There were five other men in the cell.

Once Thomas had slammed the door shut, one of the men came forward and introduced himself as George W. Twells, formerly a lieutenant in the Ben McCulloch Rangers. One by one the other inmates stepped forward and made the acquaintance of Lewis and Scully: Charles Stanton, a New York sailor suspected of being a spy; a Mississippi River pilot named J. M. Seeds charged with disloyalty; a German baker accused of the same offense, and a Richmond blacksmith by the name of Saunders, indicted on theft.

Some of the men were garrulous, eager to pump Lewis and Scully for news from the outside. Was it true about Nashville? Had McClellan launched his offensive? Lewis said little, claiming to be an Englishman ignorant of American affairs. In reality he suspected "that probably one of them had been placed there to note my actions and conversations."

---

* The exact number of prisons at the time is almost impossible to determine as the city's authorities often used converted warehouses to hold prisoners, sometimes for just a few weeks, but an official report into the condition of Union prisoners in Richmond in 1863 listed nine prisons. However, this figure didn't include jails in which civilians or Confederate soldiers were imprisoned.

Instead he coaxed his new companions into telling their own stories. Twells hailed from Philadelphia. Before the war he'd worked for Charles Morgan's Southern Steamship Company, the line that operated between New Orleans and the Texas ports. When war broke out he'd enlisted in the Confederate army only to desert a while later, the reason for his incarceration.

Stanton described to Lewis how he and Twells had escaped from the jail six weeks earlier by working a hole through their cell wall, then scaling the wall and stealing out of Richmond. They'd been recaptured as they tried to cross the Chickahominy, the river that ran east to west above the city, as effective a defense as a moat to a castle. But Stanton appeared unperturbed by their failure, promising Lewis that the next time he would get across over the Chickahominy.

Seeds and the German baker said little, but Saunders explained without bravado that he had previous spells in prison for theft and for forgery, though the latter was a clear case of injustice as he'd swallowed the evidence—a handful of dollar bills—while Winder's men searched his smithy. This time Saunders was in for stealing, and though he made no secret of the fact he supported the Confederate cause, he bore no animosity toward the North.

Someone produced a pack of cards, and they killed time playing whist in the long minutes before lunch. When the time came to eat, the prisoners were escorted one at a time from their cell to the kitchen on the first floor. A bored jailor named Staples, a stout and jolly-looking man, supervised the collection of the food. It was the same fare every day, a mug of soup and a plate of pork, vegetables and bread.

After lunch the prisoners were conducted into the inner yard for half an hour's exercise. The yard was bare save for a small tobacco shed in one corner and an ash heap in another. Lewis took Scully to one side and confided his fears about there being a spy in their midst. Scully just shrugged and began complaining about the food. Lewis told him to get a grip, but Scully wandered away across the yard "very much downcast."

Later that afternoon Winder's men arrived at the jail and removed Scully. Lewis shouted after his colleague to keep his spirits high. Then he watched from the window as Scully was led across the courtyard and out into the street.

Over the next few days Lewis settled into prison routine: awoken in the morning at seven thirty for a roll call; breakfast of corn bread and coffee; confined to cells for the morning; lunch around one o'clock; half an hour's exercise; back to the cells; roll call at five o'clock; half an hour's exercise; supper; back to the cells. The evening was when the prisoners deloused themselves. Lewis watched perplexed on his first night as his cellmates pulled off their shirts and began examining the seams with great care. The ritual eased his fears about a spy; clearly they had all been rotting in Henrico for several weeks and were who they said they were.

To his fellow prisoners Lewis remained an enigma. All they knew, all he told them, was his name, his nationality and the fact he'd been arrested in Richmond. He said nothing about the reason for his arrest. His skill at cards led some of his cellmates to speculate that perhaps he was a professional gambler, but on Tuesday, March 4, the mystery ended.

Lewis had been badgering his jailors for several days for a newspaper, waving one of his gold coins under their noses. George Thomas took the money and returned the next day with a copy of the *Richmond Enquirer*. He tossed it into the cell, along with a quip that the prison now had an infamous inmate. Lewis found the story under the headline YANKEE SPIES.

The report, a mix of fact and fabrication, described how "John Scully and Pryce Lewis were arrested at the Monument Hotel on Friday last [*sic*], and are now in prison . . . officers in pay of our Government were immediately put upon the track, and discovered them in a private house [*sic*] . . . they became so much confused that they hastened away to the Hotel, leaving their overcoats behind . . . it is clearly shown, by evidence not prudent to detail in this place, that they are paid hirelings of the enemy."

The *Enquirer* explained that the arrest came about because of the actions of a true patriot, a young woman from Washington, who recognized Lewis and Scully as she passed them on the street, and went at once to tell General Winder. What the men were doing in the Monument Hotel, the paper didn't say. Nor was there any mention of the name Webster.

The *Enquirer* also revealed to Lewis the whereabouts of John Scully. He was in Castle Godwin, which the paper described as a "snug institution, hitherto known as McDaniel's negro jail . . . located in an obscure alley on Franklin Street . . . it contains thirteen clear and well ventilated

Pryce Lewis as he would have appeared to General Wise in Charleston. This photograph was taken shortly after his return from his daring mission. (Pryce Lewis Collection at St. Lawrence University in Canton, New York)

Allan Pinkerton during the early days of the war, when he was in the field with General McClellan. (Pryce Lewis Collection)

Sam Bridgeman (left), who played the part of Lewis's servant, seated next to Seth Paine and sixteen-year-old William Pinkerton in 1862. (Pryce Lewis Collection)

This photo of Timothy Webster, taken at the start of the war, shows the spy at his handsome best. (PRYCE LEWIS COLLECTION)

Henry Wise, the politician turned soldier who was fooled by Pryce Lewis and paid the price a few days later. (LIBRARY OF CONGRESS)

General Jacob Cox, on the other hand, put his faith in Lewis and was rewarded with the prize of Charleston. (LIBRARY OF CONGRESS)

It was the legal probity of Confederate secretary of state Judah Benjamin that saved the lives of Lewis and John Scully. (LIBRARY OF CONGRESS)

The beguiling Rose Greenhow, a seductive spy whose powers failed to charm either Pinkerton or Lewis. (LIBRARY OF CONGRESS)

The bar of Richmond's Spottswood Hotel was where Webster liked to cultivate his rebel contacts. (LIBRARY OF CONGRESS)

Richmond's Capitol Square, where the well-to-do strolled during the day and the thieves and prostitutes congregated during the night. (LIBRARY OF CONGRESS)

The Exchange and Ballard Hotel, with the covered walkway that linked the two buildings.
(LIBRARY OF CONGRESS)

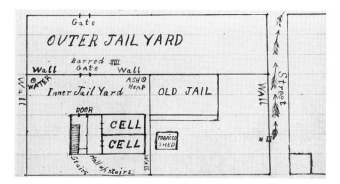

The sketch Lewis drew to show how he and eight others broke out of Henrico County Jail. (Pryce Lewis Collection)

The exterior of Castle Thunder prison, where Lewis and Scully spent more than a year. (Library of Congress)

Old Capitol Prison housed rebel spies such as Rose Greenhow, and was Lewis's first port of call when he returned to Washington. (PRYCE LEWIS COLLECTION)

Pryce Lewis's ordeal turned his hair gray, as can be seen from this photo taken in early 1864. (Pryce Lewis Collection)

Maria Thwaites, Lewis's wife, not long after their marriage in 1868. (PRYCE LEWIS COLLECTION)

Elizabeth Van Lew was the Union's
answer to Rose Greenhow, only much
more effective. (VIRGINIA HISTORICAL
SOCIETY, RICHMOND, VIRGINIA)

It was Lewis's daughter, Mary, seen here as a child in the
mid-1870s, who did so much to honor her father's memory.
(PRYCE LEWIS COLLECTION)

Pryce Lewis in the early 1880s, not long before he sat
down to write the memoirs that he hoped
would set the record straight. (PRYCE LEWIS COLLECTION)

The World Building in New York, where Pryce Lewis ended his life in December 1911.

rooms, which have been provided with comfortable beds and other conveniences, far surpassing in cleanliness and in comfort, the accommodations offered at nine-tenths of the cheap boarding houses of Richmond." However, added the *Enquirer*, despite the impressive amenities available, the spy Scully can expect to "receive all attentions due to his calling and position."

Lewis was now "a big man" in the eyes of his cellmates, the leader of the group and allowed to choose the best spot for his cot. His status as a daring spy soon reached the ears of those in the other cells, and in the exercise yard the following day Sam Tatum, an oyster fisherman in Baltimore before the war, took Lewis to one side and revealed that he and Charles Stanton, the New Yorker whose first escape attempt foundered in the Chickahominy River, had a plan drawn up. Back in their cell Stanton whispered to Lewis that the difficulty wasn't so much escaping from the jail, nor getting past the city line, it was surmounting what lay north: the Chickahominy, the pine forests, the swamps and the flat meadows. When they had bust out in January, Stanton explained, it was during one of the wettest winters in recent memory. The Chickahominy had been swollen fit to burst and impossible to ford. But the rains had abated. In a couple more weeks it should be possible to negotiate the Chickahominy. With that done, they would head north until they encountered the Union army.

So what was the plan? asked Lewis. Stanton presumed that Lewis had already seen how lax security was in the jail; how the jailors frequently wandered off to a saloon for an hour or two, leaving them in their cells; how it was possible to pick the lock of the inner door of their cell with a knife; how the jailors, if asked courteously, would leave the thick iron outer door of their cell unlocked at night to increase the ventilation; how once the outer door was left open, the jailors would head home for the night.

Lewis admitted that he was rather surprised by the blasé attitude of the jailors. Well, said Stanton, that just leaves one obstacle, "the main entrance to the jail, consisting of two doors, the interior one made of thick round iron bars and fastened with a Chubbs English patent lock, celebrated for its security, [and] the exterior door . . . a heavy wooden one fastened on the outside with an ordinary padlock."

Stanton continued, explaining how Seeds, the Mississippi pilot, had examined the wooden door and declared that if they sawed through one of the bars at a certain place they "could wrench it off leaving an opening large enough for all of us to creep through." And the outer door? No problem, said Stanton, grinning. During the afternoon exercise a prisoner would "cover himself up in the ash heap in the corner of the inner prison yard . . . and remain hidden there until night when he would unlock and remove the padlock of the wooden door."

Stanton finished describing the plan and looked at Lewis. Well, what did he think? Lewis thought it foolhardy but worth a try. They had nothing to lose, after all. The prisoners had already purloined a number of table knives, and Saunders the blacksmith had got his hands on a small file. For nearly two weeks they worked every night on the main door, sawing at the iron bar in a relay system while another man on his hands and knees removed all trace of iron filings from the stone floor. As dawn approached they hid all evidence of their industry with "a lump of soap mixed with ashes rubbed into the cut on the bars . . . the lump was the same color as the iron and completely concealed the work."

During the day when they were confined to their cells, the prisoners discussed what they would do once they were over the wall. The newspapers had told them about the declaration of martial law, warning that anyone found on the streets after ten o'clock at night without a pass would be arrested. The location of the jail, however, was in their favor. It was in the northeast of the city, close to the railroad. All they had to do was run along the tracks until they were outside the city line, then head cross-country, using the darkness to slip past the fortifications that encircled Richmond.

On Saturday, March 15, the job was nearly complete. A few minutes more the following night, and the bar would be severed. They agreed to go on Sunday, though Saunders the blacksmith and another prisoner named Pitcher announced they wouldn't be going. Pitcher didn't feel strong enough to make the bid, and Saunders had learned he was soon to be paroled. The Negro prisoners asked if they could come. Lewis didn't see any reason why not as they'd helped in the sawing. Are you mad? retorted one of the white prisoners, who "asserted that if we took them with us and were recaptured, we would certainly all be hanged as John Brown was." Lewis accepted the wishes of the majority and apologized to the black prisoners. One begged Lewis to let him go with them, saying he could act as their guide through the rebel lines, but Lewis turned him down.

They were in luck! Staples was on duty on Sunday, and even among a herd of bovine jailors, his stupidity was special. Under a cold drizzle he took the roll call in the inner yard, then told the men that as it was the Sabbath they could exercise for an hour. The prisoners crowded around the guard, and old man Seeds spun Staples a complicated story about being owed money by General Winder. Can we talk about it in private, he asked the jailor, in the outer yard away from the other inmates? As Seeds maneuvered Staples out of sight of the ash heap, "Stanton wrapped himself in a blanket, lay down in the excavation and was covered up by the others." Earlier in the day Tatum had given Staples a few cents and asked him to buy a new straw tick for his cot as his present one was worn out; now he appeared with his old tick and threw it ostentatiously on top of the ash heap.

Lewis, meanwhile, slipped back inside the jail and "rigged up a broomstick in blankets so as to resemble the figure of a man and placed it in a corner to deceive the jailor in case he should come to the door and count us."

When the exercise hour was over, Staples ordered the men inside for their supper. It was dark and drizzling when he locked the prisoners in their cells. As usual Staples agreed to leave the outer cell doors open to increase the flow of fresh air. Lewis heard Staples pull the main door to the jail shut; then he and Twells stepped on the bench in their cell and watched him walk across the moonlit inner yard. Suddenly "the jailor's eye caught sight of the heap of straw in the corner, and going over to it he took a match from his vest pocket." Lewis stifled a curse as Staples scratched the match against the wall, once, then again, until the match broke. The brickwork was too damp and Staples too tired for a second match. The straw could wait till the morning.

After waiting fifteen minutes Stanton burst from the heap. He brushed the ash from his eyes and then ran across the yard to the prison door. There Stanton discovered the extent of Staples's ineptitude: he'd failed to lock the padlock's hasp into its body. Stanton waited while Lewis and the other prisoners picked the locks of their cell doors, and soon they were facing each other on either side of the iron door. It took just a couple of minutes to cut through the bar and wrench it off, and they were all but free. Seeds had the honor of going first, as it had been his idea to saw through the bar. He plunged his head through the gap, squeezed through one shoulder, then the other, but no, his second shoulder "positively refused to follow his body." Seeds wriggled like a fish on the end of a hook, but it was no good, he was stuck. For several minutes there was "cursing, intermingled with expressions of disgust and indignation . . . at our own folly." Eventually they tugged Seeds's "foolish head back into the prison where it now seemed all of us were to remain until Mr. Jailor came along the next morning."

A voice from behind spoke up, a calm, rather amused voice. It was Saunders the blacksmith. Don't worry, boys, he said, he'd soon have the door open. He asked for some tools—a knife, the file and a leg from the stove—and then set about unlocking the door. While Saunders worked, the Negro prisoners sang and clapped and praised the Lord, drowning out the bangs and thumps as the blacksmith broke the lock. In a few minutes the door was open. Lewis thanked the Negroes for their spirit of true camaraderie, shook hands with Saunders and then joined his fellow escapees in the inner yard.

Tatum and Stanton set the heavy stepladder against the tobacco shed, and one by one the nine men climbed up onto its roof, pulled themselves onto the top of the prison wall and dropped down over the other side. It was now nearly ten o'clock at night, and the drizzle had stopped. It was a clear, frosty, moonlight night, far from ideal for a gang of fugitives. But Richmond was deserted, and soon Lewis and his friends had "passed the last house in the suburbs and were making our way across the fields."

CHAPTER SEVENTEEN

"Trust for a Favorable Outcome"

P RYCE LEWIS AND HIS EIGHT ACCOMPLICES were traveling north, hoping to soon encounter the advance parties of General McClellan's Army of the Potomac on their way south. Unfortunately for the prisoners, the only soldiers moving in their direction in the first half of March 1862 were elements of General Joseph Johnston's Confederate army.

For months Johnston's men had been entrenched in Manassas, thirty miles southwest of Washington, and for most of that period an increasingly despairing Abraham Lincoln had been exerting pressure on McClellan to go on the offensive, drive the rebels from Maryland and then, as the popular cry went, "On to Richmond!" An assault planned for the start of the New Year had to be canceled when McClellan was stricken with ty-phoid and spent a month in bed. The general's critics in the government— and there were many—accused him of malingering, of avoiding a battle because his Democrat principles aligned him more with the government in Richmond than with the one in Washington.

Lincoln rose above the squabbling, waiting until McClellan was on his feet before telling him he expected a spring offensive. The plan the president was finally presented with wasn't one that inspired much con-fidence. McClellan intended to ferry his army south across the cold wa-ters of Chesapeake Bay as far as the mouth of the Rappahannock River, seventy-five miles southeast of Manassas and sixty miles east of Richmond. Then, predicted McClellan bullishly, it would be a question of either capturing Richmond before Johnston's rebels had time to rush south, or taking the capital once the Union army had surprised and smashed the retreating Confederates. There was a flaw in this plan, however, which Lincoln was quick to point out. What if Johnston, on hearing of McClellan's move south, chose to head north? Who would defend Washington from the rebels?

As it turned out, General Johnston preempted the Unionists by withdrawing from Maryland into Virginia. On March 12 the *New York Times* gloated of "the precipitate flight of the rebels . . . [they] retreated in a most excited and disorderly manner," but in truth it was a far more disciplined extraction. Though Johnston's men were forced to destroy or discard a quantity of supplies, they calmly pulled back forty miles, to just below Fredericksburg, and dug in on the southern side of the Rappahannock River, where they could better defend Richmond from the assault they knew was coming.

Hundreds of rebel troops continued south toward Richmond, arriving either by rail or on foot along the Mechanicsville Turnpike. On Saturday, March 15, the day before the jail break, John Beauchamp Jones noted in his diary that "for several days troops have been pouring through the city, marching down the [Virginia] Peninsula. The enemy are making demonstrations against Yorktown." In fact Jones was misinformed about Yorktown, a strategically important port on the York River, seventy miles east of Richmond. It was still in Confederate hands, a fact which only exacerbated the chagrin of Abraham Lincoln.

The president, like his people, had been led to believe by McClellan that Johnston had nearly one hundred thousand soldiers at Manassas. When Northern troops took over the newly vacated defenses it soon became evident that the rebels had numbered half the figure, if that. On March 13 the correspondent for the *New York Tribune* described how a tour of the former Confederate positions had left him "utterly dispirited, ashamed and humiliated . . . their retreat is our defeat." Lincoln reduced McClellan's authority, so that he was no longer general in chief but responsible only for the Army of the Potomac. In addition, Lincoln—without prior discussion with McClellan—appointed four corps commanders to the Potomac army. Before the month was out, Lincoln had also instructed General John

Frémont to head a new military department in West Virginia, and agreed that a division from McClellan's Army of the Potomac should augment Frémont's nascent force.

Despite his relegation, McClellan defied Lincoln's recommendation to launch an overland attack on Virginia and continued with preparations to mount a waterborne offensive. Hundreds of vessels and artillery pieces were assembled, and thousands of men underwent training for the long-awaited push into Southern territory. Never far from McClellan's side during this fraught period was Allan Pinkerton. He strove to aid his general as best he could, even while McClellan's "secret enemies were endeavoring to prejudice the mind of the president against his chosen commander; when wily politicians were seeking to belittle him in the estimation of the people; and when jealous-minded officers were ignorantly criticizing his plans of campaign." Pinkerton described his team as being "taxed to its utmost" as he and his operatives interrogated captured Confederate soldiers, Southern refugees and runaway slaves to try and ascertain the number, condition and location of the rebel army. Pinkerton also inquired of some of those he examined if they were familiar with the names Webster, Scully and Lewis. Perhaps they'd heard talk of these men during their wanderings.

Four weeks had passed since his two operatives set out south, and no news was forthcoming. The silence was a bad omen. Had Lewis and Scully been arrested on the way to Richmond? Or in Richmond? Or on their return journey? Perhaps they hadn't been caught; perhaps they were inching their way north hiding from militia patrols and avoiding retreating soldiers. And what of Webster? Where was he? How was he? Not a day passed without Pinkerton being "tortured by the uncertainty of their fate."

Tim Webster had hardly seen his wife in the past twelve months. His real wife. Hattie Lawton was the woman with whom he had shared his life since the start of 1861. The intensity of their existence, its precariousness, its pressure, had brought them together in a way Webster had never experienced with Mrs. Charlotte Webster. Hattie Lawton had acted the adoring wife well enough to fool everyone in Richmond.

The day after the arrest of Lewis and Scully, Samuel McCubbin knocked on the door of the Websters' room in the Monumental Hotel.

The greeting with Hattie Lawton was coolly cordial. He pulled up a chair alongside Webster and wondered at the strange events of the previous night. Webster told McCubbin he didn't follow, so the detective, watching the sick man closely, explained how Lewis and Scully had been arrested on suspicion of spying.

Webster could hardly believe it. On what evidence? McCubbin couldn't go into specifics, but he asked for the letter that they'd delivered. Of course, said Webster, by all means. He told his wife to look for it; it was somewhere in the room. Lawton found the letter and gave it to the detective, who tucked it into his pocket and left with a curt "good day."

In the following days none of Winder's men appeared at Webster's door to make inquires about his health. Only polite Mr. Price still popped by. Webster knew the danger he was in; they were on to him, of course, but what was their proof? Pinkerton's idea to send a letter had been crass and injudicious, but on its own it couldn't damn him. Webster spent hours sitting up in bed, reviewing the past year, searching for lapses that might prove pivotal to his enemies, and fatal to him. While Webster agonized, Lawton acted the devoted companion, telling him to "trust for a favorable outcome."

CHAPTER EIGHTEEN

"We Have All Your Companions"

Half an hour after scaling the prison wall, Pryce Lewis and his eight companions "found ourselves on elevated ground outside the city. Here the earth was freshly dug in all directions and we knew we were on a line of fortifications . . . glancing about we saw the flare of hundreds of camp fires."

Away to their left they saw Academy Hill silhouetted in the moonlight. They paused to let a sentry pass out of sight. Stanton crouched beside Lewis and whispered that Fort Johnson was ahead and to their right. There were also some artillery batteries, he warned, but he wasn't sure of their exact location. They "moved cautiously on, passing at last beyond the earthworks whose irregular windings confused us considerably as to the direction we were taking." Several times Stanton stopped to check his bearings before creeping forward into a mass of underbrush and felled trees which were penetrated with muttered curses.

By the time they'd fought their way through the worst of the foliage, one or two men were whining they would be better off back in jail. Others, Lewis included, drove the party forward into a copse. For the first time since the breakout the men had time to catch their breath. Some of the prisoners chewed at the lumps of corn bread they'd brought with them, and others licked the damp leaves to moisten their dry mouths. Someone asked Stanton if the Chickahominy was close. Not too far, he replied.

Anyone know the time? Lewis looked at his watch. It was midnight. Suddenly they heard the "tramping of horses hoofs and men talking and we knew we were not far from the highway [the Mechanicsville Pike]."

They got to their feet and pressed on. Soon they felt the ground turn soggy, and every step required a greater effort than before. Their thighs burned as they squelched toward a flooded field of cornstalks. By now "the water was quite deep, in some places up to our waists, and very cold." Seeds, the shortest of the men, plunged forward and disappeared up to his neck. He was pulled free, and someone made a quip about Seeds's habit of getting stuck.

The joke raised the men's spirits. So did the sight not long after of the Chickahominy. It wasn't as broad as Lewis had feared,* and in among "the tall pines [that] grew along the banks . . . we found a spot where a tree trunk had fallen across." They forded the river only to endure another demoralizing struggle through swampland on the northern banks. Finally the ground underfoot became firmer. Several of the men demanded that they rest a few minutes. Lewis said they must press on. A prisoner turned on Lewis. It was all right for him, he hissed, he'd only been a captive for a couple of weeks. But they'd been locked up for months. They must rest. Lewis relented, but more strong words were exchanged when someone proposed a campfire. Stanton and Lewis called it a foolish risk, but no one else cared what they thought.

They headed north for the rest of the night and at dawn hid under some heaps of brushwood. Lewis and Stanton hunkered down together, both frozen stiff, but nonetheless pleased with the first few hours of their escape. What awaits us? Lewis wanted to know. Stanton told him that the next big obstacle was the Pamunkey River to their north. They remained hidden for the rest of the day. Apart from the "beating of distant drums, reminding us that we were not many miles distant from a camp," the prisoners passed an uneventful day. They dozed, ate the last of their soggy corn bread and giggled at the thought of Staples arriving at the jail to find them gone.

---

* The men almost certainly crossed the Chickahominy at a point between Meadow Bridge and Mechanicsville Bridge. Farther east the river widened, although there were three fording places known to the rebel troops.

They were on the move at dusk, none of them much invigorated by the day's rest. Soon the wind strengthened, and the rain arrived. The men went into camp and built another fire. Now everyone "crowded around it in a desperate mood, careless of consequences, if only we could get warm." They carefully picked out every last crumb of corn bread from their pockets and savored the fleeting taste in their mouth. It seemed only to intensify their hunger. Lewis fell asleep and woke when he felt his feet on fire. The soles of his shoes were badly scorched but at least they no longer resembled blocks of ice.

The storm had passed by one o'clock on the morning of Tuesday, March 18. There was no relief. Lewis led them into "such a thick growth of underbrush that we could make little progress. We forced the twigs away from our faces [but] they seemed to be interlaced like a mat. We finally emerged from this labyrinth just before daylight."

Up ahead, three hundred yards distant, was a large farmhouse and a scattering of outhouses. Noiselessly they approached the outhouses and searched them one by one for food. There was none. The weaker men were now flagging, saying they'd had enough and wanted to surrender. Lewis, Stanton and Twells insisted that they push on to a piece of timber, where they could camp for the day. Despite the enormous risk, they built a little fire, and the men removed their socks and warmed their numb feet. Suddenly they heard the sound of wood being chopped. The fire was stamped out, and the prisoners crouched down, listening, hardly daring to breathe. When the chopping continued, one of the men crept forward to investigate. Suddenly all was silent, then they heard the sound of horse's hooves. A couple of minutes later their comrade reappeared with bad news. A black slave had been chopping wood when his master appeared and told him to saddle up his horse.

They agreed "at once that the white man had seen us and was mounting his horse to go and give an alarm." The men staggered to their feet and hurried north into some woods. Half a mile later they saw a cluster of log cabins.

They discussed what to do. Should they avoid the cabins, or go begging for food? Fearing they'd already been detected, the prisoners decided to seek out some breakfast. Lewis and Stanton volunteered and stole noiselessly forward. As they emerged from the woods they saw a group of black and white children playing among the cabins. There didn't appear to be a man in sight. Lewis knocked on the door of the first cabin. It was opened "by a white woman with a kindly face." Lewis removed his felt hat and explained that they were detectives from General Winder's office looking for deserters. Had she seen any suspicious characters in the past twenty-four hours? The woman said she hadn't, but her husband might have. He was out in the fields, but she could go and fetch him.

Lewis said that wouldn't be necessary. Then he asked if she had something to eat as tracking fugitives was hungry work. Of course, he would pay her for it. The woman told Lewis she didn't have much but "gave us a cheek of bacon and filled my handkerchief with corn meal." Lewis handed her two dollars in Maryland money and thanked her warmly.

When the pair returned to the woods they found no trace of their comrades. Had they come to the wrong spot? They looked around, agreeing that this was definitely where they'd left them. They surmised that their companions had scattered, perhaps alarmed at the sight of a passing farm laborer. Lewis and Stanton weren't too bothered; in fact they were glad to get rid of one or two whiners. They sat down against a tree and ate their breakfast. With their morale replenished as well as their appetite, they felt confident in crossing the Pamunkey River and reaching Northern lines.

Soon they were up and off, moving far quicker as a pair than they had done as a group. It was midafternoon when they saw the river, in front of which "was a little red brick house lying in a little hollow." Between them and the house was an upturned tree, its exposed roots resembling the hands of a clock. Underneath was a hollow that Stanton suggested would make a good place in which to rest till dusk.

As they walked toward the tree they heard a noise from the woods behind. Lewis turned and "saw not far off, three men, two with muskets on their shoulders, coming directly toward us." The men weren't in uniform, and for a moment Lewis thought they might be hunters. But he shuddered at their swaggering approach.

One of the men with a musket asked what they were doing. Lewis replied that they were looking for a place to rest. The man laughed and so did Lewis, though his was "a sort of laugh that relieves the nerves." The man pointed the musket at the hollow and said that looked an ideal spot. Lewis and Stanton agreed. Then he asked where they intended to head once they'd rested. Fredericksburg, said Lewis. At this moment one of the other men lost patience and, raising his musket, told Lewis and Stanton that they knew who they were because "we have all your companions." Lewis and Stanton were escorted through the woods until they reached a house. Inside they found their comrades sitting around an open fireplace and finishing the remains of a bountiful supper. One of the men joked that they'd missed a feast, and everyone found it funny. Lewis "joined in the laugh, a thoughtless, healthy, good-natured laugh, inspired by the blazing fire and signs of food." More food was produced, and Lewis and Stanton ate until their whiskers glistened with pig fat. As the captured men gorged themselves, their captors commended them on their daring escape, telling them they were twenty miles from Richmond and headed in the right direction for Fredericksburg. They might have made it, they were told, were it not for their imprudence in lighting a fire.*

The next morning, Wednesday, March 19, Lewis and the eight escapees were loaded into two covered wagons and driven back to Richmond. When they arrived in the city there was quite a crowd to see the recaptured men. Boys and girls cowered behind their parents' legs as the wagons approached, having "learned to dread and fear the Yankees above all tame or wild animals." Stanton and Twells, seasoned escapees, enjoyed the attention and lapped up the notoriety, but Lewis didn't. He dared not show his face in case " 'Old Wise' or some of my West Virginia acquaintances might be in the crowd and recognize me."

General Wise was indeed in Richmond at this time, having arrived in February after the fall of Roanoke Island in North Carolina, a defeat that cost the life of his son, Obadiah Jennings. He remained in the city until April 25, when he was ordered into the field. Also in Richmond was Colonel George Patton, who had been the beneficiary of a prisoner exchange with the Northern army. The shoulder wound he had suffered eight months earlier had all but healed, and he was looking forward to resuming command of his regiment.

* The *Baltimore Sun* reported on April 9 that "among the prisoners were Tajem, Geming, said to be from Baltimore, and J.M. Seeds, of Ohio." Tajem was in all probability a misspelling of Tatum as records fail to show any prisoner in Richmond by the name of Tajem. On May 15 Tatum, Twells, Seeds and Stanton were transferred from Castle Godwin to Salisbury Prison in North Carolina.

CHAPTER NINETEEN

"Hanged by the Necks Until We Were Dead"

T HE CONVOY OF WAGONS HALTED outside General Winder's headquarters. This time there were no warm handshakes or polite greetings. The provost marshal general ordered every prisoner to be returned to jail and clapped in irons.

They arrived at Henrico to find a new door and new jailors. As the prisoners were kicked and shoved inside their cells they "learned that jailor Staples and keeper Thomas were both under arrest charged with conniving at the escape." For two or three hours the escapees sat on the cold stone floor pondering their fate. They'd had no breakfast and still wore the damp, ragged clothes in which they'd escaped. Presently the outer iron door of their cell was opened, then the inner one, and a jailor appeared. He dragged out one of the prisoners, who reappeared a few minutes later wearing irons about his wrists.

Lewis's turn came last. He was taken to the adjoining cell in which stood three or four men in with fixed bayonets. One of them swore at the "Yankee Abolitionist." Sitting at the table were the sheriff, a blacksmith and his Negro assistant. In the middle of the table was a pile of rudely made handcuffs. The jailor forced Lewis's wrists into the iron rings, and then the blacksmith riveted the rings together. Lewis turned to go, but the jailor told him General Winder's orders were that he be cuffed hands and feet. When Lewis was pushed back inside his cell it was empty. Later the prisoner named Pitcher, the man who had stayed behind during the escape because of ill health, was put into the cell and instructed to help and feed Lewis.

Within a couple of days Lewis's wrists and ankles had been rubbed raw by the shackles. Even the smallest movement was painful. He spent his time lying on the floor of this cell, pulling himself to his feet only when nature demanded. Pitcher collected his food and tended to him.

On the eighth day Lewis received a visitor, George Clackner, the enigmatic detective from Baltimore. He cursed when he saw the irons and demanded they be removed immediately. Apologizing for the indignity, Clackner helped Lewis to his feet and explained that he was to be tried by court-martial.

Outside the prison gate two armed guards were waiting to escort Lewis to the City Hall, but Clackner dismissed them, saying he could manage the prisoner on his own. Clackner marched Lewis along Broad Street toward the City Hall. There was a bit of small talk, a brief description of the prison break, and then Clackner mentioned that he had a little errand to run before they went to the City Hall. They turned down a side street and entered a hardware store. Clackner told his prisoner to wait at the entrance while he attended to some business. Lewis did as he was told as Clackner chatted with the owner, seemingly unconcerned about the prisoner at the door. Lewis was puzzled at the lax security, and "it occurred to me that here was an opportunity to escape." But was it a trap? Were the two armed guards waiting around the corner to shoot him as he fled? Had he felt stronger, Lewis might have run the risk and bolted. But eight days chained hand and foot had stripped him of his strength. He stood by the door and waited.

Clackner finished his errand and handed Lewis to the City Hall authorities without another word. After a few minutes Lewis was taken upstairs to a large room, where he was introduced to William Crump, the judge advocate of the court. He asked Lewis if he wished to have a counsel. No, said Lewis. Crump advised him to think about it, particularly as "your friend Scully employed counsel." The remark threw Lewis, who had no idea Scully had already been tried.

Lewis accepted the proposal and was given Scully's counsel, a Mr. Gilmer. When the lawyer arrived from his office at the corner of Bank and Main streets he showed the prisoner into a side room and came straight to the point. He wasn't cheap. From Scully he'd received "one hundred dollars in gold," and he expected the same from Lewis. He could have it, replied the Englishman, provided he told him what had happened to Scully. Gilmer gave a brief account of the trial, how "Scully admitted that he had been in the United States government service, but becoming disgusted and being a foreigner, he had left." Gilmer advised Lewis to adopt the same defense. One further thing, added Gilmer, beware the Morton family. They would be called as witnesses, and they "were very bitter."

The trial began the following day, after Lewis had been given time to rest, eat and wash. He stood before a court-martial consisting of the judge advocate, a colonel acting as the president of the court and six field officers of lower rank.

There were several charges laid before the defendant, the principal accusations being that Pryce Lewis was an enemy alien in the employ of the Lincoln government and that he been "found within the fortifications of Richmond taking a plan thereof." Lewis pleaded not guilty to all charges.

Over the following three days the prosecution called a number of witnesses to prove otherwise. Mrs. Morton, her two daughters, and her two sons took the stand, all testifying that the man in the dock was the same man who had led the search of their former home in Washington. Yet far from exacting revenge, Mrs. Morton wished to emphasize that Lewis "had behaved gentlemanly in her house."

Next General Winder testified, followed by his detectives, including Samuel McCubbin, Philip Cashmeyer and George Clackner. The latter confirmed to the court that he'd seen the letter brought to Timothy Webster by the defendant, and that its writer, Scott from Baltimore, was known by Clackner to be loyal to the South. The claim surprised Lewis, who looked hard at Clackner and wondered once more "if he had left me near the store door to give me an opportunity to escape."*

When Lewis was called to the stand his counsel asked him few questions. Instead Mr. Gilmer confined himself to the "theory of defense."

---

* Lewis was never able to unravel the enigmatic Clackner. In November 1862 Winder reorganized his force, and Clackner was fired. He finished the war as a lowly warden at Libby Prison.

He told the court that it was well known in Richmond that following the Union army's calamitous defeat at Manassas (Bull Run) the previous July, many of their officers had deserted to the Confederate army. And that, blazoned Gilmer, waving a finger at Lewis, was what the accused had done. But Lewis knew he was wasting his breath. After the prosecution had rattled off a few perfunctory questions, the prisoner was marched from the court to await his fate.

Lewis was escorted to Castle Godwin prison and left in a cell with his wrists shackled. The next day he was taken downstairs to a comfortable room with a fire. Lying listlessly in a cot in front of the fire was John Scully, who looked up at Lewis and "burst into tears." One of the jailors removed Lewis's handcuffs and told him his companion needed succor. Lewis was shocked at what he saw. Scully was "haggard and woe-begone [but] suffering more from mental anxiety than bodily pain." He wanted to go home to Chicago, he said, weeping, to kiss his wife, and hug his children, little Lizzie and Tom. It would be Tom's first birthday soon. The thought tortured him. He didn't want to die.

Don't talk nonsense, said Lewis, trying to console his friend, "they could not hang us on the ridiculous charge of taking plans of fortifications." They sat up most of the night talking, and by dawn on Tuesday, April 1, Scully was thinking more positively. Lewis had convinced him that within a matter of days McClellan would be marching through the streets of Richmond, followed no doubt by Pinkerton holding the general's hat. Scully raised a smile. We'll be all right, Lewis reassured him.

After breakfast the pair dozed in front of the fire. They were woken sometime later by the arrival of their jailor, accompanied by two men they didn't recognize. One was tall and athletic with sandy-colored hair and a goatee of the same hue. He introduced himself as Captain Archibald Godwin, provost marshal of Richmond, after whom the prison had been named. The second man was Captain George Alexander, assistant provost marshal, short but stocky with an olive complexion and an elegant black mustache.

Captain Godwin removed a document from the pocket of his uniform. He asked John Scully and Pryce Lewis to confirm their names, then pronounced that both men were "to be hanged by the necks until we were dead on the 4th of April between ten and two o'clock."

The condemned men were told they could have anything they wished in the remaining three days of their life, and then Godwin and Alexander departed. Lewis put a consoling arm around his friend's shoulder and told him they were in this together and must bear up. Scully rebuffed his companion, saying Lewis could not know how he was feeling for he didn't have a wife and children.

Scully was soon seized by a manic energy. He would write, yes, he would write letters to everyone who had the power to help. To the Catholic bishop of Richmond, to Gilmer their lawyer, to the British consul. He told Lewis he had written to the consulate a week earlier but had received no reply. Scully suggested Lewis write, too, and the Englishman thought it worth a try. He called for some paper and a pencil; then he wrote to the British consul stating his case and asking to see him immediately. He entrusted the letter to Father McMullen, a priest at the city's St. Peter's Cathedral, who made daily visits to Castle Godwin to offer spiritual relief to some of the 250 inmates. McMullen gave his word that he would deliver the letter to the consul. Then he asked if he could be of assistance in a more spiritual way. Lewis declined the offer, explaining that he was not a religious man. For Scully, however, the appearance of Father McMullen was a balm for his anguished soul.

Once the priest had departed, Scully and Lewis sat before the fire and talked about the past and future. A subject that troubled them was Tim Webster. Scully told Lewis Webster had given a statement in his defense during his trial. How had he looked? inquired Lewis. Scully explained that Webster had been too ill to attend the court-martial in person, so he and the court-martial had gathered around Webster's sickbed to hear his evidence.

Webster had been staunch in his defense of Scully, describing him as a friend from Baltimore who "was always in the company of known Secessionists, and was considered by them to be a good friend to the South [and] so far as he had any knowledge . . . he was what he assumed to be, and that his appearance in Richmond was a surprise to him." When it was put to Webster that Scully might be in the employ of the Federal government, the sick man had dismissed the idea as impossible.

Lewis told Scully the news was encouraging because "suspicion that would naturally attach to Webster from the circumstances of our arrest" remained for the moment only that, suspicion. Winder and his men still lacked the hard evidence to bring Webster before a court.

CHAPTER TWENTY

"Keep Your Courage Up"

B Y APRIL 1862 a semblance of order had been restored to the British consulate in Richmond. Acting Consul Frederick Cridland was no longer besieged by dozens of fretful Britons demanding permits, money and safe passage home. Most had long since left Richmond, and Cridland was toiling less hard for his monthly wage of twenty-one pounds.

He had indeed received a letter from a Mr. John Scully on March 28, though it was a rather vague, poorly written correspondence with no mention of an imminent execution. Nevertheless, Cridland "sought and obtained an interview with the officer presiding at the Court Martial which had condemned Scully and became convinced that the evidence produced against him left no doubt of his guilt."

The letter handed him by Father McMullen on Tuesday, April 1, was altogether more alarming. Not only had it been written by an educated, articulate man, but one under the sentence of death. Cridland, reluctant as he was to interfere "in the cases of persons who had evidently violated Her Majesty's Proclamation," nonetheless considered he would be failing in his duty as acting consul if he did not follow up the letter. Cridland had applied to see the prisoners the day he received the letter, but the request was refused. On Wednesday he tried again, with more insistence, and he was granted an appointment on Thursday, April 3, the day before the execution.

As the acting British consul strode to Castle Godwin, a mile and a half to the west laborers began erecting a gallows under a grove of oak trees on the Camp Lee Fair Grounds.

Cridland was shown to the cell occupied by Lewis and Scully, and introductions were made. Neither Lewis or Cridland made any reference to the letter that Lewis had written to the consul from Charleston nine months earlier asking for a pass to Richmond; in all likelihood Cridland never received the letter. The diplomat soon got down to business, explaining that he had discussed their case first with the court-martial officer, then with Gilmer. It wasn't good. They'd repeated to Cridland the report of General Winder: that the two spies had been under surveillance from the moment they arrived in Richmond and that the detectives had judged "their movements very extraordinary and suspicious." To sum up, declared Cridland in a pompous tone, "there is enough evidence against you to hang a hundred and eleven men."

Lewis was flabbergasted at Cridland's attitude and asked if he'd seen the evidence. The consul admitted that he hadn't, though he had asked. The confession riled Lewis, who accused Cridland of not doing enough to help them. Cridland, impressed with the clarity of Lewis's outburst, adopted a more conciliatory approach, and soon they were deep in conversation, reviewing in detail every circumstance that had brought Lewis and Scully to this woebegone moment.

"Keep your courage up" were the last words Cridland said to Lewis and Scully before departing. For their part, the two prisoners begged him to keep his word and seek an immediate interview with the Confederate government. They had less than twenty-four hours to live.

Cridland walked a few blocks west from Castle Godwin to the secretary of state's office in the front part of the Treasury Building devising his strategy. There was no time to ask Lord Richard Lyons in Washington to intercede on the men's behalf, nor did Cridland consider that he alone possessed the diplomatic weight to exert sufficient pressure on the Confederate government. He must tread carefully but firmly; diplomacy of the highest order was required. No threats, but perhaps he might employ one or two subtle hints apropos Her Majesty's government and its relations with the South.

Judah Benjamin, the secretary of state, and George W. Randolph, the secretary of war, rose when Cridland was shown into the room by the chief clerk. Cridland expressed his gratitude for the extraordinary interview and then set out the nature of his call. He had come straight from Castle Godwin, where two British subjects, "John Scully and Pryce Lewis acknowledged to me that they had been employed as spies in Washington and paid as such by the Federal Government." That point was indubitable, Cridland emphasized, adding that he was well aware of Her Majesty's Proclamation of Neutrality in which the queen had warned all British subjects from interfering in the American conflict. That wasn't the issue. What concerned Cridland was the revelation that "the prisoners had been tried and condemned to death at a moment when it was utterly impossible for either of them to obtain any evidence in their favor from Washington." He, too, had requested to see the evidence against the two men, but this had been refused. Surely this went against all judicial protocol? Cridland would be happy "to write to Lord Lyons in order to obtain evidence should the execution be postponed," but of course that was a decision to be made by the Confederate government.

The interview concluded with "no promise" from either Randolph or Benjamin. Cridland thanked the men for their time, and they in return were grateful that the matter had been brought to their attention.

To his friends, the fifty-year-old Judah Benjamin was "the brains of the Confederacy"; to his enemies he was "the hated Jew." John Beauchamp Jones, who had worked as Benjamin's clerk when he was secretary of war, despised his religion but respected his "intellect, education, and extensive reading, combined with natural abilities of a tolerably high order."

When Cridland sat before him on the afternoon of Thursday, April 3, 1862, Benjamin had been secretary of state for a mere six days, having succeeded LeRoy Pope Walker. His replacement as secretary of war, George Randolph, was thus similarly inexperienced in his new position. While Randolph was considered a competent lawyer, Benjamin's brilliance bordered on genius. He had been elected to the Senate in 1852,

rapidly gaining a reputation as one of the Democratic Party's most elo-
quent and powerful orators. The Southern Anti-Semites may have detested Benjamin, but he was a favorite with President Davis, who admired
his blunt honesty and valued his cool judgment.

Benjamin enjoyed his work. Sixteen-hour days weren't unusual, with
or without a war, and the question of the two British prisoners must have
appealed to his legal mind. Having been born in the West Indies to English
parents, Benjamin was an Anglophile, but he, like everyone else in the
Confederate government, was losing patience with the British.

In the months following Queen Victoria's Proclamation of Neutrality, the
British government had maintained a discreet distance on the "American
war question" and made no attempt to lift the Union blockade of Southern ports. Not so the country's press, which was overwhelmingly inimical
to the North. The spectacular failure of the Union army at Bull Run in
July 1861 was greeted with thinly veiled glee by most newspapers with
the London *Times* describing it as a "cowardly rout, a miserable, causeless panic, and disgraceful to men in uniform."

American papers in the North retaliated with splenetic attacks of their
own. *Harper's Weekly* told its readers to ignore the "short-sighted selfish-
ness" of Britain, while reminding them that the London *Times* was "the
exponent of that British public opinion which allowed George Third to
hire Hessians to fight his battles against the sons of Englishmen."*

The *New York Times* warned Britain that "a profound indignation is
felt by the larger part of the American nation, and it is not likely to be al-
layed for years to come." The insults traded across the Atlantic delighted
those in the South. Mary Chesnut, the wife of a Confederate soldier and
politician, told her diary on July 5, 1861, "The [London] *Times* reflects
the sentiment of the English people. How we do cling to the idea of an
alliance with England."

Yet just a few weeks later, on August 26, Chesnut was rebuking
William Russell, the *Times'* august war correspondent, for his antislavery

---

* The Principality of Hesse-Kassel (part of modern-day Germany) supplied many of
its soldiers to King George III during the American War of Independence. Its ruler,
Frederick II, was a cousin of the British monarch.

polemic. Russell was the most influential reporter of the day on either side of the Atlantic. Since March 1861 he had been traveling through the Southern and Eastern states, filing regular dispatches on what he found. Russell was an impartial observer; he admired the determination and courage of the Confederate army, while questioning similar attributes in the Northern forces; he liked the hospitality he encountered in the Southern states and felt intimidated by the hectoring that emanated from certain Union politicians. But what Russell detested above all else was the institution of slavery. Reaching one Southern plantation, he had found it run like "a hideous black harem." How was it, Russell asked, that one could have anything but contempt for a man who "holds his head high and poses as the model of all human virtues to these poor women whom God and the laws have given him, [and] from the height of his awful majesty he scolds and thunders at them as if he never did wrong in his life?" Russell's antislavery polemic touched a raw nerve with educated Southerners like Mary Chesnut, many of whom knew of the depravities practiced on plantations, but who had chosen to purge their consciousness of such thoughts. They didn't take kindly to an outsider reminding them of the evil that lay among the tobacco plants and cotton fields.

As summer turned to autumn, the Confederacy's desperation for British assistance deepened. Cotton hadn't brought "England to its knees," as one Southern paper had so confidently envisaged earlier in the year, and Northern newspapers seized every opportunity to remind the rebels of the fact. In September 1861 *Harper's Weekly* reported that the viceroy of Egypt had notified the British government that the productive cotton capacity of the country would be "increased to an unlimited extent," while "the Nicaraguan Embassador [*sic*] in London offers it free grant of land in Nicaragua to settlers who propose to raise cotton."

President Davis resolved to send two more emissaries to London to plead with the British government once again to recognize the Confederate States as a sovereign nation. The men chosen were James Mason, former chairman of the U.S. Senate Foreign Relations Committee, and John Slidell, a respected lawyer from New Orleans. Some considered Mason a curious envoy to send to England. The Virginian-born Mason was not a born diplomat, but he was a fierce proponent of slavery and a driving force behind the Fugitive Slave Law of 1850, a bill that allowed slave owners to cross state lines in order to retrieve their goods.

On October 12, 1861, Slidell and Mason ran the Union blockade at Charleston, South Carolina, and reached Havana without incident. In the Cuban capital they boarded a British mail steamer, the *Trent*, bound for the English port of Southampton. The two diplomats traveled with secretaries, and Slidell was also accompanied by his wife, son and three daughters. As the purser of the *Trent* later related in a letter to the London *Daily Telegraph*, it wasn't long after leaving Havana on November 8 that they observed ahead a large steamship in the narrowest part of the Bahama Channel. The vessel displayed no flag, explained the purser, and the first intimation of its nationality was "a round shot being fired across our bows and at the same moment by her showing American colours." The British steamer held its course, and the next instant the American ship, the *San Jacinto*, "fired a shell from a swivel gun of large caliber on her forecastle, which passed within a few yards of the ship, bursting about a hundred yards to leeward."

The *Trent* hove to, and within a few minutes "between twenty and thirty men, heavily armed, under the command of the first lieutenant," boarded the ship. As Lieutenant Donald Fairfax stood on deck demanding to see the ship's passenger list, he was confronted by the *Trent*'s skipper, Captain James Moir, who informed the American that this was a British vessel and his actions were tantamount to piracy. Fairfax eyed the captain and demanded a second time the manifest, saying he had reason to believe the ship carried two enemies of the U.S. government and his orders were to remove them. Moir again "indignantly refused" to cooperate, at which point, said the purser, "Mr. Slidell himself came forward . . . but appealed to the British flag, under which they were sailing, for protection."

Fairfax ignored the petition and ordered the seizure of the two envoys and their secretaries. Slidell and Mason asked that they be permitted to pack a few belongings, a request that was granted. It was at the moment, related the purser, that "a most heart-rending scene took place between Mr. Slidell, his eldest daughter—a noble girl devoted to her father—and the lieutenant. It would require a far more able pen than mine to describe how with flashing eye and quivering lip she threw herself in the door-way of the cabin where her father was, resolved to defend him with her life, till on the order being given to the marines to advance, which they did with bayonets pointed at this poor defenceless girl, her father ended the painful scene by escaping from the cabin by a window, when he was immediately seized by the marines and hurried into the boat, calling out to Captain Moir, as he left, that he held him and his Government responsible for this outrage."

Outrage was the word used in the *Daily Telegraph*'s headline of November 30 when it heard of the drama on the high seas. The *Manchester Guardian* declared that "the American government are determined to test to the utmost the truth of the adage that it takes two to make a quarrel," and not one British newspaper deviated from the line that in boarding a British vessel, the American government had violated international law and abused Britain's position of neutrality. The Northern newspapers saw it differently. Commodore Charles Wilkes, skipper of the *San Jacinto*, was a hero, a man to be exalted and promoted. *Harper's Weekly* was of the opinion that "the arrest of the rebel Commissioners was fully justified . . . and that Commodore Wilkes would even have been justified in taking the *Trent*, and bringing her into the harbor of New York as a prize, for carrying rebel officers and dispatch."

The *New York Commercial Advertiser* was one of the few Federal newspapers to quietly draw attention to the fact that "Wilkes has done the very thing in principle for which we went to war with England for doing. It is true that the right of search exists in a time of war, and rests in the belligerent; but this forcible seizure of political prisoners when under the protection of a neutral flag is unjustifiable and ought to be repudiated by the United States government."

The "war" referred to by the *Advertiser* was the one of 1812 against Great Britain, a conflict in which the roots lay in part in America's actions throughout the Napoleonic Wars. Britain had done its utmost to prevent all neutral countries trading with the French in the early years of the nineteenth century, issuing in 1807 an order compelling neutral vessels to submit to an inspection by its naval authorities. Any captain who failed to comply would have his vessel boarded and his cargo impounded. With its superior navy Britain was able to enforce the order, much to the fury of American seamen, who saw no reason why they could not continue to trade with France. But Britain justified its "Right of Search" on the fact that it was at war. To emphasize the point, the crew of a British naval vessel boarded the American ship *Hercules* in 1810 just before it left Sardinia for America, taking into captivity Lucien Bonaparte, younger brother of Napoleon. By 1812 the United States was unable to further tolerate British naval aggression. War was declared. Half a century later, another war appeared inevitable, though this time it was Britain complaining of American hostility.

On November 30 the British government sent Queen's Messenger James Haworth-Leslie across the Atlantic to deliver Dispatch no. 444 to Lord Lyons in Washington. The dispatch contained the conditions Lyons was to set before the American government if it wished to avoid war. On the same day Britain began its preparations to send troops to Canada. The *Blackburn Times* reported that the Admiralty had telegrammed Portsmouth ordering "the fifty-one gun screw frigates *Shannon* and *Euryalus*, and the *Stromboli*, 6 guns, to be in readiness for immediate commission . . . an addition was made to the cargo of the transport *Melbourne*, viz., 2,500,000 rounds of small arms' cartridges, 30,000 stand of arms, and accoutrements."

A bellicose cartoon appeared in *Punch* on December 7 showing a burly but unarmed British sailor warning his pistol-toting American counterpart to "do what's right, my son, or I'll blow you out of the water." But as the jingoism increased and the clamor for war intensified, one or two newspapers began to draw back. The *Daily Telegraph*, while it expressed outrage at the actions of the *San Jacinto,* also called on its compatriots for a period of reflection. "We are, indeed, too strong a nation to be hot-tempered . . . to draw that sword which cannot go up unbloody into its scabbard. All the horrors of war are aggravated when war is between men of one civilization and language . . . [and] let it be remembered that the officers of the *San Jacinto* must either have acted under orders from head-quarters or they officiously exceeded their orders, and in either case we must await explanation, if not repudiation."

The *Telegraph* also probably knew what most informed members of the British establishment knew: that the British lion was a weary beast, weakened by recent conflicts in the Crimea and India. The roar was still there, and from a distance the lion looked as menacing as ever, but up close the coat had lost its shine and the claws their sharpness. The call to arms issued by the British government was a snarl, but in reality the wish was to resolve the crisis peacefully.

On the other side of the Atlantic similar moves were afoot to steer a way through the stormy diplomatic waters. President Lincoln and Secretary of State Seward allowed passions to cool on both sides, and Charles

Adams, the United States' minister to Britain, blamed their silence on the paucity of communication links between the two countries, though some encouraging news came from Alexander Galt, Canada's minister of finance, who was in Washington and secured an interview with Lincoln. Galt reported that the president assured him the United States had no intention of attacking Canada, and as for the *Trent* affair, his only comment had been "Oh, that'll be got along with."

On December 18 Lord Lyons received the official dispatch from London sent nearly three weeks earlier. It was delivered by James Haworth-Leslie, who was in such haste to reach Washington that he hired a private train to bring him south from New York, having learned that the next regular service wasn't until the following day. The dispatch instructed Lyons to obtain the release of the two Confederate envoys along with an apology from the U.S. government. He was to allow the Americans seven days' grace. Also included in the instructions was an unofficial directive from Lord John Russell, Britain's foreign secretary, explaining that while the freedom of Mason and Slidell was imperative, the apology was less so. In other words, America was being given a chance to save some face.

On December 19 Lyons met Seward and apprised him of the dispatch's contents. Seward asked how long his government had to respond. Lyons concealed the seven-day deadline. On December 25 Lincoln and his cabinet agreed to release the two envoys and crafted a communiqué that was in places contradictory and disingenuous but defiant enough to please the American public. Though Commodore Wilkes had been justified in his actions, because the Confederates were contraband of war, he had broken international law by not bringing his booty into an American port for trial by a prize court. As a result, James Mason and John Slidell would be allowed to resume their passage to England. No apology was forthcoming.

The British were satisfied with the response, and Lyons commented that "the preparation for war . . . has prevented war." With honor intact on both sides of the Atlantic, everyone was happy, except the Confederate States. A representative of Jefferson Davis's government already in London, Henry Hotze, wrote that "the *Trent* affair has done us incalculable injury." In particular, the revelation by the *Trent*'s purser that Slidell's last words as he was taken from the ship were a reminder to Captain Moir that "he held him and his Government responsible for this outrage" proved to the British people that the two Confederates were agent provocateurs desirous of dragging Britain into their war. Hotze also reported the London *Times'* view of Mason and Slidell (who finally reached the English capital on January 30) as "the most worthless booty it would be possible to extract from the jaws of the American lion . . . so we do sincerely hope that our countrymen will not give these fellows anything in the shape of an ovation."

When news of the *Trent*'s violation had first reached Richmond, men and women from the grand drawing rooms of the palatial houses on Clay Street, to the barroom of the Monumental Hotel, eagerly anticipated the day, surely not far off, when Britain would declare war on the Union. Thus the news that a compromise had been reached distressed those in the Confederacy who had pinned their hopes on Britain. A front-page editorial in the *Richmond Dispatch* of March 12 declared that "Frenchmen fight for glory, Englishmen for gain. England will not recognize our independence or raise the blockade until it is in her interests so to do." The paper returned to the attack on March 25, saying that the "controlling motive of the British government . . . through the abolition of slave labor in the south [is] to cripple and destroy the cotton culture in America as to make the world dependent for its manufactures upon the cotton productions of British colonies."

Judah Benjamin was conscious of such Anglophobic sentiment; but he was also aware of the enduring resentment felt by many in the British Parliament toward the Federal government. In February the venerable Earl of Carnarvon had clashed with Lord Russell on the issue of the North's attitude toward citizens of Great Britain. Carnarvon thought it preposterous that "three British subjects were at this moment detained in prison in the Federal States, where they had been between four and five months, on secret charges without a single allegation of any sort being made." Russell countered that the U.S. government was engaged in a civil war and extreme measures were thus required, but he assured the Right Honorable Member that he would "always be ready to instruct Lord Lyons [the British ambassador to the United States] to bring the case under the consideration of the authorities of the United States Government." The Earl of Carnarvon was not placated by Russell's vapid statement. After all, they had been here before, had they not, only three months earlier, when two British subjects—a Mr. Patrick and a Mr. Rahming—had been held without charge for several weeks. In that instance, when Lord Lyons had complained to William Seward about the "irregular proceedings," he had been informed that "the safety of the whole people has become, in the present emergency, the supreme law, and so long as the danger shall exist to all classes of society equally, the denizen and the citizen must cheerfully acquiesce in the measures which that law prescribes."

Yet even if Benjamin saw the fate of Lewis and Scully as an opportunity to exploit British disquiet by contrasting Northern oppression with Southern goodwill, his overriding concern was whether correct legal procedure had been followed in the case of the two spies. For such a punctilious lawyer, this was the fundamental issue at stake, and it would govern his final recommendation to President Davis as to whether the men should live or die.

CHAPTER TWENTY-ONE

"I Have Made a Full Statement and Confessed Everything"

P RYCE LEWIS SAT in Castle Godwin's "condemned cell" on April 3, waiting to die. He and Scully had been separated shortly after the visit of Frederick Cridland, and Lewis considered his new home a cruel place for a man to spend his last night on earth. It was windowless and lightless and practically airless; only "a hole cut in the door about five inches square" allowed Lewis to breathe. There was one bench and "the floor was wet . . . and smelt horribly."

Lewis told his jailor, George Freeburger, that "there is no people in the world, civilized or savage, who would consign a condemned man to a room like this." Freeburger looked around and agreed. He departed with a promise to cheer up the place and soon returned with two Negroes who between them carried a cot, blankets, a bucket, a chair and some candles. Freeburger had a pile of books under his arms. Father McMullen arrived and told Lewis that he had heard Scully's final confession. Lewis did not reply. The Father asked if he could do anything for the Englishman, but the offer was rebuffed. McMullen expressed his sorrow for Lewis and implored him to confess his sins and prepare for the next life. Lewis shook his head and asked what was the point. Face it, Father, he said, "you know nothing beyond the grave more than I do. None of us know anything about it."

McMullen was astounded by Lewis's words. He asked if he could stay

with him for a few minutes, if he promised not to preach. The pair sat in
silence for a while, and the priest then left, saying he would return at dawn.
Fine, replied Lewis, as long as he came as a man and not a priest.

After McMullen left, Lewis ate "an excellent supper, including roast
chicken," and spent the evening reading by candlelight. One of the
books he found funny, a tale of an Irish schoolmaster who fell victim to
a series of schoolboy pranks.

Lewis fell into a fitful sort of slumber but soon awoke and spent the
rest of the night reviewing his life. He hadn't lied to Father McMullen.
He had no fear of death and considered "that the physical pain would not
be greater than an instant's sharp toothache." And as for the hereafter
Lewis "believed in a just God. I was in His power. If He were not just, I
could not help it."

At eight o'clock Captain Freeburger arrived with Lewis's breakfast.
He thanked the warden and asked if the hammering he could hear was
the gallows being erected. No, Freeburger assured him, just some new
bunks being installed in the guards' room.

Not long after Lewis had finished his breakfast Father McMullen
entered the cell. He said nothing but gazed at Lewis for a few seconds.
Then, matter-of-factly, he conveyed the news that the execution had
been respited. Lewis gave a small nod of his head. McMullen placed a
couple of religious volumes on the bench and walked out.

Judah Benjamin had granted the two men a "spontaneous" respite in the
name of President Jefferson Davis. The first Frederick Cridland knew of
the decision was when he read "in the public papers that the execution
had been postponed to the 12th day of April." Benjamin's decision did
little to endear him to his critics, particularly to the newspaper editors
who were vexed at his show of mercy. "For reasons satisfactory to ourselves," ran a report in the April 5 edition of the *Richmond Dispatch*,
whose editor, James Cowardin, was personally acquainted with the two
spies, "the principal one being the fact that the authorities were averse to
any publicity being given to the affair, we have refrained for several days
past from mentioning that two men, Pryce Lewis and John Scully, had
been tried before the Court Martial now sitting in the City Hall, and
condemned to be hung as spies. The execution was to have taken place
yesterday at 11 o'clock, at the New Fair Grounds, the gallows having

been erected there, and all needful preparation made for carrying into effect the sentence of the court. The execution has been postponed for a short time on a respite granted the parties by the president, but we are assured it will come off at an early day."

There was a curious end to the *Dispatch*'s report, a twist that must have tantalized Richmond's citizens as they sat at their breakfast tables drinking their coffee substitute. The newspaper revealed "that the condemned have made disclosures affecting the fidelity of several persons, one or more of whom have been apprehended. Rumor had it yesterday that one of the parties thus implicated was an officer holding a place under the Government. If rumor speaks the truth, he will find himself, no doubt, in an uncomfortably hot place."

After Webster had spoken up for John Scully, the Confederates knew they had their man. The "style of his evidence," and his avowal that Scully "was a good friend to the south" was a lie. It was arranged that William Campbell, the government contractor with whom Webster had journeyed to Nashville in January, should insist that the sick man finish his convalescence at his house. There would be less risk of him absconding from Richmond during the dead of night. Webster, who had celebrated his fortieth birthday earlier in the month, raised a feeble protest, but Campbell insisted and in late March Webster was moved from the Monumental Hotel.

Not long before sundown on Thursday, April 3, at around the time Cridland was shaking hands with Benjamin and Randolph, there was a knock at the Websters' door. Standing outside was Campbell who, in a detached voice, announced that a policeman was on his way up the stairs.

Philip Cashmeyer was one of the younger members of the military police, a cunning man with a "blarney smile" whose favorite phrase was "you can always catch flies with molasses"; in other words, grease his palm, and he might turn a blind eye. But not in Webster's case.

Cashmeyer entered the room and announced that it was his "painful duty" to arrest both Mr. and Mrs. Webster and convey them to Castle Godwin prison. There was the sound of heavy boots running up the stairs, and then two soldiers with bayonets fixed appeared. Hattie Lawton exclaimed that Webster was in no fit state to be moved, but Cashmeyer had his instructions.

The *Richmond Dispatch* reported a few days later that eleven people were committed to Castle Godwin on April 3. Mike Fitzgerald from New Orleans was imprisoned because of "fighting," John Fallon for "a breach of discipline" and J. T. Reed had been "disloyal." The paper made no special reference to the two suspected Union agents; it simply stated: "Tim Webster, Mrs. Webster, Kentucky, spies." The Websters were put in a cell on the second floor of Godwin, in which were "several females accused of disloyalty and giving aid to the United States government." On the floor above the Websters was a thirty-four-year-old Virginian named George Washington Frosst, a machinist in a woolen factory arrested on suspicion of "disloyalty." Over the coming days Frosst saw Webster several times and noted that "he was greatly suffering from rheumatic pains in his limbs . . . and was compelled to use crutches."

On the day of his reprieve Lewis was moved from the condemned cell to a furnished room on the first floor with a window. There was a table and chair, writing material and plenty of books. Lewis was shackled at the wrists, which made writing impossible and reading tiresome, so he spent hours at the window enviously watching people go about their business outside the prison's walls. Still unnerved by the morning's events, Lewis leaped to the door whenever he heard footsteps and peeped through the keyhole. In the afternoon he thought he recognized the squat frame of General Winder climbing the stairs to the second floor.

The next day, Saturday, April 5, Lewis's guards brought him the newspapers. He read about the postponement of his execution, and then he came to the final paragraph. "The condemned have made disclosures affecting the fidelity of several persons." Lewis slumped into a chair and read the words again, hoping that perhaps he had imagined them. He hadn't. It was several minutes before his head stopped spinning. Then he began to think. He must get a message to Scully. When a Negro arrived to collect his breakfast tray, Lewis asked if he might deliver a message to John Scully on the top floor.

The servant looked doubtful, but Lewis persuaded him with two dollars slipped into his hand. The message asked Scully what he had told the authorities. The reply came in a note hidden under Lewis's lunch plate. "I have made a full statement and confessed everything and it would be better for us if you would do the same."

The news upset Lewis for reasons, initially, unrelated to Tim Webster. At that point self-preservation was Lewis's priority. By saying he had "confessed everything," was Scully referring just to their trip to Richmond or to their entire espionage career? In particular Lewis was terrified that "Scully had told about my visit to [Henry] Wise's camp." Lewis had heard it said that Wise was in Richmond at this very moment. If there was any proof he had spied on Virginian soil, he would hang.

Lewis passed an anguished night. The next morning he handed the Negro another dollar bill, folded around a note that asked Scully if he had mentioned anything about his trip to West Virginia. Lewis knew the note might be intercepted, but "my mental suspense was such that I was desperate enough to take the risk."

A different man brought Lewis his supper, so it wasn't until the morning of Monday, April 7, that he received Scully's reply. It was a terse note, one which studiously ignored Lewis's question. It simply exhorted Lewis to tell Winder everything he knew. In the afternoon Father McMullen appeared and advised the Englishman "to make a statement to the authorities."

Lewis brusquely dismissed the suggestion. McMullen sighed and reminded Lewis that he was in a bad fix, one that only a full and frank confession could remedy. On Tuesday Lewis was taken from his cell into the guards' room. There was a group of men sitting around a table on which "were a couple of large, leather-bound account books or ledgers." He recognized George Alexander, assistant provost marshal, and Judge Advocate William Crump. The latter spoke first, saying he understood Lewis "desired to make a full statement." Lewis said he wished to do nothing of the sort.

Crump asked for another chair and beckoned the prisoner to sit. Lewis removed his felt hat and did as instructed. Then Crump, "in a soft and gentlemanly manner," told Lewis that he was an Englishman, caught up in a conflict that had nothing to do with him. He was in this predicament because the Washington government "recklessly led you into this trouble without caring a snap what became of you." What loyalty could he possibly harbor for Abraham Lincoln?

Lewis listened impassively as the judge tried to snare him with civility, aware that "his line of argument was a powerful one in my condition of mind." When Crump had finished he looked in expectation at the disheveled figure across the table. Lewis raised his head and said, "Judge, I have no statement to make."

No one spoke for two or three minutes; then Crump asked Lewis what he knew of Timothy Webster. Lewis repeated his earlier assertion, that he barely knew the man and was just passing along a letter to him. Crump shook his head wearily, called Lewis a "foolish man" and ordered him to be taken back to his cell and "put in double irons."

Lewis was returned to his cell, and his feet and hands were shackled. All the furniture supplied by Captain Freeburger was removed; even the books were confiscated. His food was thrown in through the small hatch in the cell door, and, except for a few hours a day, he sat in darkness. Lewis felt "entombed [and] began to devise some scheme to get out of this torture chamber." If Scully had made a full confession and the rebels knew everything, concluded Lewis, it was pointless to maintain his silence. They knew he was a Northern detective; if he said nothing about his adventure in western Virginia, and nothing that they didn't already know about Tim Webster but instead fed his inquisitors scraps of harmless information, it might appease their vengeful souls.

On the morning of Thursday, April 10, Lewis told his guards he wished to see Judge Crump. The judge arrived in the afternoon, and he and the prisoner sat down across a table in the guards' room. Crump asked if now he would make a statement. Yes, he would, replied Lewis, rubbing his red wrists as the manacles were removed. Crump smiled and told Lewis he was a sensible man. The statement should be written, he added, as "Scully had done." The Englishman refused, saying he would answer any questions put to him but he wouldn't put pen to paper. Crump accepted the compromise and for nearly an hour plied Lewis with questions. When did he leave England? How long had he worked for Allan Pinkerton? So what did he do before becoming a detective? A traveling book salesman. For which company? The titles of the books? There were inquiries about Rose Greenhow, Eugenia Phillips, and more information was demanded about his role in the search of the Morton home.

Crump listened intently to all Lewis's answers. Suddenly he asked him about his trip to Tennessee, information that could only have come from Scully. Lewis told the judge about the murder case, including his purchase of the novel about Eugene Aram. It had nothing to do with the war, Lewis stressed, offering to furnish the judge with the names of several people in Jackson who could testify to that effect.

Eventually Crump brought up Timothy Webster, and Lewis replied, yet again, that he had never met him prior to handing over the letter. Crump refused to believe it. Lewis shrugged and said it was true. What more could he say? Crump leaned back in his chair and considered Lewis for several long, dragging seconds. The Englishman felt sure the judge was building up to his final question, the one about Charleston and the Kanawha Valley, but then Crump expressed his "astonishment." At what? inquired Lewis. The judge said it appeared Lewis did indeed have nothing to hide. Lewis was unsure if the judge was being sincere or sarcastic. But then Crump told the guards to return the prisoner to his cell and to remove his irons. The judge left Castle Godwin and reported his findings to the officers of the court-martial; having spoken at length to Mr. Lewis, Crump related, he was satisfied that he was who he said he was, nothing more than a minor detective working for Allan Pinkerton, and not "an emissary between the Union people of Richmond and the Government of Washington . . . [who] could give information that would expose the secret political affiliations of hundreds of people in Richmond."

That same day, Thursday, April 10, John Beauchamp Jones wrote in his diary about the facts gleaned from the newspapers: "The condemned spies [Lewis and Scully] have implicated Webster, the letter-carrier, who has had so many passports. He will hang, probably. Gen. Winder himself, and his policemen, wrote home by him. I don't believe him any more guilty than many who used to write by him."

CHAPTER TWENTY-TWO

"I Suffer a Double Death"

THE CHARGE WAS LAID before Timothy Webster by Colonel Nathaniel Tyler, president of the court and also the co-owner and editor of the *Richmond Enquirer*.* The defendant stood accused of "lurking about the armies and fortifications of the Confederate States of America," and it was the court's intention to prove two specifications.

First Specification: That on the 1st of April [1862], being an enemy alien and in the service of the United States, he lurked about the armies and fortifications of the Confederate States in and near Richmond.

Second Specification: That about the 1st of July 1861, prisoner being an enemy alien and in the service of the United States, did lurk in and about the armies and fortifications of the Confederate States at Memphis, in the State of Tennessee.

---

* The transcripts of Webster's trial, and of Lewis's and Scully's, were never found. In all probability when Richmond fell to Union troops in April 1865 and Judah Benjamin ordered stacks of wartime documents to be burned, they were among them. None of the Richmond papers carried extensive reports on the trial (held in camera), but the *Dispatch* summarized the court's proceedings in its edition of April 30, 1862.

The court summoned John Scully, who confirmed that the accused was Timothy Webster, an employee of the Pinkerton Detective Agency. He also told the court that he had come to Richmond to collect information from Webster and to take this information to Washington.

The next day Pryce Lewis was called. The Englishman looked across at Webster and noticed how much he had changed. He was gaunt, worn-out, a man who no longer had the strength to keep up the act. Webster acknowledged Lewis with a bow of his head. When Lewis was asked if he knew the accused, he replied in the affirmative. And what else do you know of him?

Very little, said Lewis. Was he aware Webster carried mail between Richmond and Washington? Lewis had never seen him carry any mail.

Well then, had he heard any rumors to that effect? Yes, replied Lewis. It was rumored that he carried mail. But he couldn't swear upon it because he had never seen him do it.

For several minutes the prosecution skirmished with Lewis, pressing him again and again on the subject of Webster's role as a letter carrier. But the witness stuck to what he'd already said, reemphasizing that he had never seen Webster in possession of Richmond mail. Webster's defense counsel, James Nance, asked Lewis to elaborate on what he'd already said: he came to Richmond to deliver a letter to Webster. No, he knew neither the contents of the letter nor why it had to be handed over in person. And that was correct, prior to delivering the letter he had never met the accused.

Lewis was returned to his cell in Castle Godwin. More than a week had now passed since the postponement of his execution, and he was being tolerably well treated, though not as well as Scully if Father McMullen was to be believed. His cell, so the priest said, "might be termed elegant." Lewis wrote again to Frederick Cridland but received no reply. He passed the days reading or standing on the bench looking out of the window. One day Lewis saw Tim Webster in the prison yard below, "sitting down on a step, very pale and weary-looking."

Webster's trial concluded on Saturday, April 19. Three days later the *Richmond Dispatch* reported that "the result has not transpired." However, added the newspaper, a guilty verdict was assured because "the proof, it is understood, was direct and positive." On Friday, April 25, Timothy Webster was taken from Castle Godwin to City Hall, where the verdict was announced by Colonel Tyler, president of the court. Guilty.

Tyler then announced that with "two thirds of the Court concurring, it was adjudged that the accused suffer death by hanging . . . that the sentence should be executed under the direction of the provost marshal on the 29th of April, between the hours of 6 and 12 o'clock."

It was the *Richmond Dispatch*'s report of April 5 that first alerted the Federal authorities to the fate of Lewis and Scully. The next day Captain Gustavus Fox, assistant secretary of the Union navy, received a telegram at his headquarters at Fort Monroe, on the tip of the Virginia Peninsula, signed by C. C Fulton. It read: RICHMOND PAPERS MENTION THAT TWO MEN NAMED PRICE [SIC] LEWIS AND JOHN SCULLY HAVE BEEN CONVICTED AS SPIES AND WERE TO HAVE BEEN HUNG YESTERDAY, BUT THAT A SHORT RESPITE HAS BEEN GRANTED. THE MEN CLAIM TO BE BRITISH SUBJECTS AND LOYAL.

Word was quickly passed to Pinkerton, who was on the Virginia Peninsula with McClellan. Two days earlier, on April 4, McClellan had begun to push west toward the Confederate-held port of Yorktown. McClellan arrived outside Yorktown on the fifth, the same day he learned that President Lincoln had rescinded his order to General Irvin McDowell to move his thirty-five-thousand-strong corps from northern Virginia to the peninsula.*

McClellan was apoplectic when he found out, petulantly fuming that he was the victim of political intrigue on account of his Democratic leanings. He still had fifty-five thousand men under his command, however, as he drew closer to Yorktown. Entrenched around Yorktown were no more than fifteen thousand poorly equipped rebels. Most other generals would have invested the port in a matter of days, but not McClellan. He recoiled from an all-out assault, preferring to wait for his artillery to

---

* Lincoln's decision was prompted by the revelation that far from the seventy-three thousand men McClellan claimed to have left in Washington to defend the capital, there were fewer than thirty thousand. McClellan had included in his wildly inaccurate figure the twenty-five thousand men of Major General Nathaniel Banks's army stationed in the Shenandoah Valley, and he had also blatantly deceived his president, counting some divisions twice.

arrive so he could blast the rebels from their trenches. It was Lincoln's turn to rage. IT IS INDISPENSABLE TO YOU THAT YOU STRIKE A BLOW, the president telegraphed his general, warning that THE COUNTRY WILL NOT FAIL TO NOTE—IS NOW NOTING—THAT THE PRESENT HESITATION TO MOVE UPON AN ENTRENCHED ENEMY, IS BUT THE STORY OF MANASSAS [THE BATTLE OF BULL RUN] REPEATED.

Confronted with the gravest crisis of his military career, General McClellan had more pressing matters than the fate of two spies,* but Pinkerton sought clarification from the harbormaster at Fort Monroe. The thought that one or all of his operatives might be dead left him "almost prostrated" with anxiety.

Subsequent intelligence was confused. The harbormaster confirmed that it appeared the men were indeed still alive. But then on April 16 the *Boston Herald* ran an article headlined A SPY HUNG BY THE REBELS in which it said that "Price [*sic*] Lewis late of Wolcottville, Con; was a few days since hung at Richmond, having made several trips to the enemy's camp successfully was caught at last and manfully paid the penalty."

After hearing his verdict, Webster was returned to Castle Godwin and moved to the condemned cell lately occupied by Pryce Lewis. Hattie Lawton, whom the Confederates still believed to be the real Mrs. Webster, had been found guilty of complicity and sentenced to one year's imprisonment. Although she was now separated from her companion, Lawton was allowed a few minutes each day with Webster, and she was also granted permission to petition President Jefferson Davis. Her plea for clemency was rejected.

Webster wrote to no one. What was the point in writing to Frederick Cridland when he had long since renounced his British citizenship? Tim Webster was a Yankee. He couldn't even write to his real wife, Charlotte, six hundred miles northwest in Onarga, for fear of exposing Hattie Lawton as a Pinkerton operative.

---

* Pinkerton later claimed that when he told McClellan about Lewis and Scully, "his sympathy and sorrow were as acute as though the men had been joined to him by ties of blood." Given that the general—who had met neither Lewis nor Scully—had the fate of tens of thousands of men in his hands, it seems unlikely he would have lost much sleep over the pair.

On the evening of Monday, April 28, Lawton called on Webster for the final time. He gave her his possessions, including "plenty of gold and C.S Treasury notes," and then they embraced. Webster's last visit was from the Reverend Dr. George Woodbridge, the fifty-one-year-old rector of Richmond's Episcopal Monumental Church. Woodbridge was an avuncular figure, father to four children and a much respected preacher.

Webster prayed with Woodbridge; then they talked for many hours. The rector left a Bible with the prisoner and promised to return the next morning. Webster passed the night reading the Bible. One psalm in particular gave him solace, it was psalm 35, David's psalm, and contained within it were the following lines.

> *Plead my cause, O Lord, with them that strive with me:*
> *fight against them that fight against me.*
> *Take hold of shield and buckler,*
> *and stand up for mine help.*
> *Draw out also the spear,*
> *and stop the way against them that persecute me:*
> *say unto my soul, I am thy salvation.*
> *Let them be confounded and put to shame*
> *that seek after my soul:*
> *let them be turned back and brought to confusion*
> *that devise my hurt.*
> *Let them be as chaff before the wind:*
> *and let the angel of the Lord chase them.*
> *Let their way be dark and slippery:*
> *and let the angel of the Lord persecute them.*
> *For without cause have they hid for me their net in a pit,*
> *which without cause they have digged for my soul.*
> *Let destruction come upon him at unawares;*
> *and let his net that he hath hid catch himself:*
> *into that very destruction let him fall.*
>
> *False witnesses did rise up;*
> *they laid to my charge things that I knew not.*
> *They rewarded me evil for good to the spoiling of my soul.*

· · ·

The Reverend Dr. Woodbridge returned at six o'clock the next morning, Tuesday, April 29. Webster was dressed in a white cotton shirt and a black coat. The two men prayed and talked, and together read some passages from the Bible. The rector implored Webster to be strong, reminding him that he had nothing to fear from a just and loving God. Woodbridge remained with the condemned man for an hour. When the time came for him to depart, he shook Webster's hand and suggested he spend his final minutes in prayer.

Soon a carriage driven by Winder's men arrived, and Webster was taken from his cell by George Freeburger. Without the aid of crutches, Webster had to lean heavily on his jailor for support. They rode west along Broad Street, following the course of the railroad toward Camp Lee. It was a fine day, and the air was scented with violets and hyacinths. Daffodils burst from the roadside verges, and the meadows beyond the hedges of ailanthus that lined the mile-long route were golden. Behind the carriage the sun climbed above the spires of Richmond's thirty-three churches.

The carriage passed a guard of soldiers and pulled up outside the headquarters of the camp commandant, Colonel John Shields. In prewar days the headquarters had been the office of the president of the Richmond Central Agricultural Society. Eighteen months earlier the society had hosted the Prince of Wales during his visit to the showground. To the rear of the headquarters was a long building occupied by quartermasters, surgeons and drillmasters, and the enclosed space in front of this building was where the officers played marbles in the cool of the evening. Enlisted soldiers lived in tents and washed in a creek on the edge of the camp.

Inside the headquarters Webster's manacles were removed, and he was left alone with the Reverend Dr. Moses Hoge, the padre of the camp. They prayed and talked, and at ten minutes past eleven Freeburger returned. Webster was shackled once more, and then Hoge and Freeburger assisted him into the carriage. It was a short ride to the gallows, no more than 250 yards, but it took five minutes because the ground was still soft from the spring rain. From inside the carriage Webster saw the wooden coffin at the foot of the scaffold.

A large crowd of Richmonders had gathered, and soldiers pushed them back as Webster climbed down from the carriage. He mounted the scaffold steps unaided. In the branches of the oak trees that overhung the gallows perched a gang of boys, their young eyes wide with curiosity. Waiting for Webster on the scaffold was the hangman, a fearsome fellow with a "white beard, long and flowing . . . face hard, features large and firm, eyes gray, cold and cruel." His name was John Caphart, once a hunter of runaway slaves and now the city's executioner. In Richmond and throughout Virginia they called him "Anti-Christ Caphart." He bound Webster's feet as Hoge invoked the Divine Mercy. The rope was adjusted around the prisoner's neck, under his brown beard flecked with gray. George Freeburger asked Webster if he had anything to say. Webster looked at Hoge and thanked him for his kindness.

Caphart removed Webster's silk dress hat and slipped a black cap over his head. He stepped back three paces, grasped a wooden lever and pulled. The trap opened, and Webster fell. There was a heavy thud, then gasps and shouts from the crowd. Caphart looked through the trap and saw the empty noose and underneath Webster twitching on the ground. Two soldiers pulled Webster to his feet and dragged him up the gallows steps as the prisoner moaned, "I suffer a double death."

Caphart adjusted the cotton noose, looped it once more around Webster's neck and tightened it with a brutal jerk. Webster gave an anguished cry: "You are going to choke me this time." Caphart stepped back and pulled the lever. There was no thud. The mute crowd watched as Webster kicked the air in his death throes. Caphart removed his hat and wiped his brow with his lucky red bandana. For fifteen minutes the correspondents of the Richmond newspapers stood and chatted in front of the gallows as Webster's body gently swung to and fro. Then they began to move away. It was nearly luncheon, and they had to write their copy for the morning issue.

The newspapermen had agreed that Webster's gallant death would not be edifying for their readers. The people of Richmond expected a Yankee, particularly one as perfidious as Webster, to die with more disgrace.

The *Richmond Examiner* related how Webster had arrived at Camp Lee "making use of horrid oaths and treating the subject of his approaching death with scorn and derision." Then in the final few minutes his bluster vanished and instead "he wept constantly and his strength seemed to fail him utterly. He trembled like an aspen and was unable to stand alone." The paper added: "It is said, on taking leave of him, Webster's wife exhorted him 'to die like a man'; in how far he obeyed her exhortation our readers can judge."

The *Dispatch* concentrated less on the manner of Webster's death and more on his profanity, describing how he had insisted Reverend Woodbridge "read the psalm of David, invoking vengeance on his enemies. He [Woodbridge] refused and Webster grew indignant, causing the clergyman to take an early departure." The *Enquirer* also published details of this final prayer meeting, during which Woodbridge's "endeavors to bring about a pious state of mind in the unmitigated villain only met with ill-mannered responses, [and] the only approach he made towards resignation was a request that the Rev. gentleman would read him that psalm of David which invoked curses upon his enemies."

The Reverend Dr. Woodbridge read the newspapers with mounting irritation. Having deliberated on the response, he retired to his office and wrote a letter to William B. Allegre and Nathaniel Tyler, the owners of the *Richmond Enquirer*.

Gentlemen:

Will you please allow me to correct a statement in your paper respecting Webster, the spy. I ask it for the sake of his wife. In all my interviews with him he was uniformly grateful and respectful . . . the psalm to which reference is made is the 35th. He pointed it out to me the day before. Considering it as indicating a state of mind not desirable, I told him that if he entertained any unkind feelings towards the others he must abandon them, as an indispensable qualification for forgiveness from God. He said, however, that the Psalm suited his state of mind, not that he wished any evil to others; and that he freely forgave others their offences against him as he wished forgiveness from God. This Psalm he did not ask me to read on the morning of his execution, though I noticed that the leaf was turned down.

Geo. Woodbridge

Will those editors in the city please to publish this who have given similar accounts.

CHAPTER TWENTY-THREE

"It Was Not War, It Was Murder"

MOST OF THE NORTHERN PAPERS carried the belated news of Webster's death, the first execution of a spy by either side in the war. The *New York Post* noted the fact and asked the rhetorical question: "What if the federal government should commence hanging spies?" The *Burlington* (Iowa) *Hawk Eye* related the facts surrounding the case, boasting that Timothy Webster was well known in Iowa, having helped solve many cases over the years, and that some people might remember his charming wife and children. With breathtaking irresponsibility the paper then told its readers that "the report that he had his wife with him, and that she was in Richmond with him at the time of Webster's execution, is a matter very easily understood and explained by those who understand the workings and intricate machinery of the secret police service. We doubt not that some female, passing as his wife, was with him, and that when it became known to him that his fate was sealed, he revealed his true name, that his friends would know him."

The *New York Times* and *Chicago Tribune* reprinted the report from the *Richmond Dispatch*, the same one in which Webster was alleged to have imprecated all manner of curses on the heads of every Southerner. Contained toward the end of the *Dispatch*'s spurious article—and also reproduced by the Northern papers—was a paragraph concerning the fate of the other three detainees. Mrs. Webster, "arrested along with her

husband as a spy," was still in Castle Godwin but would "no doubt be
sent out of the Confederacy" before long. Not so Pryce Lewis and John
Scully whom, the paper said, could expect to remain imprisoned for a
good many more months. The *Dispatch* mocked the two poltroons,
claiming that they were to blame for Webster's death because "they let
the cat out of the bag on him after their conviction."

In the same week that the Northern newspapers were publishing news
of Webster's death, a copy of the *Boston Herald* dated April 16, 1862,
reached the pretty market town of Shrewsbury, just inside England's
border with Wales. It had been six years since Elizabeth Lewis last saw
her favorite son, Pryce, but she exchanged the occasional letter with him
and knew he was working as a detective. Nevertheless, she had no idea as
to the exact nature of his work, even less that he was actively engaged
in the Civil War. And now she read the crushing news that, according to
the *Boston Herald*, Pryce had been executed.

She had lived in Shrewsbury for a couple of years, just her and Thomas,
who had risen above his rank to become a solicitor. It was Thomas who,
on May 14, wrote on his mother's behalf to Charles Adams, the United
States' minister to Britain. On a sheet of paper banded in black as a sign
of mourning, Thomas Lewis repeated the erroneous claim made in the
Boston Herald of April 16 that his brother had been executed and pleaded
for more information. He then asked Adams to "kindly inform me how I
am to act in the matter and if my poor brother has left any personality [*sic*]
behind him (which I have no doubt he has), how I am to obtain it. He has
left a poor broken-hearted (widow) mother to lament his loss. Hoping you
will excuse me for the liberty I have thus taken."

John Scully's brother was closer at hand when he heard that his sib-
ling was in rebel hands. From his home in Carlisle, Indiana, P. B. Scully
wrote to Lord Lyons, the British ambassador in Washington. Lyons forwarded the letter to Frederick Cridland, along with a note instructing
him to "inquire into the matter and make a report to me upon it." It took
two months for Lyons's note to reach Cridland, but the acting consul
replied in detail, apologizing first that "the arduous duties at this office
and the innumerable cases involving the liberty of British subjects prevented my reporting the case at the time." Cridland then elaborated on
the arrests, his interview with Mr. Benjamin and Mr. Randolph, and the

subsequent commutation of the sentences. As far as he was aware, Cridland concluded, "the prisoners are still confined in jail."

Lewis read with disgust the "grossly prejudiced" accounts of Timothy Webster's execution in the Richmond papers. He knew them to be untrue because George Freeburger had delivered a detailed description of the hanging that same afternoon. Of course Webster had been afraid, but he'd gone to his death like a man. Lewis attached no blame to himself for what happened, nor did he harbor much rancor toward John Scully, with whom he was reunited a couple of days after Webster's death. Scully was young and not particularly bright. He should never have been sent South. Instead Lewis reserved his vehemence for Father McMullen, whom he believed had pressured Scully "to make a full confession to save himself," and for the man he blamed most of all, the fool who had landed them "deep in the mud." As Lewis and Scully sat in their cramped cell, sweating in the stifling May heat, the Englishman turned to his companion and laid the blame for their plight squarely at the feet of Allan Pinkerton, "for it was his downright lack of judgment, or worse, that brought us here."

A little more than a week after Timothy Webster's execution, May 8, John Beauchamp Jones penned a plaintive entry in his diary: "Norfolk and Portsmouth are evacuated! Our army falling back! The Merrimac is to be, or has been, blown up!"*

Every day rumors swept through Richmond that the Yankees would soon be at the city's gates. People promenading among the linden trees in Capitol Square wore creased brows and asked one another if there was any truth in the report that General McDowell's army was coming south to reinforce George McClellan's already vast force. The pessimistic professed solemnly that it was only a matter of time before the bell in the tower on Capitol Square tolled to warn of the enemy's arrival. Some inhabitants began to flee Richmond, at least those who could, the wealthy and the influential. John Beauchamp Jones packed off his

---

* The *Merrimac* or *Merrimack* was a United States' ship converted by the Confederates in 1861 to their first ironclad and rechristened the CSS *Virginia*. It was blown up by its crew on May 11 after a dramatic battle with the USS *Monitor*.

family to Raleigh, North Carolina, on Friday, May 9. Jones admitted he was ashamed at this "flight from the enemy . . . [but] no one scarcely supposes that Richmond will be defended."

That same evening, a courier delivered a message to President Jefferson Davis as he hosted a reception at the Confederate White House on Clay Street. He read the message in his office, then returned to the drawing room and his guests. He passed his wife, Varina, en route and whispered, "The enemy's gun-boats are ascending the [James] River."

The next morning Davis ordered his wife to North Carolina. John Beauchamp Jones's family and Mrs. Davis were among the first to leave, the first drops of a summer shower that soon became a deluge. "The panic began some days later," wrote Mrs. Davis, "and it was pitiable to see our friends coming in without anything except the clothes they had on, and mourning the loss of their trunks in a piteous jumble of pain and merriment."

For Richmond's poor there was no alternative but to remain in a city that seemed to be disintegrating before their eyes. The chins of profiteers doubled, tripled, quadrupled as they grew fat on the misery of others; few people could afford either meat or fish, so most grew thin within their summer clothes.

People took to the street to demonstrate at the injustice, but it had no effect; nor did General Winder when he tried to curtail the profiteering with the imposition of a maximum tariff for various foods. The farmers and fishermen responded by refusing to come to market, forcing Winder to back down.

Some found solace in black humor, and a favorite joke of the day was that shoppers left home with their money in their baskets and returned with their goods in their purses. In public Jones bore a look of stoic fortitude, like the others who refused to run. Men and women took their lead from John Letcher, Virginia's governor, who told his people he would never surrender Richmond. He feared no Yankee, be he McClellan or Lincoln.

Each morning Richmonders woke wondering if today would be the day the Yankees came. Every afternoon after work scores of men and women—John Beauchamp Jones included—trooped up the top of Hospital Hill, north of the city, from where the guns could be heard. Sometimes as they stood on the hill listening to the sound of battle they saw the Union observation balloon, *Constitution*, ascending in the distance.

Inside the basket was twenty-nine-year-old Thaddeus Lowe, the pioneer of aerial military espionage.

Lowe had been fascinated with aeronautics since childhood, and his first ascent in a balloon was in 1856; by the time war broke out he was rivaling John Wise as America's preeminent balloonist. On June 18, 1861, Lowe had risen from the grounds of the Columbian Armory (present-day site of the National Air and Space Museum) and from a height of five hundred feet above Washington telegraphed the White House from his basket, telling Lincoln he was indebted to him for his ENCOURAGEMENT FOR THE OPPORTUNITY OF DEMONSTRATING THE AVAILABILITY OF THE SCIENCE OF AERONAUTICS IN THE MILITARY SERVICE OF THE COUNTRY. That evening Lowe spent the night at the White House explaining to the president the potential of balloons as a reconnaissance tool. By the end of July 1861 Lowe was the chief aeronaut in the U.S Army Balloon Corps (the corps would have seven balloons, each with a mobile hydrogen gas generator), and the following month he made the first of twenty-three ascents in a thirty-four-day period, gathering intelligence on the Confederate positions on Upton's Hills and around Fairfax Courthouse, as well as the roads to Arlington and Alexandria.

McClellan was one of the first officers to go aloft with Lowe, and he made sure the Balloon Corps was used during the Peninsula Campaign. The Confederates hadn't the resources to launch their own aeronautical rival, but their reaction to the innovation was to produce one of their own: military camouflage. They disguised military encampments so they couldn't be seen from the air, and in other cases they painted logs black to look like cannons.

Toward the end of May Richmond braced itself to be invaded. The *Dispatch* did little to allay people's fear, warning in its edition of May 24 that "our Northern brethren are now engaged in an assiduous endeavor to restore the Union and set the Stars and Stripes afloat in Richmond, by laying plans to murder and rob all of our people who may wish to prevent the consummation of their dearly-cherished project." Women sat in their drawing rooms sewing sandbags, or they "gathered at St. Paul's Church to prepare bedding for the hospitals." Plans were drafted for the evacuation of all women and children should the city come under bombardment; it was agreed to burn all tobacco and cotton stocks to prevent their falling into Yankee hands. On May 28 George Randolph, secretary of war, ordered the removal of official documents to the railroad depot, and the following day General Winder had the temerity to close the city's gambling houses to prevent the soldiers straying from their posts.

The information given to President Jefferson Davis on the evening of May 9 had been erroneous. The Union gunboats that were reportedly steaming up the James River didn't appear until six days later. And when they did, a Confederate artillery battery at Drewry's Bluff, seven miles below Richmond, repulsed the vessels in a fierce exchange. But McClellan's army continued to edge closer to the city until it was six miles distant, close enough to hear the Reverend Dr. Woodbridge's church bells.

General Robert Lee had been absorbing the gravity of the situation since the moment McClellan had landed on the Virginia Peninsula at the start of April. McClellan had one hundred thousand troops at his disposal, with a further thirty-five thousand to come when General McDowell arrived. Lee had approximately seventy thousand. McClellan, he could handle, but McDowell had to be prevented coming south.

Lee ordered General Stonewall Jackson into the Shenandoah Valley, instructing him to harry and hound the enemy, stretching them this way and that so they wouldn't know if they were coming or going. Jackson was the ideal man for the job. He led by tyranny, pushing his men to the limits of their endurance, punishing them severely if they erred. He was pious and cheerless, but he inspired respect because he demanded of himself what he demanded of his men. He endured their hardships, and he shared their danger. He was also a master strategist. Throughout May Jackson tore through the Shenandoah, winning victories against General Frémont's army at McDowell (a hamlet in Virginia), Front Royal and Winchester.

The moment President Lincoln heard of the defeats he suspended General McDowell's move south and ordered him to crush the impertinent rebels. McDowell protested, but obeyed, and led his army west instead of south. For a fortnight they chased Jackson's exhausted army all the way to the Blue Ridge Mountains, where, on June 9, there was a bloody but indecisive clash at Port Republic. Then Jackson withdrew through the mountains, out of the reach of the Union troops.

While the seventeen thousand soldiers of Stonewall Jackson's army were causing trouble for the Yankees in western Virginia, those troops belonging to Joseph Johnston went on the offensive at Seven Pines. (The Union army called this battle Fair Oaks, after the nearby railroad station.) Not only had McClellan taken an inordinate amount of time to move up the Virginia Peninsula, but once he got within striking distance of Richmond "Little Mac" foolishly split his army. Two corps were ordered to establish positions on the southern bank of the Chickahominy, and these were the troops attacked by Johnston.

As John Beauchamp Jones and others listened to the battle from the top of Hospital Hill, seven miles to the east young American men fought each other to the death among the Judas trees and white dogwood flowers close by the Chickahominy. A Union lieutenant in the Twentieth Massachusetts Regiment, Henry Ropes, who fought at Seven Pines, later recalled how "we again took the double quick step and ran through deep mud and pools of water toward the battle. The whole field in the rear of the line of firing was covered with dead; and wounded men were coming in great numbers, some walking, some limping, some carried on stretchers and blankets, many with shattered limbs exposed and dripping with blood. In a moment we entered the fire. The noise was terrific, the balls whistled by us and the shells exploded over us and by our side; the whole scene dark with smoke and lit up by the streams of fire from our battery and from our Infantry in line on each side."

When the fighting stopped, neither side could celebrate a resounding victory. Among the six thousand Confederate casualties was Johnston himself, shot in the shoulder. Robert Lee replaced Johnston as commander of the Army of Northern Virginia, and the first half of June was spent stiffening Richmond's defenses and reconnoitering the enemy's positions. By the middle of the month Lee had his plan: he would attack the Yankees head on and hit their right flank north of the Chickahominy. Lee ordered Stonewall Jackson south, and on June 25 the offensive began. It raged for seven sanguinary days, leaving thirty thousand Americans dead and wounded.

On July 1, the final day of the slaughter, at the Battle of Malvern Hill, General Daniel H. Hill watched six thousand of his men destroyed by Union artillery, and later wrote that "it was not war, it was murder."

McClellan's army triumphed at Malvern Hill, but the general quailed at the thought of pushing on to Richmond. He still put faith in Pinkerton's reports that the rebel army was "near to 200,000 men."*

Richmond had been saved, for now, at least, and while McClellan's army tended to its wounds, dysentery, malaria and typhoid began to ravage his men throughout the hot and humid July. At the end of the month, an exasperated Lincoln instructed McClellan to withdraw his army north from the Virginia Peninsula.

By the beginning of July Richmond reeked no longer of tobacco but of death. When Varina Davis returned to her husband she wrote how "the odors of the battlefield were distinctly perceptible all over the city." More than five thousand wounded soldiers were brought to one of Richmond's sixteen army hospitals that were "crowded with ladies offering their services to nurse." Many of the ladies fastened purple calycanthus flowers on their chest to combat the stench, and they propped up their gallant menfolk on cushions taken from the city's churches.

When the army hospitals overflowed six private hospitals and thirteen emergency hospitals received the stricken soldiers, and when they were full citizens opened up their houses and looked on impassively as young men dripped blood over their carpets. Even the basement of the Spottswood Hotel, where once eager volunteers of the Richmond Howitzers had been initiated into the art of soldiering, became a temporary hospital.

The lucky ones, the able-bodied, staggered into town with wild eyes and black lips from the powder of the cartridges that they had bitten off in their haste to kill McClellan's Yankees. They were greeted "by a string of girls, children and Negroes, each carrying dishes, trays of popcorn,

---

* Pinkerton arrived at this figure through a combination of inexperience and incompetence, and his touching naïveté in putting faith in the accounts of escaped slaves whom he interviewed. As James Horan wrote in his biography of the Pinkertons, "Though [the slaves] were incapable of giving realistic information about what was happening on a grand scale behind Confederate lines, it is evident that Pinkerton believed everything they told him." If Pinkerton learned of a presence of a rebel regiment, he assumed it was at full strength and part of a division, also at full strength. Such was his devotion to McClellan that he preferred to err on the side of caution.

buckets and pitchers of sorghum and vinegar and water, the 'Confederate lemonade.' " There were shrieks of delight and tears of joy as "mothers found sons, and sisters brothers, whose fate had for days been uncertain." Other women ran among the ranks of the returning, looking frantically for the face they loved. "Some were not found," recalled one bystander, "and, oh, the woe of it."

One woman who didn't deign to dirty her hands in Richmond hospitals was Rose Greenhow, who had been deported from Washington on May 31. She had expected to be released in April, and when she hadn't been she sent a truculent letter to Washington's military governor demanding to know the cause of the "unnecessary delay." The reason was the sentence of death hanging over Lewis and Scully; the Federals weren't going to release a woman who had caused far more harm to the enemy than either of their two spies if there was any chance of their being executed. (Webster had been a different matter. His life wasn't exchangeable. He was a double agent, and the Confederates were in a position to claim that they were hanging a traitor, one of their own.) What brought about Greenhow's eventual release was an assurance that in return for her freedom, she would work to secure the release of Pryce Lewis and John Scully the moment she reached Richmond.

Greenhow never kept her promise. She arrived in the city on June 4 and "was taken to the best hotel in the place, the Ballard House, where rooms had been prepared for me." She was then visited by General Winder, who, if Rose was to be believed, prostrated himself at her feet and swore to the sparkling heroine that he would "dispense with the usual formality of my reporting to him." The procession of male pilgrims continued late into the day, and Greenhow was particularly humbled when "the President did me the honor of calling upon me, and his words of greeting 'But for you there would have been no battle of Bull Run' repaid me for all that I had endured."

In the ensuing weeks and months Greenhow embroidered herself into the pattern of Richmond life, dancing regally at "Starvation Balls," gracing the theater with her presence and promenading in Capitol Square. She did nothing for Lewis or Scully, ignoring their letters petitioning her to intervene. Instead she began to write a book about her life as a prisoner of Abraham Lincoln.

The news of McClellan's withdrawal north confirmed to Lewis and

Scully that their release might be a long time coming. It also had the effect of canceling a proposed transfer from Richmond to Salisbury Prison in North Carolina, a far more salubrious establishment than Henrico County Jail or Castle Godwin. In Salisbury the prisoners' food was prepared by captured cooks from the Union army and consisted of boiled beef, rice and wheat bread. Vendors from local stores were allowed to visit the camp and sell such luxuries as sweet potatoes, onions and coffee, and a large wall enclosed sixteen acres of grounds on which the prisoners amused themselves with games of baseball. Lewis and Scully were told they would be transferred to Salisbury on May 15, but the order was rescinded, as was a second command on June 5, when it became clear the Union army wouldn't be marching into Richmond.

There was, however, one face familiar to Lewis and Scully in the city that month, though they only discovered his presence when they read the *Richmond Whig* on Wednesday, June 18. The paper described how a Yankee spy named Dennis had been relaxing in the parlor of the Exchange and Ballard Hotel when "he was recognized by the little daughter of Mrs. Greenhow . . . [but] the shrewd rascal, it seems, recognized the little girl at the same time that she discovered him and when she ran to give the intelligence to her mother he disappeared." This was the Paul Dennis who had disarmed little Rose's mother when she pointed a pistol at Lewis on the day of her arrest in August 1861.

That Pinkerton had sent him to Richmond, presumably to ferret out information about his captured colleagues, was incredible, particularly as the Greenhows had been released only a fortnight earlier. Pinkerton had not learned his lesson, and only the cunning of Dennis in eluding his pursuers and returning North prevented another of his agents falling into enemy hands.

CHAPTER TWENTY-FOUR

"They Held Existence by a Frail Tenure"

O N THURSDAY, AUGUST 21, the *Richmond Enquirer* reported that a new prison had opened three days earlier, under the direction of Captain George Alexander, assistant provost marshal, and its capacity was reputed to be in excess of one thousand, more than five times the number of Castle Godwin. When Lewis and Scully had been thrown in Godwin four months earlier, it held sixty prisoners; now that number had bloated to nearly two hundred, and conditions were intolerable.

The new prison, to be "christened 'Castle Thunder,' a name indicative of Olympian vengeance upon offenders against her laws," was located on Cary Street and was converted from a tobacco warehouse. The *Enquirer*'s reporter had visited the L-shaped premises and approved of what he'd seen, though he worried the prison might be too luxurious for the sort of person to be incarcerated within.

> The general cleanliness of the place is the first object which strikes the visitor's sense of appreciation as he enters. The arrangement of the offices of Assistant Provost-Marshal [Alexander], superintendent, and police, all on the first floor in the front of the building; of the store-rooms, armory and "halls for confiscation" in the rear, and of the culinary department in the court, is as orderly, convenient, and comfortable as could be desired. The prison department is above,

and is appropriately divided into sections for males, females, citizens and soldiers respectively; and still higher up is the hospital, where everything is kept in proper condition, and the patients have plenty of breathing and sleeping room. Convalescents enjoy a promenade upon the roof of an adjoining wing of the building.

There were a couple of features the correspondent overlooked, such as the windowless "Condemned Cell" and the three six-foot-square dungeons, or "sweat houses," as Alexander preferred to call them. The stench from inside was pestiferous, worse than a pigsty.

The hospital didn't long retain its perfect condition. On October 3 Surgeon William Carrington was commissioned by Jefferson Davis to inspect all the hospitals in Richmond's prisons. When he came to Castle Thunder he was appalled, writing that there "are about 70 patients in a garret room 40ft by 80 of low pitch and very imperfect ventilation. The capacity of the room was 32 patients. There was no bath room, linen room or hospital clothing. The beds and bedding were filthy and the clothing & the persons of the patients in the same conditions."

Pryce Lewis, John Scully, and the other inmates of Castle Godwin were transferred to Castle Thunder on Monday, August 18. Waiting to greet them was George Alexander, newly promoted to assistant adjutant general. The elevation had made him even more conceited. He yelled commands at his prisoners "as though delivering them through a speaking-trumpet." He was also in the habit of regaling prisoners with stories of his own exploits earlier in the war, which while impressive enough, were burnished by Alexander's braggadocio. Alexander warned the prisoners, "There is no use, men, of trying to get out of here. It is absolutely impossible . . . you can not have a thought that is unknown to me. You might as well attempt to scale Heaven as escape from the Castle. You had better behave yourselves, and become resigned to your situation."

Each prisoner was searched for weapons, then dispossessed of money and jewelry, and given a receipt in return. Then they were escorted to their cells. Lewis and Scully were taken down the passage and up three long flights of stairs—armed guards were stationed at the foot of each staircase—to the third floor, directly beneath the garret hospital. This floor "consisted originally of two large rooms and one small room which was [their] cell." The door to the spies' cell was made from wooden boards, which with a bit of effort could be removed and replaced without drawing attention to the fact. So at night when most of the prison's fourteen guards were off-duty or relaxing on the first floor, Lewis and Scully would "squeeze out into the large rooms and enjoy the society of the other prisoners." The camaraderie among the incarcerated transcended wartime loyalties; everyone knew about the two Northern spies, but no one cared. If anything, Lewis and Scully were celebrities. The prisoners with whom they mingled represented all of war's detritus; there were dozens of Confederate soldiers awaiting trial for desertion, mutiny or murder. There were civilian men accused of disloyalty or forgery, women caught selling either liquor or sex, and there were thieves and drunkards both male and female.

The highlight of Lewis's day was the exercise hour. Not only could he escape for a few blissful minutes the stench imparted from the tubs that served as toilets on the prison floors, but he had the chance to converse with prisoners confined in "the Citizens' Room" on the second floor. Among the topics of conversation was the course of the war, which at the time was discouraging for the Northerners. Not only had the Federals pulled back from Richmond, but the rebels had chased them north, crossing the Potomac on September 5 and engaging McClellan's army twelve days later at a Maryland creek called Antietam. Unimaginable carnage ensued. By the end of the day twenty-three thousand American soldiers lay dead or wounded.

The inmates soon learned that Captain Alexander was a fair man: civil to the good, evil to the bad. Pryce Lewis struck up a rapport with the preening superintendent, who saw himself as the Confederacy's answer to Alfred, Lord Tennyson. Where the Crimean War had inspired the English poet to write "The Charge of the Light Brigade," so Alexander had been moved by the South's travails to pen verses of similar stature. Unfortunately Alexander didn't quite possess Tennyson's turn of phrase, but Lewis discovered that "by praising his poetry it was easy to keep on the right side of him." So adroit was Lewis in playing to Alexander's ego that the prison governor took to printing souvenir copies of his ballads and poems.

In Castle Godwin Lewis and Scully had been well fed, but in Castle Thunder there were just two meals a day, and they barely qualified as meals. The food was brought to them in their cells, for breakfast "a piece of wheat bread of good quality and a piece of fresh soup meat, often in an uneatable condition." The second meal was served between three and four in the afternoon and consisted of "a tin can of soup and a piece of bread. The soup was made of black beans and, if allowed to stand a little while, the maggots and winged insects would rise to the surface." Lewis and Scully fished out the insects and threw them away, but ate the maggots for their nutrition.

An acquaintance Lewis made among the prisoners on the second floor was Colonel Thomas Jordan (not to be confused with the Thomas Jordan who was Rose Greenhow's spymaster), Ninth Pennsylvania Cavalry, who had been captured in Kentucky the previous July. Subsequently Jordan was accused of having orchestrated a campaign of robbery, rape and murder throughout the state of Tennessee a few weeks before his capture. George Randolph, the Confederate secretary of war, had ordered an inquiry into the allegations, the results of which were pending.

Jordan and Lewis "exchanged little notes on a string through cracks in the floor," and during the exercise hour they paced the yard in each other's company. Toward the end of November Jordan learned that the charges leveled against him had been dismissed; also, eyewitnesses told the inquiry Jordan had been "very humane and kind to citizens." He was ordered to be returned to Washington on a flag-of-truce boat, along with "two hundred and forty five Abolition prisoners of war, and ninety-eight citizen prisoners of the North." The prisoners departed Richmond on November 29, and Jordan had secreted on him a note from Lewis written the night before, which was addressed to Allan Pinkerton.

Among the ninety-eight civilian prisoners liberated along with Colonel Jordan was Hattie Lawton. As early as June 1862 the *Richmond Dispatch* had speculated that "Mrs. Webster," as everyone in Richmond still described her, would soon be released. But she remained confined throughout the long hot summer. In August she too had been transferred from Castle Godwin to Castle Thunder, and while her new abode had horrified her, she was resilient enough to write Jefferson Davis on October 13. The letter was a heartfelt plea from a grieving widow.

My Honorable President

I come to you, a poor weak woman whose future looks, oh, so cheerless. I come to you the relic of him who has paid the penalty of his wrongdoing, if wrong he did, of which I know nothing. I come to you begging. I wish to go home. It was hinted an exchange. Oh sir, exchange me, Southern born, a South adoring woman . . . I have suffered. Oh, you can feel for the suffering; let me go home where I may seek some sot, and unnoticed pass the remainder of my dreary, dreary days. I will pray for you, do you no harm and my Holy Mother knows my heart; but I have ties in Maryland, interests there. Please let me go home.

Very respectfully, your obedient servant
Mrs. T Webster

The letter was forwarded to General Winder, who by now suspected there was more to Mrs. Timothy Webster than first met the eye. He returned the letter with a recommendation that the prisoner "would compromise many friends in Maryland" were she to be released. Eventually, however, the authorities in Richmond relented, and Lawton was sent North, to make her report on the sorry saga of Timothy Webster.

Colonel Jordan delivered Lewis's letter as promised, but by now Pinkerton knew nearly all the events surrounding Webster's death, and it appeared from the letter he dictated to one of his subordinates that he attached no blame to Lewis. The letter reached Castle Thunder early in the New Year of 1863.

Pryce Lewis Esq,
Castle Thunder, Richmond, Va
Dear Sir

I am requested by Mr. Allen [Pinkerton's nom de guerre] to write you, and to acknowledge the receipt of your letter of No. 28th 1862, the first direct news from you. He requests me to say to you that he is very glad to hear directly from you and hopes still that you will improve other opportunities of writing to him, letting him

know of any and every want so that if in his power, he may supply
it to you. That he regrets your arrest, your sufferings, your long
confinement, and that his efforts thus far, have not proved successful in your liberation . . . Mr. Allen, also directs me, further, to say
that sometime since, he has received through the American Legation
in London, a letter from your brother, saying that your relatives there
had heard of your arrest and supposed execution, and desiring to
know of your effects; and that he replied to the letter, through the
same channel, giving your brother the facts of the case, and of the
assurance had from the Confederate authorities, of your safety and
probable release . . . I hardly need add that everyone in the employ
of Mr. Allen, shares with him in the deep feeling on account of
your long and dreadful suffering; and all alike, desire to express the
wish and hope of your early deliverance.

Around the same time as Lewis received the letter, Captain Alexander
underwent the first real test of his authority at Castle Thunder. On the
night of Monday, January 26, 1863, a group of Confederate prisoners contrived to make firebombs from the prison stove, which they then hurled
from the windows of their cells toward the building opposite. Inside were
scores of captured Union soldiers. Their screams brought out the guards,
and it was several hours before the fire was brought under control. In the
opinion of the *Richmond Examiner* the arson "best illustrates the amount
of hellish recklessness and devilry which is congregated within the walls of
Castle Thunder." It called for swift retribution, and Alexander obliged.
Lewis looked between the cracks in the wooden planks across his window
as the culprits were "marched down into the prison yard and there they
were kept in the wind and rain without shelter for six days."

Complaints were made, but Alexander was unrepentant, as he demonstrated in April 1863 when he was summoned to appear before the committee of the House of Representatives of the Confederacy to answer
charges of cruelty within the walls of Castle Thunder. Even some of the
staff condemned the practices of their superior. A hospital steward named
T. G Bland told the hearing that in his view the prisoners were "most
barbarously and inhumanely treated." One of General Winder's detectives, Robert Crow, singled out John Caphart, Timothy Webster's hangman, as the most sadistic.

The committee published their report on May 1. In it George Alexander was found to have employed "improper" methods at times, but, because Castle Thunder "embraced among its inmates the most lawless and desperate characters," they recommended that no further action be taken against either the superintendent or any of his guards.

Lewis had been "subpoenaed as a witness in [sic] behalf of Captain Alexander and though I enjoyed two trips under guard to the Capitol my testimony was not called for." Not long after, Lewis fell ill. Fortunately it wasn't smallpox, the disease men feared above all others. An epidemic had swept the city at the end of 1862, and the authorities ordered every house to display a white flag if there was a carrier of the disease within. Superintendents of Richmond's prisons covered their floors with loam and lime, considered to be an effective deterrent against bacteria, but men still succumbed from time to time. Mumps, measles and typhoid were also prevalent, but when the prison surgeon, Coggin, was fetched to attend to Lewis he diagnosed dysentery. As the hospital was full, Coggin handed Lewis "three most powerful pills" and told the Englishman he would soon feel better. Lewis "swallowed only one of them [and] the effect of this was so prostrating that I was satisfied that if I had taken the entire dose, I should have died immediately."

Weeks passed, and Lewis lay festering in the stale air of his cell, at times convinced "life was slowly ebbing away." The cumulative strain of the past twelve months had turned his hair gray, and his once bold brown eyes had drawn back into the sockets of his pallid face. Lewis spent his days huddled under his threadbare blanket, a pitiable shadow of the man who, two years earlier, had traveled through Virginia as an impeccably attired member of the English aristocracy. Lice swarmed over his body, but he had neither the energy nor the strength to repel them. Occasionally he felt a rat scamper across his whiskers.

By the early summer of 1863 the fever had broken, and Lewis was on the mend. His psychological well-being improved when he received a letter from Allan Pinkerton. Lewis had written to his boss to ask for news of their possible release. Since the end of 1862 he and Scully had believed their freedom was pending, but each time something had gone awry, either the intervention of General Winder or a newspaper editorial such as the one that appeared in the *Richmond Enquirer* on December 11:

"We understand that Scully and Lewis, who have been confined in Castle Thunder, under sentence of death, as spies, in co-partnership with Webster, who was hung, have been pardoned, and are to be sent North. It is difficult to comprehend the meaning of such kindness on the part of the Confederate authorities."

Now Lewis was desperate for at least a glimmer of hope. "I regret much that you were not exchanged," wrote Pinkerton, who this time used the alias of "T. H. Hutcheson." He promised Lewis "that no effort of mine or your friends will be left untried to effect your speedy release," and he mentioned that he had written Lewis's brother in England "to let him know how you are situated." In addition, could Lewis "please say to Mr. Scully that I called on Mrs. S a few days ago—and that her and all the family were well, in fact, I may say all looking well."

Finally, Pinkerton said he wanted to put Lewis's mind at rest. Yes, he was now familiar with all the facts of Webster's arrest, trial and execution, and the Englishman "may rest assured that my mind is perfectly unprejudiced and that you have my most sincere commiseration with you in the great sufferings you have endured . . . and I assure you that never for an instant has my faith or confidence in you wavered. And in this all your friends fully coincide."

Pinkerton was true to his word; he was working feverishly to secure the release of his two operatives. At the end of May it appeared their release was imminent, but then for some reason it was canceled again at short notice. On May 25 Lieutenant Colonel William Ludlow, Federal agent for exchange of prisoners, wrote an angry letter to his Southern counterpart, Robert Ould, in which he brought "to your mind the cases of Lewis and Scully. You distinctly and without reservation told me that these men should be delivered on the day following the delivery to you of a large number of citizen prisoners; their names were especially mentioned and I have not yet received them. I shall deliver to you no more political or citizen prisoners except at 'our own pleasure' and no such agreement or understanding such as you propose will be for a moment entertained."

The threats failed, however, and Lewis and Scully remained stewing in Castle Thunder as the summer arrived. If anything, their nationality now counted against them as the Confederate authorities no longer had any reason to curry favor with the British.

.   .   .

At the outbreak of hostilities, the Confederacy had acted with greater alacrity in dispatching to Great Britain emissaries to speak on its behalf; in other words, to propagandize. Men such as William Yancey and Pierre Rost had secured audiences with Lord John Russell, the foreign secretary, to plead the Southern cause, while the Union had procrastinated in appointing an American minister to London, one of their own, as opposed to George Dallas, a Buchanan appointee who, while capable, wasn't wholly trusted by the new president. Finally Charles Adams had been assigned, but when he arrived in London in the second half of May 1861, he had a lot of ground to make up on his Southern rivals.

By the time Adams took up his new post, several dozen Union-supporting Negroes had taken it upon themselves to hold public meetings to counter the Confederate point of view, taking their lead from the most celebrated Negro to visit Britain, Frederick Douglass. He had been a leading member of the abolitionist movement since the 1840s and was a gifted writer and orator. Douglass was a friend of John Brown, but he had wisely refused to take part in the Harpers Ferry assault because he knew it would achieve nothing. Nonetheless the authorities claimed letters had been found among Brown and his men incriminating Douglass, so he fled to Canada and thence to England, arriving in November 1859. For six months he undertook a lecture tour of Britain for the American Anti-Slavery Society, playing to packed houses and captivating them with the eloquence of his oration on behalf of the enslaved. In May 1860 Douglass was about to leave for France on a similar tour when word reached him that his youngest daughter had died. He returned to the States and ended the war as a special adviser to President Lincoln.

Into Douglass's shoes stepped other Negroes, many of whom had fled to Britain a decade earlier after the passing of the Fugitive Slave Law of 1850. Others, such as the Reverend J. Sella Martin from Boston, came specifically to preach the message of emancipation. Martin toured the churches and chapels of England and Scotland, telling the congregations all about the iniquities of slavery.

The Confederate emissaries thought it wise to eschew public meetings and instead ingratiated themselves with selected editors of newspapers and journals in the hope of receiving a sympathetic press. The *Irish Times*, the London *Standard* and the London *Herald* all ran articles written by Southern agents. But these papers were read in the main by the middle classes, and they didn't carry the influence of the workingmen and -women. It was they, ultimately, who would determine British government policy, and for a while the Confederate emissaries believed they would come down on their side, particularly as the Union blockade began to bite and the cotton ceased to come. From December 1861 to May 1862 only 11,500 bales of cotton arrived in England from the United States, less than 1 percent of the amount for the same period the previous year. Cotton workers in the north of England began to lose their jobs and applied for Poor Relief (the equivalent of today's state benefits); in the county of Lancashire, 61,207 people out of a total population of 2.3 million asked for official handouts in November 1861; by March 1862 this figure had risen to 113,000, and by December it had soared to 284,418.

The working classes were suffering, but they weren't starving, thanks to government aid (motivated by a fear of revolution) and donations from private charities. Ironically, the hardships endured by the mill workers in the north of England because of the Union blockade only strengthened their support for the North's cause. They believed that no one, regardless of his color or creed, should be oppressed, and they were willing to suffer so that others wouldn't have to. In this belief they were delighted by Lincoln's Emancipation Proclamation of September 22, 1862, in which he declared that unless rebel states returned to the Union by January 1 their slaves would be considered as free men. Attendance at antislavery meetings in cities such as Liverpool, Leeds and Manchester shot up in the months that followed, and a typical resolution was the one passed at an assembly in Sheffield on January 10, 1863: "Resolved: that this meeting being convinced that slavery is the cause of the tremendous struggle now going on in the American states, and that the object of the leaders of the rebellion is the perpetuation of the unchristian and inhuman system of chattel slavery, earnestly prays that the rebellion may be crushed, and its wicked object defeated, and that the Federal Government may be strengthened to pursue its emancipation policy till not a slave be left on the American soil."

The London *Times*, still at best ambivalent toward the North, dismissed these meetings as being attended by "nobodies," but Charles Adams reported to Washington that "these manifestations are the genuine expression of the feelings of the religious dissenting and of the working classes." The British government, he predicted, would not be so foolish as to do anything to enflame the passion of the workingman, not with memories of the Chartist movement still alive. Adams was correct in his estimation. Britain refused to change its position of neutrality on the question of the American conflict, even refusing a French idea to help broker a peace plan in November 1862. The United States didn't need outside help to resolve its disputes. Then in 1863 a dispute arose between Denmark and the German Confederation over Schleswig-Holstein (a peninsula between the North and Baltic seas), giving the British government a convenient excuse to turn its attention from the west to the east.

Lincoln never forgot the benevolence of the British working class, nor their support for his cause, and on January 19, 1863, he wrote to the people of Manchester, telling them that he could not "but regard your decisive utterances upon the question of slavery as an instance of sublime Christian heroism, which has not been surpassed in any age or in any country."

In the mind of Allan Pinkerton, Abraham Lincoln had diminished in stature following the dismissal of George McClellan as commander of the Army of the Potomac on November 7, 1862. McClellan had gone because Lincoln was no longer able to tolerate his prevarication, "delaying on little pretexts of wanting this and that . . . I began to fear he was playing false—that he did not want to hurt the enemy." Lincoln believed that but for McClellan's cautiousness at Antietam the previous September, the bloody stalemate would have been a comprehensive Union victory. McClellan's successor was General Ambrose Burnside.

Pushing his personal feeling aside, however, Pinkerton wrote Lincoln on June 5, 1863, telling him about the execution of Webster and asking for his help in securing the release of Lewis and Scully. "Pryce Lewis is an Englishman and has no one in this country dependant upon him," wrote Pinkerton to the president, "but I have been and still am supporting the families of Webster and Scully. The death of the former precludes the possibility of any interference in his behalf, but the latter, fortunately, can still be benefitted by such interference . . . my object in writing to you is to appeal to you, in the name of these men and of their friends, to see that Justice is done to those who have so long suffered for having risked everything, even life itself, to Serve their country; and to ask that such disposition may be made by you of the matter, by referring it to whoever may have the more immediate charge of such arrangements or in such other manner as may best ensure the release and return to their homes of men who cannot but appear to me, under all the circumstances, as having a peculiar claim upon their Government for protection and relief."

When Pinkerton's letter elicited no response from the president, he organized the dispatch south of twenty dollars in gold and some smart clothes for his two operatives. Lewis still had on the same tatty shoes he'd worn during his escape from Henrico County Jail, so he was delighted when a brand-new suit and boots arrived from Chicago. Scully was less requiring of the footwear, and to Lewis's disdain "he made a present of his new boots to a nephew of Captain Alexander who was an officer in the Confederate army . . . it had good results for the captain took Scully twice to drive in Richmond soon after."

Alexander scrupulously husbanded the money and allowed Lewis and Scully access to it whenever they wished. Intoxicated by the novelty of sudden wealth, the pair for several days drew upon the fund to buy food, "but it cost so much—six dollars a meal—that we gave up such extravagance."

Alexander also moved the two men from their cell on the third floor to the more spacious Citizens' Room below. Lewis found the transference wryly amusing, proof of "what a difference money makes, even in the case of condemned prisoners." The Citizens' Room contained "a different class of prisoner: men connected with the sanitary commission, correspondents of newspapers, merchants captured on the coasts [but] with enough of the poor to act as substitutes for scavenger duty." Here the windows were glazed, half barrels were used as chairs and there was even a stove in one corner. Among the denizens of the Citizens' Room was J. T. Kerby, an Englishman living in Niagara, Canada, who had been arrested in November 1862 on the charge of spying. Kerby claimed he had come to Virginia on a business trip, but in reality he was a Union spy, though not in Pinkerton's employ. The two most prominent newspaper reporters held in the Citizens' Room were twenty-nine-year-old Albert Richardson and thirty-seven-year-old Junius Browne of the *New York Herald Tribune*. They had been captured at Vicksburg in May 1863, along with Richard Colburn of the *New York World*. Colburn was soon released (the Confederates didn't much mind his newspaper), but the

Tribune was considered one of the most bilious organs of the North. Richardson and Browne were thrown in Castle Thunder as punishment for the poison that flowed from their pens.

Richardson and Lewis soon got to talking and discovered they had common ground. The reporter had been with Cox's army two years earlier during the Kanawha Valley campaign. Richardson rated Cox "an excellent officer," and they shared fond memories of the camp at Poca and the river trip to Charleston.

Privately, Richardson was appalled by the appearance of the two spies, disclosing in his diary that "they held existence by a frail tenure . . . long anxiety had turned Lewis's hair gray, and given to both nervous, haggard faces." The arrival of Browne and Richardson aided Lewis's rehabilitation for they shared Lewis's eye for the absurd, and nothing was more absurd in Castle Thunder than Captain Alexander. Richardson giggled behind his hands at the sight of Alexander strutting around the prison in "pompous attire that included gauntlets and a red sash," but it was his verse that had the men weeping tears of laughter.

At nighttime the Citizens' Room was lit with gas, so the men kept late hours playing checkers or whist, reading, talking and smoking. They composed lighthearted verses, obviously nowhere near the quality of Alexander's offerings. Their favorite was "The Castle Song."

At the head of the Richmond Post they have placed a Marylander
And like a Devil in Regions lost there sits old Gen. Winder
He snaps & snarls & rips & swears when he's sober & when he's tight
The old villain's heart's as black as his head is white
All through this vicinity they hate him as hard they can
But never do as they slander him by calling him a decent man
Yet as mean as he's a patriot that may be understood
For when he left the Yankee Country twas for that country's good

In the door of the Castle like a stopper in a jug
To shut the mouth of the prison they've stuck a bell plug
It is Capt Alexander, who's so cross & spunky
He's not fit for a commander of an oyster pungy
The capt. is such a case as may often be seen

Who thinks he's smart but is very green
He's a thundering blower but would dare not fight
As dogs that bark the loudest are seldom known to bite

One September day Lewis read in a Richmond paper that Brigadier General Humphrey Marshall had arrived in the city. Marshall was a large man, "too heavy to mount a horse," but he was a doughty commander and a brave soldier. In May 1862 his forces had defeated those of General Jacob Cox at Princeton, Virginia. The report Lewis read related that the fifty-one year-old Marshall had now resigned from the army and was in Richmond to serve the Confederacy in a civil capacity. There was also a throwaway line that among the general's friends was Robert Ould, the Southern agent for exchange of prisoners. Lewis "suggested to Scully that as he was intimate with Captain Alexander to speak to him about Marshall and see if he could not be retained to do something for us." Scully thought it worth a try. So did Alexander, who liked to boast he had the ear of everyone in Richmond.

For a few days nothing happened; then one morning a guard came to fetch Scully from the Citizens' Room. When the Irishman returned he told Lewis that he'd spoken to Marshall, who promised to investigate their plight. Marshall reappeared a couple of days later and informed Scully that "he had seen Commissioner Ould about our case and he thought an exchange could be accomplished."

Scully had two or three further interviews with Marshall, and at each one the general's jowls wobbled as he nodded his head and told the prisoner that he saw no reason why their release couldn't be effected. The tension was excruciating. Lewis and Scully refused to allow themselves to believe they might soon be free. They played cards, read, slept; they did everything but speculate on their liberty.

On the morning of Saturday, September 26, 1863, the pair were summoned from their cell and led downstairs into Captain Alexander's office. Humphrey Marshall told Lewis and Scully that he had obtained their release.

Before either Lewis or Scully had time to mumble a thank-you, Marshall added that their freedom came with a price: five hundred dollars each. Lewis's heart sank. He detected the malevolent hand of General Winder; it was another of his cruel psychological torments. Lewis asked how they could possibly find such a sum, explaining that the only money they had was what remained of the cache sent by the Pinkerton agency.

Marshall casually replied that if the pair gave him a joint note for one thousand dollars he would trust them to honor it once they had their freedom. It was a deal. Marshall wrote a receipt, Lewis and Scully signed it, and they "began at last to take breath, it looked as if we were really going to get away."

The next forty-eight hours took an age to pass. They told each other that they wouldn't believe they were going home until the moment they saw their first Stars and Stripes fluttering in the breeze. What they expected to see at any moment was the leering face of Winder or one of his Plug-Uglies laughing at their evil prank.

Then on the afternoon of Monday, September 28, Caphart entered the Citizens' Room and ordered the two spies to collect their belongings. They asked why. Caphart told them to shut up and do as they were told. Lewis had hardly any belongings to gather. He put on his tatty felt hat, slung his coat over his arm and at the last moment remembered Captain Alexander's ballad, the "Virginia Cavalier." He must take that to show the boys.

Lewis and Scully then "said goodbye to our fellow prisoners, including the newspaper correspondents, for whom we carried messages to their friends," and followed Caphart downstairs. They were taken to Libby Prison, just a couple of hundred yards along Cary Street from Castle Thunder, and ordered to stand in line with some other prisoners and sign their parole. When it was the turn of Lewis and Scully, the officer behind the desk read the names on the form and looked up at the two shriveled men before him. If it had been up to him, he told them, they would have hung with Webster.

They remained in Libby Prison overnight, and just before dawn on Tuesday, September 29, they and the other paroled prisoners were marched west along Cary Street, which ran parallel to the James River, to the Richmond and Petersburg Railroad Depot, at the corner of Byrd and Eighth streets. It was no more than a mile, but it exhausted Lewis and Scully. With what strength Lewis had left he "got up on a box freight car for fresh air. It tasted delicious."

At ten minutes to six the train began to move. It was true, they really were going home. They arrived in Petersburg at seven thirty A.M., changed trains and continued their journey to City Point on the James River. The flag-of-truce boat was waiting for them, and there hanging limply from the mast in the cool morning air was the Union flag. Lewis turned to Scully and said, "If before this I had any English feelings left, I've been turned into a complete American now."

Scully and Lewis arrived at College Green Barracks, Annapolis, in Maryland on the morning of Wednesday, September 30. There they encountered Major S. E. Chamberlain, First Massachusetts Cavalry, in charge of the parole camp. He was a "full-dressed, pompous, heavy official" who declined Lewis's request for help in reaching Washington, citing a recent order issued by the War Department denying transportation to civilians. But we're not civilians, retorted a furious Lewis, who in response to Chamberlain's continued indifference "told him something of the service [we] had rendered the government . . . that we had been prisoners for nineteen months, under sentence of death part of the time, and chained hand and foot." The outburst failed to move the officer, so Lewis turned to Scully and suggested they walk the forty miles to Washington. But Scully had a better idea. Why not pawn Lewis's coat and with the money buy two train tickets to Washington? That required a pass, however, which Chamberlain at first refused. Eventually he relented and on a scrap of paper wrote out a permit: "The bearer Lewis Price [sic], a citizen of England, arrived this morning from Richmond by flag of truce boat. The guards and patrols will allow him to pass. S. E. Chamberlain, Maj 1st Mass. Cav., comd'g A,G,B."

Lewis and Scully walked into town and pawned the coat for three dollars. They found a saloon, "lunched on bread and cheese," and caught the evening train west to Washington, arriving at nine o'clock at the Baltimore & Ohio station. It felt strange to be in the capital again. So what do we do now? they wondered. Pinkerton had moved his headquarters back to Chicago, they knew that from his letters, but who else remained in the city who could help them? They remembered Colonel William Wood, superintendent of the Old Capitol Prison, to whom they had delivered the odd Confederate sympathizer. He would be of assistance. They trudged to Old Capitol Prison, a three-story brick building on the corner of Pennsylvania Avenue and East First Street (site of today's

U.S. Supreme Court). There they told their story to a guard, who fetched Wood, but when the superintendent arrived at the prison gate he looked upon the two men with suspicion. Don't you know me, Colonel? asked Lewis. Wood squinted at the gray-haired, middle-aged man. He shook his head. It's me, said the Englishman. Pryce Lewis.

For a few moments Wood was speechless; then "he uttered an exclamation of astonishment and indulged in considerable profanity to express his feelings of surprise." He ushered the men inside to his office, fed them and listened to their tale of woe. Wood then summoned the captain of the guard and told him to have two cots made up. In the morning Dr. Ford, the prison doctor, inspected the men, and Wood telegrammed Pinkerton, who was in Philadelphia.

Pinkerton replied on the same day, October 1: MANY THANKS FOR YOUR KIND INFORMATION. TELL SCULLY AND LEWIS TO COME HERE. I CANNOT POSSIBLY LEAVE JUST NOW. SHOULD THEY REQUIRE MONEY TO COME PLEASE LET THEM HAVE IT AND I WILL RETURN IT TO YOU. GIVE THEM MY ADDRESS HERE AND TELL THEM TO AVOID ALL PUBLICITY OF THEIR AFFAIRS UNTIL THEY SEE ME.

CHAPTER TWENTY-FIVE

"Lewis Remained Staunch, and Did Not Confess"

PINKERTON HAD RESIGNED as chief of the secret service of the Army of the Potomac on November 7, 1862, the day McClellan had been relieved of his command. In his memoirs Pinkerton said he quit because he was McClellan's man and considered his treatment unjust. The thought of working for his successor, General Ambrose Burnside, wasn't an option, though there was no evidence that the new commander urged Pinkerton to remain.

For months Pinkerton had railed against the "Washington Cabal," men such as Edwin Stanton and Henry Halleck, the army's general in chief, sending regular reports from Washington to McClellan's head-quarters on all the intrigue. It was the opinion of Pinkerton, as well as McClellan, that Washington was deliberately withholding supplies and munitions and thus making it impossible for McClellan to pursue the Confederates across the Potomac. Munitions might have been slow in arriving from the east, but then as Lincoln—furious that his general hadn't gone after the rebels—had written McClellan in late October, "Will you pardon me for asking what the horses of your army have done since the battle of Antietam [on September 17] that fatigues anything?"

But there were other factors at work that probably contributed to Pinkerton's decision to resign. Since his installation in Washington re-porting to McClellan, Pinkerton had encountered a reluctance on the part of the government to settle the agency's accounts. On several occasions, the Scot had been forced to telegraph George Bangs in Chicago requesting drafts so he could pay his detectives, who received ten dollars a day, as well as settle other expenses incurred in the line of duty. In October 1862 matters came to a head when Peter Watson, the assistant secretary of war, questioned Pinkerton's bill for the months from July to September. He also insisted Pinkerton reveal the full names of his operatives in his accounts, not just their initials. Pinkerton, understandably, refused. It was sensitive information, and also invaluable to the South, which still had informers within government departments. Pinkerton told Watson that one of his men had already been hanged; he didn't wish another to go to the scaffold.

Pinkerton was also influenced by what had passed in Richmond. Webster and Lewis had been his most trusted and effective detectives. Their absence immeasurably reduced the potency of his agency. Those who remained were competent at counterintelligence, but when it came to gathering positive intelligence ("actionable intelligence," as it is now known), none possessed the guile, wit and charisma of Webster or Lewis. And how much had the execution of Webster frightened Pinkerton's operatives? In the first year of the war neither side had hanged spies, and there was an unwritten understanding that that would remain the case throughout the war. A spy preparing to penetrate the enemy's line might expect a bit of roughing up if caught, and a few months in a dirty prison, but not death. Webster's fate had changed all that. Even before the tragedy one of Pinkerton's operatives, Charles Rosch, had refused to accompany Lewis to Richmond because he considered it too dangerous. And now, why would anyone volunteer to head south if there was a strong possibility they would end up in the hangman's noose? It might have been that Pinkerton ran out of spies willing to risk their lives, and McClellan's departure allowed him to remove his agency from the field without losing face.

That's not to impugn the courage of Pinkerton's operatives; the fact was that by the autumn of 1862 the nature of the war had changed considerably during a year and a half of fighting. The first few months of the war had been chaotic, with neither side able to cope with the vast number of recruits that flocked to the cause. Local militia units added to the confusion, as did the initial short term of enlistments that saw men come and go with bewildering frequency. Penetrating an army in the field is the hardest task for a military spy, but in the commotion of 1861 it was easier for a spy to go about his work unobtrusively.

There was also an innocence, a naïveté, to many combatants whose romantic notions of warfare had yet to be blasted to shreds by reality. Would Colonel Patton, for example, have trusted Pryce Lewis so implicitly a year later? Would he have wined and dined him, offered to show him around the camp? More likely the cynicism of the hardened soldier would have led Patton to suspect something wasn't quite right about the quirky Englishman.

Furthermore, throughout 1862 the static warfare of the previous year had been replaced by more fluid conflict, in which the Confederates proved more adept. In May General Stonewall Jackson had ripped through the Shenandoah Valley, defeating General Frémont's forces in several encounters, and then it was the turn of Robert E. Lee's Army of Northern Virginia to push north after July's Seven Days Battles. Victories for Lee at the Second Battle of Bull Run (August 28–30) and Chantilly (September 1) heralded the rebel drive into Maryland and further bloody encounters at Harpers Ferry, South Mountain and Antietam. Thus the Confederate forces were continually on the move, far more transient than they had been for much of 1861 when they and the Union army, once they had organized the recruits into a semblance of regiments, dug in and waited to see who would make the first move.

In short, the glamorous heyday of the Civil War spy had come and gone by the end of 1862. There would be no more Websters or Lewises, spies who were masters of gathering positive intelligence from the heart of the enemy, certainly none who were as successful. Espionage in the rest of the war took on a more prosaic nature, if one draws a distinction between the civilian spy and the soldier spy, men such as the Confederate captain John Beall and Major Harry Young of the Union army. They were trained soldiers who led small bands of men through enemy territory, wearing their foe's uniform, not just gathering intelligence but also waging guerrilla war and bringing back prisoners.

For the civilian spy, espionage in the second half of the war focused more on counterintelligence, with the positive intelligence being undertaken not by infiltrators but by people long established within their community. The most skilled of these was Elizabeth Van Lew, who hailed from one of Richmond's most respected families and lived in a grandiose mansion on Church Hill. Van Lew, a cultured woman in her late forties, was a proud Virginian but a vehement abolitionist and staunch Unionist. Her views were common knowledge, and while they incurred the opprobrium of her neighbors, no one thought she was anything other than an old maid with a kind heart, who made frequent trips to Richmond's prisons, doling out parcels of food and clothing to the inmates.

As the war lengthened, Van Lew began smuggling coded messages to the North through a network of informants, mostly pro-Union Virginians like her, farm laborers, storekeepers and factory workers. The messages contained details of rebel troop strength and fortifications, some of which came from her contacts within the Confederate administration and some from the mouths of captured Northern soldiers held in Richmond's jails. Though Winder began to suspect Van Lew's sympathies extended to more than just mercy missions to prison, he could never catch her in the act despite having her put under surveillance. Van Lew was the antithesis of Rose Greenhow, not just in looks but in personality. She was discreet and cautious, and as courteous to the enemy as Greenhow was disdainful. As she once said of General Winder, "I can flatter almost anything out of old Winder, his personal vanity is so great."

Van Lew reported to General George Sharpe, head of the Union's Bureau of Military Intelligence, an organization formed in the spring of 1863 to plug the hole left by Pinkerton's resignation. Sharpe was a lawyer turned diplomat turned soldier turned spymaster, and he was adept at all four roles. Major General Joseph Hooker had instructed Sharpe, then his deputy provost marshal, to establish an intelligence unit, and a year later there were around seventy agents working as "guides"; some interrogated rebel prisoners, others trawled battlefields for information on dead Confederates and at least ten were killed in action as they roamed the front lines observing enemy positions. Sharpe was later promoted to Grant's intelligence chief, and his Bureau of Military Intelligence was the model for the U.S. Army's Military Intelligence Division that was founded in 1885.

Sharpe described Van Lew as "energetic and active and wise," an accurate assessment of the Civil War's most efficacious female spy. Rose Greenhow and Belle Boyd (a comely young Southern spy whose looks far surpassed her ability) might be the best-known spies, but that was because in the decades following the war writers and historians mythologized the pair, portraying them as beautiful women who ran rings around the hapless enemy. Unfortunately, the glamour masked the truth. Boyd's main achievement, in the words of one contemporary newspaper, was to have been a particularly energetic "camp follower"; a prostitute in other words. Greenhow had the potential to be a dangerous and destructive spy, but her undoing was her contempt for the enemy and her arrogance. The two traits coalesced to make her believe she was invincible. Her legacy was perhaps best summed up by Judge Edwards Pierrepont, a member of the wartime military commission that examined the cases of Federal prisoners (he was also the attorney general in the 1870s). Greenhow's espionage activities weren't treasonous, he declared, merely "mischief." Such a dismissive assessment would have broken Greenhow's heart.

Though his skills as a military spy had been found wanting, Pinkerton and his agency were still valued for their detective work by Lincoln and Stanton. Throughout 1863 he was employed by the government on various cases of a nonmilitary nature, such as unmasking those responsible for large-scale cotton frauds. Pinkerton also reestablished his links with the railroad companies, and one, the Philadelphia and Reading Railroad Company, hired him to root out an employee who had embezzled nearly twenty thousand dollars in government bonds. Pinkerton caught the man, a conductor, and he was successful in several other cases passed to him by the same railroad company. Pinkerton was happy; not only was he able to spend more time with his family (his eldest son, William, now seventeen, was working alongside his father) in Chicago, but he had rediscovered his métier. He was a criminal detective, not a military one.

As Lewis and Scully took a cab from the Philadelphia rail terminus to Pinkerton's headquarters, Lewis crackled with retribution. He had longed for this moment for months; the thought of it had sustained him throughout the days spent shackled hand and foot, the nights curled up in the pitch black of the condemned cell, and the weeks when he hovered close to death under his lousy blanket in Castle Thunder.

Pinkerton had perhaps been expecting a show of gratitude. After all, he reminded them, he'd done his best to get the men released. And what about the money, the clothes, the shoes, the visit to Mrs. Scully, the letter to Thomas Lewis? Anyway, let bygones be bygones; he was mighty pleased to see them safe and sound.

Lewis erupted and spewed out nineteen months of torment and rancor. He gave Pinkerton "a hot interview . . . and did not spare him for his carelessness in getting us into the enemy's hands." What exactly Lewis said he never revealed, though doubtless they were fiery words.

Pinkerton was unaccustomed to rebuke. His conceit led him to retaliate. He had read the reports in the Richmond papers, he shouted, and he knew that Lewis and Scully had "let the cat out of the bag." He had also listened to Hattie Lawton's jumbled version, some of which had been given her by General Winder and his Plug-Uglies. Were it not for the treachery of Lewis and Scully, Timothy Webster would still be alive. Oh no, snarled Lewis, there was but one man responsible for the death of Webster. It wasn't President Davis or General Winder or Anti-Christ Caphart, and it certainly wasn't Pryce Lewis or John Scully. It was Allan Pinkerton!

Pryce Lewis never again came face-to-face with Allan Pinkerton after the furious altercation in Philadelphia on the afternoon of Friday, October 2. He returned to Washington and secured an interview with Edwin Stanton, the secretary of war, the man whom Lewis had ejected from Rose Greenhow's house more than two years earlier. If Stanton remembered the incident, he didn't hold it against Lewis, as he didn't hold any prejudice for the events in Richmond, despite Pinkerton's assertion that he had refused to intercede on Lewis's and Scully's behalf "because they had betrayed their companion to save their own lives."

Stanton arranged for one thousand dollars in Confederate notes to be sent south to Humphrey Marshall and then instructed Superintendent Wood to find Lewis a position at Old Capitol Prison. Wood was only too happy to oblige and gave Lewis a job as a bailiff and detective, responsible for escorting prisoners to and from court. It was menial work, but it allowed Lewis to reintegrate himself into civilized society.

Despite his rupture with Allan Pinkerton, Lewis remained on good terms with the Scot's eldest son, William. They exchanged the occasional letter, and in January 1864 the teenager wrote Lewis: "I hope your situation [at Old Capitol] will be of long continuance. You may stand a chance of repaying some of your old Southern friends for some of the many *kind favors* you received whilst in there [*sic*] hands. You are now in a position to pay it back with interest. Mrs. Webster called today and she looks very well . . . the Old Man [Allan Pinkerton] is not here. All the men send Best respects as also does my mother. Wishing you every success. Remains Ever Your Friend, William Pinkerton."

Lewis's rehabilitation was completed in June 1864 when he was recruited by Colonel Lafayette Baker into the military secret service. Baker by this stage of the war was to his enemies in Washington what General Winder was to his in Richmond: a man to be feared, a man who believed any method was permissible if it was in the best interest of the war effort. Born in New York in 1826, the red-bearded Baker had drifted west and become a member of the San Francisco Vigilance Committee, a brutal organization that boasted it kept the city clean of human vermin. Baker was back on the East Coast in early 1861 and convinced General Winfield Scott that the Union army needed better information on the enemy. He undertook several missions in the South of his own accord, but none was particularly successful, so Baker turned from positive intelligence to counterintelligence. This was his forte, though his methods were unscrupulous and both Colonel William Wood and Allan Pinkerton deemed him a "doubtful character." Thomas A. Scott, assistant secretary of war, shrugged off the concerns, saying expediency must sometimes ride roughshod over principle.

Following the resignation of Pinkerton, Baker's star rose in Washington, and by 1863 he had over thirty employees working for his National Detective Police, known colloquially as "Lincoln's Secret Police." Later he was appointed special provost marshal for the War Department. One of the Southern sympathizers arrested by Baker was Belle Boyd, a woman whose relationship with veracity was as shaky as his, as both would later prove in their overblown memoirs.

Lewis never ventured South again during the final year of conflict. His time was spent in Washington working for Baker's secret service, where he was "authorized to arrest deserters, blockade runners and perform such other duties as may legitimately belong to his department." He had no contact with John Scully, who had returned to Chicago, fathered another child and enlisted in the city's police force.

In late 1864 Lewis left the secret service after becoming disillusioned with the corruption he encountered. Too many agents accepted bribes from those they caught trying to carry goods across the Potomac into Virginia, and when he brought this problem to the attention of Baker he was brushed off. When the news broke of Lincoln's assassination, Lewis was staying with his brother in Connecticut.

Pinkerton was in New Orleans when he heard of the outrage. Exactly a year earlier he and his operatives had been transferred to the city on the orders of Stanton to investigate widespread cotton fraud. It was an astute move on the part of Stanton, and Pinkerton secured the conviction of numerous venal brokers, in the process retrieving tens of thousands of dollars of government money.

Through it all, Pinkerton had kept in regular correspondence with McClellan. The Scot still believed that McClellan, who had retired to a quiet life in New Jersey, could be the savior of the Union cause, and in the spring of 1864 others came to share the view. The catalyst was the Battle of the Wilderness in May, the opening salvo in General Grant's "Overland" campaign against Lee's Confederate Army of Northern Virginia. The Wilderness battle was a failure, and a bloody one at that, with thirty-two thousand Union soldiers killed, wounded or missing (compared to eighteen thousand on the rebel side, though proportionally the losses were similar). The atmosphere within the Union turned despondent, but Grant continued with his campaign for a further month in what became a brutal war of attrition. Though Grant had scored a strategic victory—one that led to the Richmond-Petersburg campaign and the eventual capitulation of Richmond in April 1865—the cost of the seven-week struggle had been ruinously high for many in the North, with sixty-five thousand of their soldiers listed as casualties. With factions in the government unhappy with the way Lincoln was conducting the war, the Democrats sensed the president could be ousted from power in the autumn election, if the right candidate could be secured. McClellan stepped forward, eagerly supported by Pinkerton, among others, and on August 29 the former general was nominated as the Democratic candidate at the party's Chicago convention.

For the next three months Pinkerton championed McClellan's cause at every available opportunity, but gradually his initial optimism in his friend's chances of success diminished. The Democratic Party was split between those who favored immediate peace and those who wished to continue war, and McClellan's political inexperience proved fatal in trying to bridge the gulf. While Lincoln and the Republicans' aims were unequivocal—"Peace through Victory"—those of McClellan's appeared to be just peace. This wasn't what the Union soldiers wanted to hear, not after so much bloodshed, and just 34,000 voted for McClellan while 120,000 put a cross by Lincoln's name. Civilians shared the soldiers' view, and Lincoln enjoyed a crushing victory over his former general. Pinkerton had no doubt hoped that if McClellan had won the presidency his loyalty would have been rewarded with an important role within the administration. Instead, Pinkerton returned to New Orleans to continue hunting perpetrators of frauds.

Despite having been a supporter of Lincoln's rival in the 1864 election, Pinkerton was nevertheless stunned when he learned of his murder. Immediately he sent a wire to Secretary of War Stanton: HOW I REGRET THAT I HAD NOT BEEN NEAR HIM PREVIOUS TO THAT FATAL ACT. I MIGHT HAVE BEEN THE MEANS TO ARREST IT. IF I CAN BE OF SPECIAL SERVICE, PLEASE LET ME KNOW. THE SACRIFICE OF MY WHOLE FORCE, OF LIFE ITSELF, IS AT YOUR DISPOSAL. Stanton sent a brief reply, instructing Pinkerton "to watch the western rivers" for the assassin. By the time Pinkerton received Stanton's note, John Wilkes Booth was already dead.

At the war's end accusations that he had played a part in sending Webster to his death continued to cling to Lewis. Small wonder he decided to return to Britain for a few months in the summer of 1865.

He crossed the Atlantic to Liverpool and from there caught a train south to Shrewsbury, where his mother wept at the sight of her back-from-the-dead son. Perhaps he took the time to visit his elder brother Arthur, a sad bachelor in his forties still working as a weaver in Newtown, which after twenty lean years was enjoying a revival thanks to the introduction of steam power in the factories and the completion of three railway lines linking Newtown to towns in England and Wales. There were other changes afoot in Britain, not as tangible as the Newtown railway but far more profound. In 1867 the Conservative government of Lord Derby introduced the Reform Bill, which in effect gave one and a half million workingmen the vote. It was a reluctant bill on the part of the government, but the Civil War across the ocean had demonstrated all too clearly the dangers of trying to suppress a man's liberty. It was, as one commentator later noted, the moment Britain changed "from a government by aristocracy to one by democracy. A new nation came into being. The friends of the North [of the United States] had triumphed."

Lewis didn't stay long in his native land. He was back in the United States in 1867, and on January 20, 1868, he married Maria Thwaites in Illinois. Lewis had met Thwaites through David Erskine, the store owner for whom he had once worked. Three years later they had a daughter, Mary, followed by a son, Arthur, in 1878.

Mary didn't see much of her father in the early years of her life. She and her mother lived in the Thwaites' family home in Waukegan, Illinois, while Lewis was based in Jersey City. On his return from Britain he and William Scott had gone into the detective business together. Scott was a former agency man—he had escorted Lewis and Scully to the Potomac on that fateful final trip—and he too had grown tired of Allan Pinkerton.

Lewis had always known that Scott liked his liquor, but it soon became clear he was more than a social drinker; whiskey sustained him. With a partner incapable of performing his duties, Lewis struggled to keep the business going. On one occasion he wrote Maria: "My dear wife, don't be discouraged. It is true that I have not met with the success that I expected but it might have been worse. There is one thing that I have learned and that is how to love you."

By the late 1870s Scott was no longer part of the business; instead Lewis was in partnership with a man named William Oldring, a far more competent (and sober) man, and business boomed. They moved into premises in New York City on 169 Broadway, and Lewis now had enough money to bring his family East and buy his own property. In 1878 Pryce Lewis's name was once more in the papers when his detective agency became embroiled in a bitter dispute over the will of Alexander Stewart, one of New York's richest men who, before his death two years earlier, had owned huge tracts of the city's real estate. With the controversy arising from that case, as well as all Lewis's other work, the name Allan Pinkerton faded into a distant, if still disagreeable, memory.

In his letter to Abraham Lincoln on June 5, 1863, requesting his help in liberating Pryce Lewis and John Scully, Pinkerton had referred to

Webster as "one of my best and oldest employees." That was all; there were no fulsome eulogies or mawkish laments for the dead man. In a war that was reaping a bountiful harvest of dead, what was the life of one more unfortunate? In his letters to Lewis and Scully in Castle Thunder, Pinkerton never even mentioned Webster, not because it was a difficult subject to broach but because he was dead and it was the living who mattered.

In the years after the war Pinkerton's grief for Webster underwent an astonishing transformation. Perhaps now that the guns were silent, he was able to reflect with solemn piety on a brave man's sacrifice, or perhaps guilt was gnawing at Pinkerton's conscience. In 1871 Pinkerton ordered George Bangs to Richmond to bring back Webster's body. The perennially reliable Bangs located the remains in a pauper's grave in Oakwood Cemetery in the northeast of the city.

On June 7 the *Onarga Courier* reported that "the body of T. Webster, who was hung in Richmond, Va. in 1862, as a Union Spy, was brought home to Onarga on Thursday of last week and interred in the cemetry [sic] at that place. Mr. Webster was well known to many of our readers."

Webster was buried alongside his son, who had fallen while fighting as a Union soldier, and Pinkerton paid for the double headstone. He got his former operative's date of death wrong; it should have been April 29, 1862, not April 26. Pinkerton also fabricated the epitaph, ordering the engraver to carve into the foot of Webster's headstone: HIS LAST WORDS "I DIE FOR MY COUNTRY."

That still wasn't enough for Pinkerton. He wanted people to know about the sacrifice of Timothy Webster, the fearless man who had died at the hands of the wicked rebels. He commissioned a cenotaph to be erected in Chicago's Graceland Cemetery and spent many hours choosing the stone and deciding the wording, but less time on researching his facts. When the cenotaph was erected people flocked to read the somber inscription.

TO THE MEMORY OF TIMOTHY WEBSTER

THE PATRIOT AND MARTYR

BORN IN 1821 IN NEW HAVEN

SUSSEX CO. ENGLAND

EMIGRATED TO AMERICA IN 1833 AND ENTERED

PINKERTON'S NATIONAL DETECTIVE

AGENCY AT CHICAGO IN 1856.

ON THE NIGHT OF FEBR. 22, 1861

ALLAN PINKERTON

TIMOTHY WEBSTER

KATE WARN

SAFELY ESCORTED

ABRAHAM LINCOLN

A CONSPIRACY HAVING BEEN DISCOVERED

FOR HIS ASSASSINATION FROM

PHILADELPHIA TO WASHINGTON

WHERE HE WAS INAUGURATED

PRESIDENT OF THE U.S. ON

MARCH 4TH 1861

HE WAS THE HARVEY BIRCH OF THE WAR OF

THE REBELLION AND WAS EXECUTED AS A SPY

BY THE REBELS IN RICHMOND ON APRIL 28, 1862.

HE ENJOYED THE CONFIDENCE OF

ABRAHAM LINCOLN

AND SEALED HIS FIDELITY WITH THE BLOOD.

Pinkerton still couldn't get right the date of execution, neither the date of Webster's birth nor the year he emigrated from England. Kate Warne's name was misspelled, and there was no mention of the other people who had helped uncover the craven "plot" to kill Lincoln.

To further bring Timothy Webster to wider attention, Pinkerton decided to write a book. He called it *The Spy of the Rebellion*, and in the preface he explained that he had been "tempted to the recitals which follow . . . by a desire to acquaint the public with the movements of those brave men who rendered invaluable service to their country, although they never wore a uniform or carried a musket." In reality what followed were mostly half truths and falsehoods, wrapped in maudlin prose.

Pryce Lewis had been warned that the *Chicago Times* contained an article about a book Pinkerton was writing. The newspaper finally fell into Lewis's hands on February 29, 1884, and on page 11, under the headline THE FINAL CLEW, was a thrilling summary of Pinkerton's impending book. It was mostly laughable guff, but what infuriated Lewis was the fifth paragraph. "Near to Webster's grave is that of Price Lewis, but the other actor in the tragedy, John Scully, is still living, and is now employed at the [Chicago] city hall." Lewis wrote at once to Pinkerton.

Dear Sir

In an article first published in the Chicago Times Oct 9th 1883 entitled "The Final Clew," which is still going the rounds of the press I find myself dead and buried in the Pinkerton burial plot, and the reporter claims he gets his information directly from you. If this was the first time such statements were published I should say nothing about it, but it is not. Under the circumstances I don't think it is fair treatment to bury a man in Chicago and resurrect him as occasion requires to brace up statements which are only in part true, when you ought to know he is still in the flesh. I think it is only fair to ask that you have the Times make the necessary correction.

Respectfully Yours
Pryce Lewis

Pinkerton's reply was a flippant dismissal of his former employee's concerns. Lewis was incensed. He knew Pinkerton and the way his mind worked; he had circulated the scurrilous rumors to put a rival detective agency out of business. On March 21, 1884, Lewis wrote again to his former boss.

Mr. A Pinkerton Esq.
Dear Sir

Yours of the 3rd was received and contents noted. From your stand point you are doubtless right in thinking that the publication of my death was not material but when such a story as published in Chicago is reprinted in this locality I assure you it is of vital importance to me, as I have been engaged in some very important cases in this city, and it is not at all agreeable to me to be under the suspicion of being other than whom I claim to be. The facts regarding the circumstances that led to the capture and execution of Tim Webster are best known to myself and the time might come when I will give them to the public. If daring exploits should be the stock in trade of our business, it is but fair that those who passed through the ordeal should reap the benefit, particularly while in this world. I fully appreciate your goodwill, but nevertheless I realize that in this progressive age business is business and if one would live to have a fair share of the earth's products he must blow his own horn.

Please have the inclosed inserted in the Chicago Times and forward me a copy

Yours very truly
Pryce Lewis

The enclosed, whatever it was, was never published in the *Chicago Times*. Six weeks later *The Spy of the Rebellion* was published. It was 666 pages, illustrated, and the cost was $2.50. The *Chicago Inter Ocean* called it "more profoundly interesting and exciting than any romance of the year." The book beatified Timothy Webster, lionized Allan Pinkerton and mortified Pryce Lewis.

Pinkerton had all but single-handedly saved the president from assassination ("I had informed Mr. Lincoln in Philadelphia that I would answer with my life for his safe arrival in Washington, and I had redeemed my pledge"); his description of Timothy Webster bordered on the homoerotic ("The mouth, almost concealed by the heavy brown mustaches which he wore, and the square, firm chin evinced a firmness that was unmistakable. His nose, large and well-formed, and the prominent cheek bones all seemed in perfect harmony with the bold spirit . . . his shoulders were so broad, his feet and hands so shapely, and the lithe limbs so well formed . . . [that] a casual observer on meeting this man would almost immediately and insensibly be impressed"). George McClellan was unrecognizable from the dithering neurotic who had so frustrated Lincoln ("Self was his last and least consideration . . . McClellan pursued his course with unflinching courage and with a devotion to his country unsurpassed by any who have succeeded him, and upon whose brows are entwined the laurels of the conqueror").

Pinkerton misspelled Lewis's name throughout the book, a curious oversight for someone so meticulous. "Price" Lewis's mission into western Virginia was well chronicled, though with one or two alterations. The Lord Tracy persona was carried through right to the end, and there was a romantic interlude when Lewis fell for the ravishing daughter of Judge Beveridge, though in fact these people existed only in Pinkerton's fertile imagination. Pinkerton related how Lewis had saved the young woman from certain death after her horse had taken fright and bolted. That evening Lewis was invited to take supper with the Beveridges, and the beautiful woman greeted her gallant "with rare grace . . . and her expressions of thankfulness were couched in such delicate language that the pretended Englishman felt a strange fluttering in his breast, which was as novel to him as it was delicious."

Such flights of fancy just made Lewis laugh, but then the calumnies began to mount. Pinkerton told how Lewis and Scully had accepted the mission to Richmond "without the slightest hesitation"; a couple of pages later he added, "I had made extensive enquiries . . . and learned that Mrs. Morton and her family had departed for their home in Florida." Everyone in Washington had known the Mortons were estranged.

But it was what Lewis read on page 529 that made him reel. Pinkerton had described on the previous pages how Scully unburdened himself to Father McMullen, who in turn persuaded the Irishman to make a statement. Then Pinkerton wrote that "finding that the worse had occurred, and that further concealment was of no avail, Lewis, too, opened his mouth." But Pinkerton didn't blame them; oh no, how could any Christian gentlemen "express an unjust sentence? They were simply men who, after having performed many brave acts of loyalty and duty to their country, failed in a moment of grand and great self-sacrifice. I cannot apologize for them—I cannot judge them."

It had taken Pinkerton twenty years, but he had got his revenge for the "hot interview." Lewis was devastated. But Pinkerton didn't survive long to gloat over his victory. A month after the publication of his book the already poorly Scot fell and bit his tongue. Gangrene set in, and for three weeks the devout Pinkerton lingered, each day getting closer to his own Judgment Day. On July 1, 1884, Pinkerton died at age sixty-five. He was buried in Graceland Cemetery, and in time a towering obelisk was erected over his grave on which was inscribed: A FRIEND TO HONESTY AND A FOE TO CRIME.

· · ·

Lewis's business declined as Pinkerton had hoped. He still took odd jobs around the country, but his heyday was over. He was getting old, too, though he retained his strong physique and lively mind. One January afternoon in 1888 Lewis left his New York office and caught the ferry boat across the Hudson to New Jersey. He got to talking—as was his custom—to a well-dressed gentleman of around the same age. His name was David Cronin, an artist and writer now but a former officer in the First New York Mounted Rifles. They swapped war stories, and suddenly Cronin clicked his fingers and exclaimed, "I heard the story of your escape from Henrico County Jail!" Cronin told Lewis he should write his memoirs. Lewis didn't like to blow his horn. Damn it, said Cronin, it's time you did. He offered to edit them, and soon an agreement was drafted and signed for "Pryce Lewis: his adventures as a union spy during the war of the rebellion. A historical narrative."

Cronin paraded the manuscript around publishing houses for the first six months of 1889, but there was little enthusiasm. Civil War stories were now a little passé, unless they came from the pen of a general or a statesman. One publisher after another turned down Cronin, but then a house appeared to bite. Cronin was called for an interview and informed by the company that it was interested in publishing but there needed to be some "padding." What sort of padding? The book would be a greater success if Lewis portrayed himself as one of Lincoln's bodyguards during the tumultuous days of 1861. Cronin relayed the conversation to Lewis, who angrily retorted that he was not prepared "to include a lot of lies about his experiences with Lincoln . . . he never met the man." The publishers decided not to pursue the project.

As Lewis's manuscript gathered dust at the family home in New Jersey, he continued to take whatever detective work he could find despite being in his sixties. In 1892 the New York Life Insurance Company hired him to track down a gang of counterfeiters operating throughout the United States. The case took him to Texas, and across the border into Mexico, where the gang was arrested. From El Paso he wrote to his daughter, enclosing a money order for seventy-five dollars and telling her he "was very sorry to learn of ma's relapse and hope by the time this reaches you she will be better." Two years later he passed through Kansas and lodged for the night with his brother-in-law Albert.

Lewis always dropped in on his brothers, George and Matthew, whenever he was in Connecticut. Matthew, who was widowed with a grown-up son, was a successful farmer, and George had a battery of grandchildren who loved to hear their great-uncle's war stories. It was his brothers' job to fill him in on news from home: the passing of their wonderful, loving, indomitable mother, Elizabeth, at the age of ninety, in 1889; the death seven years later of Arthur, George's twin, in the Newtown workhouse, a man whose demise mirrored that of the Newtown woolen industry. By the end of the nineteenth century the great towns of Lancashire and Yorkshire dominated Britain's woolen industry; they possessed the capital and resources to mass-produce on a scale beyond the capabilities of Newtown. They also had the temerity to pass off their inferior-quality wool as "real Welsh flannel," the supreme insult to Newtonians.

Thomas, however, the brother who had sent the sorrowful letter to Charles Adams all those years earlier after reading of Pryce's "death," was a success. He lived in the south of England with his wife and four children, and earned a good living as a town clerk.

When the new century dawned the Lewis family was in troubled straits. Pryce's eyesight wasn't what it was, and his seventieth birthday was looming; he was too old to be a detective. Mary Lewis, now age twenty-nine, was teaching pottery and clay modeling and living in New York City, but twenty-two-year-old Arthur was still at home. On January 12, 1900, his frail mother wrote to William Drake, principal of Jersey City Business College, Arthur's alma mater, asking if he might be able to help Arthur find some work. By the time Drake replied, Maria Lewis was dead.

Arthur Lewis found a job, but it killed him two years later at the age of twenty-four, at least it did in the eyes of his sister, who believed he "died because he overworked in the printing business." Pryce was distraught at the loss. In the doleful months that followed, his spirit seeped out. He stopped writing to his two brothers in Connecticut and lost touch with his circle of friends.

When Lewis received a chatty out-of-the-blue letter from David Cronin in 1905, he did respond, writing that "I lost my wife 4 years ago and my son nearly 3 years ago. My daughter lives in New York City. So I am alone and I don't care how soon I shall be magnified into an angel."

The words upset Cronin, who was now living in Philadelphia. This wasn't the dauntless Pryce Lewis he so admired. In a follow-up letter he begged his friend not to get downhearted and offered encouragement: "Making allowance for what you have been through since I last saw you, I trust that you will cling to what has been written from your own lips until I am in a position to put the whole narrative in print at my own expense, and I trust that time is not far off." Cronin's letter revived Lewis, as did his promise to visit him soon in New York. Lewis wrote and told his old friend that he looked forward to seeing him and not to worry too much as "I have never needed the services of a doctor, and hope never to. I know I shall never need the service of a priest or minister. As you say they know no more about the future than we do and that's nothing. I don't believe in survival of consciousness after death of the body."

Cronin neither showed in New York nor found the money to pay for the publication of the memoirs. He did, however, put Lewis in touch with W. Anson Barnes, a lawyer friend of his in New York whom he thought might be able to help. Barnes sent the manuscript to the New York publisher Funk & Wagnalls, but it replied, "After considerable discussion the opinion prevailed that we could not secure results which would be satisfactory alike to the author and to ourselves."

Barnes pushed some odds and ends of employment Lewis's way; it wasn't much, serving subpoenas and running messages, but it paid. Barnes also cast a legal eye over the letters Lewis wrote to the War Pensions Bureau in Washington, advising Lewis to make the staff understand quite clearly his unique situation: he was not an American citizen (though he had lived in the country for more than half a century), nor had he fought as a soldier in the Civil War. Thus while he wasn't legally entitled to receive a pension, he deserved one as a reward for the outstanding service he had given the U.S. government.

But no matter how many letters Lewis sent, the response was always the same: he failed to meet the criteria for a war pension. Barnes urged Lewis to apply for American citizenship, that way he would be entitled to receive help, but the Englishman refused to countenance the idea. It would be a betrayal. "I've served this [American] government well and taken the Secret Service oath of loyalty over and over again," he told Barnes. "But when it comes to swearing that I'll take arms against my own sovereign, I'll see them damned."

There was one piece of good news that cheered Lewis, whose pride remained, if nothing else. In November 1906 Allan Pinkerton's son William, who had taken over the agency following his father's death, published a small pamphlet titled *Timothy Webster*. It ran to just a handful of pages—another paean to the dead spy—but toward the end there was a sentence that was William's way of apologizing for his father's heinous lie: "Scully made a confession, implicating Webster as the head of the Richmond Secret Service for the United States Government. Lewis remained staunch, and did not confess."

Lewis appreciated the public vindication, but it came twenty years too late. By 1911 he was drawing on his well of pride. The letters he wrote his daughter were short and rinsed of self-respect. In one, sent on August 19, he asked for a little loan, nothing much, and promised to pay it back as "my memoirs will soon be published in book or magazine form . . . I hope it will be published in a magazine, as we will get paid on its publication. I am anxious to stop the drain on you." Nothing was published.

His last letter to his daughter was written on November 25.

My Dear Mary

Yours of yesterday is recv'd. Thanks. I made no arrangement with the Salvation Army. I expect to make a new arrangement in a few days of wish [*sic*] I have written to Mr. Barnes today and the letter goes in the same mail with this.

Your affectionate Father
Pryce

There was to be no second reprieve for Pryce Lewis, no ghost of Father McMullen standing in the doorway. Instead when he returned to his lodgings on the evening of Tuesday, December 5, 1911, it was his landlady he encountered. She handed him the letter from the War Pensions Bureau, and he read the words that stared at him, cold and harsh, like the gaze of General Winder.

The next morning Lewis rose early. He put on the same dark blue suit and the same scuffed leather shoes from the night before. For a final touch he fastened a black bow tie to his white cotton shirt. It had stopped snowing, and the sky was a deep clear blue. At midmorning Lewis left the house unseen, covering his bald head with his boater, and made his way to Jersey City station. A couple of hours later Oscar Corbett heard a rushing sound. Not bothering to look up from his desk in the filing room of the World Building, he remarked to a colleague, "There goes a big slide of snow."

"A Faithful Servant to His Country"

O N T H E S A M E A F T E R N O O N that Pryce Lewis leaped to his death, a woman called at the office of Anson Barnes. She introduced herself as Mrs. Lew Gibson from Waterbury, Connecticut, and told Barnes that she had been given his address by Mary Lewis. Gibson then explained that she was the third cousin of Pryce Lewis and was in New York at the request of his younger brother.

When Pryce had stopped writing to Matthew Lewis after the death of his son a decade earlier, Matthew presumed his brother was dead. Only when he received a letter from Mary a few days earlier had Matthew realized Pryce was alive but indigent. He asked Lew Gibson to go to New York and bring his brother back to Waterbury to live with him. Barnes and Gibson arranged to visit Pryce Lewis the next day to break the good news.

But as they set out for Jersey City on Thursday, December 7, the *World* carried a report on its inside pages under the headline SUICIDE LEAPS FROM TOP OF SKYSCRAPER. It described Lewis "as a man of about fifty-five years of age" who was "bald, had a white mustache and was poorly dressed." The paper added that the business card of one of its reporters, Isaac D. White, had been discovered in the deceased's pocket, but that White was unable to put a name to the face that had been smashed on the fender of an automobile.

The *New York Times* and the *New York Herald* also covered the tragedy in their editions of December 7, with the former commenting that the first physician on the scene, a Dr. Russell, "found that the man's skull had been shattered and that practically every bone in his body had been broken."

The description of the man sounded familiar to Charles Newkirk, even though his friend Pryce Lewis was eighty years old, not fifty-five. After breakfast on Thursday morning he called at 83 Jefferson Avenue and, in the company of the landlady, entered Lewis's small and drafty room. There on the table was the note, but they found no body in the garret. Newkirk caught a train to New York City and visited the morgue of the Hudson Street Hospital. For several seconds he stood staring at the battered face "and after some hesitation declared that it was that of Mr. Lewis." Later, when a reporter from the *Herald* pressed Newkirk for more details of the dead man, he was too upset to say much, other than that Lewis was a Civil War veteran "who saw much active service as a scout." Asked why Lewis had killed himself, Newkirk told the *Herald* that his friend "had realized he had outlived his usefulness and that he was too old to continue a fight for existence."

The *World* ran with the story on Sunday, December 10, publishing a photo of an elderly Lewis along with embellished information about his wartime activities. There was no mention of Timothy Webster or John Scully, but the paper made much of the Lord Tracy escapade. The *World* also warned in its final paragraph that if assistance was not forthcoming from friends or family, Lewis, "a faithful servant to his country . . . will be buried by the city in Potter's Field with only a number to indicate where he lies."

The report left Mary Lewis in a state of great distress. She had no intention of allowing her father to be buried in an unmarked grave. She emptied her savings to pay for the funeral expenses, and Anson Barnes contributed something toward the cost. Barnes also approached the Pinkertons in the hope that as they have "established a private burial ground near Chicago for the internment of the bodies of his [Allan Pinkerton's] faithful employees the agency will aid." Nothing came of the request.

On Thursday, December 14, the *New York Daily News* reported that Lewis was to be laid to rest in Torrington, Connecticut, in a service paid for by his family, and that "in accord with his wish, flags of the United States and Great Britain were to be buried with him."

But poor Pryce Lewis was not allowed to rest in peace. On Sunday, December 17, the *New York Times* evoked the ghost of Allan Pinkerton in a shabby, idle article hacked from the pages of the *Spy of the Rebellion*. Don't believe the "glowing accounts of his service to the North," taunted the paper, because "forty nine years ago Timothy Webster, the greatest of Union spies, was hanged in Richmond after Pryce Lewis had betrayed him to save his own neck. The death of that brave man was as much on Pryce Lewis's soul as if Lewis had cut his throat . . . it is an old commonplace that such deeds do not prosper—a commonplace too often proved untrue by the subsequent history of those who perform them. In Pryce Lewis's case the old smug commonplace came true . . . the ghost of Webster, the heroic man who looked death in the eye without a tremor, and who met it at last with a tranquil smile, may have gazed upon that mass of pulp lying on the busy street and thought of retribution."

For a second time Mary Lewis was devastated by the thoughtless words of a New York paper. She wrote the *Times*, correcting its story and condemning its "lies about my father." The paper refused to print an apology, so Lewis turned to Barnes and pleaded with him to restore the reputation of a man who had been traduced in life and now in death. Barnes took on the responsibility and tried for several weeks to persuade a paper to run the truth about Pryce Lewis. No one appeared interested, until the story landed on the desk of William Inglis, a veteran reporter for *Harper's Weekly*. The tale appealed to him, not just its adventure and intrigue but also its injustice, and on January 30, 1912, Inglis's full-page exposé appeared under the headline A REPUBLIC'S GRATITUDE: WHAT PRYCE LEWIS DID FOR THE UNITED STATES GOVERNMENT, AND HOW THE UNITED STATES GOVERNMENT REWARDED HIM.

Inglis revealed what had really happened in Richmond in the spring of 1862. John Scully was the man who had betrayed Timothy Webster, not Pryce Lewis. Lewis was imprisoned for nineteen months in "loathsome surroundings" and returned to Washington "broken in health." But it wasn't Lewis's fortitude in surviving a Richmond prison that impressed above all else; it was his journey through the Kanawha Valley in July 1861. By dint of his courage and boldness he "had achieved more than a hundred soldiers" and merited the gratitude of a nation. Instead he had been neglected by the government.

In the same month in 1912 that *Harper's Weekly* published Inglis's piece, an article appeared on the other side of the Atlantic in the *Montgomeryshire Express*, a modest publication popular with the people of Newtown. Contained within the article was an extract from an American newspaper describing Pryce Lewis's wartime espionage, along with an accompanying letter from John Owen, for many decades a resident of Blackinton, Massachusetts, but a Newtown lad deep down.

Dear Mr. Editor,

As I am always interested in reading your accounts of old Newtown folks in the Express I thought you might be interested to read the clipping which I enclose. Mr. Price [*sic*] Lewis lived with his parents when a boy at the White Lion, Penygloddfa. I don't know who would be likely to remember him as a schoolmate. We were quartered in a room above the Green Tavern, and one Edward Morgan, the teetotaler, was our teacher. That was between 60 and 70 years ago. We Welsh-Americans don't think our Government did the square thing with our friend Price Lewis. If they could not pension him they could have made him a present of a few thousand dollars so that he might have ended his life in comfort.

The Baltimore Plot

The so-called Baltimore Plot to assassinate Abraham Lincoln received a blast of fresh publicity in January 2009 when President-elect Barack Obama retraced the final 135 miles of Lincoln's journey in February 1861 prior to his own inauguration in Washington. Dozens of newspapers carried stories about the putative assassination plot, with a number describing Allan Pinkerton's role in thwarting the conspirators.

Unfortunately, the weight of historical opinion agrees that there was never any plot to murder Lincoln, at least not a serious one that went beyond bravado. Colonel Ward H. Lamon, Lincoln's bodyguard, was the first to break ranks and openly cast doubt on the legitimacy of a "plot," writing in his 1872 memoirs (*The Life of Abraham Lincoln from His Birth to His Inauguration as President*), "It is perfectly manifest that there was no conspiracy—no conspiracy of a hundred, of fifty, of twenty, of three; no definite purpose in the heart of even one man—to murder Mr. Lincoln at Baltimore." Pinkerton, added Lamon, was merely "intensely ambitious to shine in the professional way . . . it struck him that it would be a particularly fine thing to discover a dreadful plot to assassinate the president elect, and he discovered it accordingly."

Pinkerton's supporters, however, accused Lamon of lying and said he was motivated by revenge, having been described by the Scot as "a brainless, egotistical fool." A decade after Lamon's biography, Pinkerton released his own memoirs in which he devoted much space (sixty pages) to detailing how close Lincoln was to death and how, but for him, the wicked assassins might have been successful.

The first serious and impartial analysis of the plot came in 1900 when George L Radcliffe, later an adviser to President Franklin D. Roosevelt and a Maryland senator, received a doctorate of philosophy in history at the Johns Hopkins University for a thesis that examined the Baltimore Plot. Radcliffe had interviewed many people present in Baltimore at the time of the incident, including Cipriano Ferrandini (who died in Baltimore in 1910), and concluded that the plot was a Pinkerton fabrication.

Fifty years later, in March 1950, the *Maryland Historical Magazine* published a long article by Edward Stanley Lanis, in which the author rubbished the idea that Lincoln's life had been in danger as he headed to his inauguration. "During the Civil War when Mayor George Brown, Marshal George B. Kane, several newspaper editors—all from Baltimore— and members of the Maryland legislature were being locked up in federal prisons on charges of disloyalty to the Union, Ferrandini remained a free man," wrote Lanis. "That these men were arrested and the barber left free was all the more remarkable because Allan Pinkerton and his agency, now working for both the State and War Departments, had assisted authorities in rounding up suspected traitors but had left the barber alone." Lanis went on to reveal that in the chaotic days following Lincoln's assassination in April 1865, Pinkerton did not disclose to General Lafayette Baker, the chief of the secret service, "Ferrandini's connections with the alleged earlier assassination plot—information which might have linked John Wilkes Booth with Ferrandini, for Booth was known to have frequented Baltimore."

There can only be one reason why Pinkerton held back the information from Baker: because Ferrandini had never been involved in an earlier attempt to kill Lincoln, except in Pinkerton's rich imagination. The definite proof cited by Landis that there was no plot was the fact that "to the end of his days, Pinkerton never permitted disinterested parties to examine the papers which persuaded [Norman] Judd and others to put pressure on Lincoln to flee from a danger largely imaginary."

Some writers have disagreed with Landis and come down on the side of Pinkerton, but this writer, having studied all the evidence, particularly

Pinkerton's long track record of distorting the truth for his own gain, takes the view that there was never any serious attempt to kill President Abraham Lincoln as he passed through Baltimore on his way to Washington in February 1861.

The Trial

While Pryce Lewis's memoirs are a fascinating and concise account of his work as a Civil War spy, there is one aspect in which they are inadequate: the trial of Timothy Webster, and who exactly said what. In Lewis's defense, one must remember that at the time of the trial he was not only physically exhausted, having spent several weeks in a small, damp prison cell, but also mentally shattered. Just days before he appeared as a defense witness for Webster, Lewis had been scheduled to die. In addition, Lewis only appeared briefly at the trial and therefore was able to describe just the events relating to his testimony. Unfortunately, the notes of Webster's trial, along with those pertaining to Lewis and Scully, were lost at the end of the war. Thus the best surviving contemporary account is the article published by the *Richmond Dispatch* on April 30, which was later reproduced by several Northern newspapers. The *Dispatch* reported that Webster faced two charges or specifications: that on April 1, 1862, "being an enemy alien and in the service of the United States, he lurked about the armies and fortifications of the Confederate States in and near Richmond" and that on July 1, 1861, "[he] did lurk in and about the armies and fortifications of the Confederate States at Memphis, in the State of Tennessee."

The first charge was clearly spurious as on that date Webster was confined to his bed in the home of William Campbell, while the second charge would have been hard to prove nine months down the line (and indeed he was acquitted on this count).

In reality, both charges were manufactured to put Webster in the dock, probably why the documents were later destroyed. The Confederates had enough circumstantial evidence from inquiries made in Baltimore to convince themselves that Webster was a double agent. And they also had the word of John Scully.

Again, the precise nature of Scully's confession was never made clear, not by the Confederate newspapers, nor Pryce Lewis, nor Allan Pinkerton. The *Richmond Dispatch* said he "let the cat out of the bag," while Pinkerton in *The Spy of the Rebellion* wrote that Scully, "yielding to the influences which he could not control, had told his story, and had given a truthful account of all his movements." Yet in his memoirs Lewis described receiving a note from Scully in which the Irishman said, "I have made a full statement and confessed everything." But later, after Lewis's interview with Judge Crump, he "concluded that Scully had not made a full statement."

In fact Scully appeared to have remained loyal to Lewis throughout his interrogation, refusing to reveal the latter's journey through the Kanawha Valley in July 1861, as well as the trip to Chattanooga that Lewis had planned to take once they had wrapped up business in Richmond.

Nor did Scully seem to tell Winder's men much about Webster, if the best the court could come up with were two specifications, one of which was risible. Did Scully also tell the Confederates about Webster's journey to Memphis in July 1861? More likely the rebels had eyewitnesses willing to testify that Webster had been in Tennessee during this time, such as the pompous army doctor named Burton, and the court-martial preferred to concentrate on one additional charge other than the one of spying in and around Richmond. To list all the Southern cities and towns that Webster had visited in the past twelve months would have been a considerable embarrassment to the Confederate authorities, and revealed the extent of the damage caused by Webster's espionage.

In all probability, Scully confessed two things: first, that he was still in the employ of the Federal secret service, and second, that he came to Richmond to deliver a letter from Allan Pinkerton to Timothy Webster. This confession, while not direct proof that Webster was a Northern spy, was enough for the rebels to hang him.

Lewis maintained in his memoirs that he said nothing to incriminate Webster, merely acknowledging to the prosecution that he came South to deliver a letter to Webster. Bizarrely, however, Lewis didn't mention if the prosecution asked who wrote the letter and what, therefore, was his response. It's inconceivable that Lewis was not asked this question, and peculiar that Lewis did not address this issue in his memoirs.

In 1945 Harriet Shoen, a friend of Mary Lewis, Pryce's daughter, sent the memoirs to Colonel Louis A. Sigaud, who, during the First World War, had commanded the Corps of Intelligence Police of the American Expeditionary Force to France, and later wrote several books and articles about Civil War espionage. Sigaud scrutinized the memoirs, describing them as "very interesting" but highlighting inconsistencies with regard to Webster's trial. Specifically, Sigaud found it "exceedingly difficult to believe that Lewis was not questioned at all as to his call upon Webster with Scully, their delivery of the letter to him, their employment by the Federal Government and the fact that the alleged Scott letter was a fake." This gave Sigaud "the impression that much is being left unsaid and perhaps deliberately." Did Lewis admit during Webster's trial that the letter came from Pinkerton? Sigaud thought he might have, though his suspicions were based on inference rather than hard evidence. Ultimately, however, Sigaud concluded that neither Scully nor Lewis was to blame for Webster's fate but that "primarily Pinkerton was responsible for he slipped up by sending men to Webster who ran the risk of identification in Richmond by Southerners who had met them in Washington."

Pinkerton's Military Espionage

When Abraham Lincoln was shot by John Wilkes Booth on April 14, 1865, Pinkerton lamented the fact that had he been in charge of the president's security Lincoln would not have been slain. It was yet another extravagant claim by Pinkerton in a war in which his detective agency had underperformed, at least militarily. Edwin Fishel, a longtime intelligence agent for the U.S. military and government, wrote in his book *The Secret War for the Union: Military Intelligence in the Civil War* that Pinkerton deserved some credit. Prior to the Civil War espionage was "not conducted by a recognizable organizational entity." Pinkerton's agency, working as part of McClellan's army, was an innovation in that sense, but it could have been so much more effective if better coordinated. As Fishel wrote, Pinkerton should "have received reports from the cavalry and the other sources [such as the Balloon Corps] not under his control and synthesized the information from all the sources into a comprehensive picture." Instead, Pinkerton placed too much importance on firsthand testimony, rambling accounts given him by fugitive slaves and rebel deserters. This information was often included in the reports Pinkerton passed on to McClellan, even though it hadn't been verified by other sources.

Pinkerton was also guilty of failing to exploit the loyalty of some of the thousands of Virginians who lived under Confederate rule but whose allegiance lay with the Union. Why, for instance, didn't Pinkerton make an approach to Elizabeth Van Lew? By the end of 1861 her sympathies were well known in Richmond, and, working with Pinkerton, she could have established a network of informants throughout Richmond and Virginia. Instead, Pinkerton tried to insinuate his operatives into rebel strongholds, the most glaring case being E. H. Stein, who spent months in the rebel capital working as a barman yet who was unable to carry out any productive espionage because he was under constant surveillance. Similarly Timothy Webster, instead of placing himself at the heart of the rebel underground, should have used his charisma and cunning to win the confidence of Northern sympathizers in Virginia, men and women whose roots were known and trusted by their Southern friends, and groom them as spies. But Webster took all the risks himself, relying on his charm to see him through. It worked for a while, but then people began to delve into his background. How long had he lived in Baltimore, this man who always evaded capture? Where did he get his money? Who were his friends in the prewar days? Pinkerton didn't appear to understand that deep roots are always the hardest to pull up, as Elizabeth Van Lew was to prove later in the war when she provided much valuable information to the Bureau of Military Intelligence.

Another of Pinkerton's grave failings concerned Pryce Lewis. Lore has it that Webster was Pinkerton's ablest spy, but that accolade should be shared with Lewis if not handed to him outright. It was he who spent three weeks traveling through western Virginia in July 1861, noting the strength and morale of Wise's men in one of the most audacious missions of the entire war. He dined with Colonel Patton, inspected military fortifications, visited rebel camps, took a hotel room opposite General Wise and drank native wine with a Confederate major. When Lewis handed this information to General Jacob Cox, it persuaded him to advance against General Wise. The result was the capture of Charleston and the Kanawha River, not only an important strategic gain but a crucial morale boost for the Union coming in the wake of the Bull Run disaster. As the *New York Times* wrote on September 18, 1861, "nowhere else on all the theater of war have the Union armies so well sustained their cause as in Western Virginia . . . Gen. Cox enjoys the unquestioned honor of winning the important valley of Kanawha for the Union . . . what is Bull Run for the rebels by the side of it?'

And yet despite Lewis's obvious talent for military espionage (he had also brought back significant information from Tennessee during his attempt to discover the bank murderer), he was removed from the field by Pinkerton after his mission to Charleston and sent to Washington to guard the likes of Rose Greenhow and Eugenia Phillips, a task Lewis undertook with "much distaste." It wasn't that Lewis was singled out by Pinkerton for this thankless job; the agency's payroll records show that between October 1861 and March 1862 only fourteen trips were made by his agents into Confederate lines, and half of those were undertaken by Webster and Hattie Lawton. It was a woeful misuse of resources, but it occurred because Pinkerton had become distracted by counterintelligence. Some of this work was important, and Pinkerton did arrest many genuine rebel informants, but a lot of it was pointless, such as the search of the Mortons' home.

The answer to why Pinkerton turned away from positive intelligence to counterintelligence in the second half of 1861 lay in his canine devotion to General McClellan. When the general arrived in Washington at the end of July to take command of the Army of the Potomac, he summoned Pinkerton from Cincinnati and asked him to establish a secret service for his army with the emphasis being on rooting out enemies within the Union. In his eagerness to follow McClellan's orders, Pinkerton lost sight of the bigger picture; he diverted the majority of his operatives to uncovering spies and sympathizers in Washington and Baltimore instead of dividing his resources between the two components of military espionage. News of arrests such as Rose Greenhow's pleased McClellan, as they did the editors of Northern newspapers, but the general should have ordered Pinkerton to send one or more of his operatives to Manassas to determine the strength of General Johnston's forces prior to the offensive that Lincoln was calling for.

That's what an aggressive commander would have done, but McClellan had by this stage of the war already established his reputation as an apprehensive leader. It behooved Pinkerton to propose the idea, but the Scot didn't. He and his men were too busy scrutinizing the movements of perfumed ladies, or worse. Pinkerton noted in his record book for the period some of the tasks that were given him by McClellan: the president of the Ohio Valley Bank demanded that Pinkerton put in a word on the bank's behalf to Salmon Chase, the treasury secretary; an army board asked him to investigate a Chicago meatpacker, whose supply of beef to the army was mainly "skeletons and steers with thirteen wrinkles on their horns"; and on one day Pinkerton was asked to find out the time of a train leaving the capital.

The bald truth is that when he moved to Washington Pinkerton became as much a bureaucrat as a spymaster. He continued to receive the Richmond mail from Webster, but even that revealed little of importance; certainly not enough to warrant the risks Webster took each time he went South. In short, Webster's espionage talents were never maximized by Pinkerton. He went on too many missions where the danger was greater than the information he brought back until eventually the Confederates suspected him. Pinkerton should have tasked Webster with collecting information on General Johnston's forces at Manassas long before that last fateful trip to Richmond. Similarly, why in the fall of 1861 didn't Pryce Lewis adopt once more the guise of the English cotton mill owner and head to Alabama or South Carolina? No one would have recognized him from his trip to western Virginia. The reason is that Pinkerton didn't possess the brain of a military espionage chief, and in the fall of 1861 he was too preoccupied with pleasing General McClellan.

Nevertheless, despite his six frustrating months in Washington, Pryce Lewis was one of the most successful spies of the Civil War, and he was certainly the most unsung. Greenhow immortalized herself in her book, as Belle Boyd did in her memoirs, and Lafayette Baker in his. In his own account of the war Pinkerton tooted Webster's horn nearly as loudly as his own. But no one lauded the achievements of Pryce Lewis.

NOTES

Prologue: *"There Goes a Big Slide of Snow"*

3 Although several newspapers covered Lewis's death, the three most comprehensive accounts—and the ones on which I base his final hours—were published by the *New York Times* of December 7, 1911, the *New York World*, December 10, 1911, and *Harper's Weekly*, January 30, 1912.

Chapter One: *"Little Molehills from the Green Sea"*

8 "As the ship is towed out": *Illustrated London News*, July 6, 1850.

8 "The laboring of the ship": Charles Dickens, *American Notes for General Circulation* (London: Chapman and Hall, 1842), 23.

Chapter Two: *"A Detective! Me?"*

13 "A detective! Me?": Pryce Lewis memoirs, xi, Pryce Lewis Collection, St. Lawrence University Library. Hereinafter referred to as PLM.

13 "earnestness, enthusiasm, heartiness": The report of the "Phrenological Description" of Allan Pinkerton, made by Professor O. S. Fowler on Thursday, December 14, 1865, is contained in the Pinkerton Papers, Library of Congress, Washington, D.C.

16 "got to sort of hanging around her": James Mackay, *Allan Pinkerton: The Eye Who Never Slept* (Mainstream, 1996), 49.

16 "had become an outlaw": James D. Horan, *The Pinkertons: The Detective Dynasty That Made History* (Crown, 1967), 10.

Chapter Three: *"Murdered in the Most Shocking Manner"*

17 "praised Lewis's appearance": PLM, xi.

17 "with a good salary": Ibid.

19 The crime had riveted the Southern states: Maroney was found guilty in June 1860 and sentenced to ten years' hard labor. The role of the Pinkerton agency in securing

a conviction led to the expansion of its operations on the East Coast (the headquarters of the Adams Express was in New York) as more and more companies called upon its services.

19 "high and honorable calling": James D. Horan, *The Pinkertons: The Detective Dynasty That Made History* (Crown, 1967), 30.

19 "It cannot be too strongly impressed": Kevin Kenny, *Making Sense of the Molly Maguires* (Oxford University Press, 1998), 154.

20 Many of the men: The only member of the agency who had been attacked was Pinkerton himself in 1853. A report appeared in the *Chicago Daily Press* describing how a gunman had fired "two slugs [which] shattered the bone five inches from the wrist and passed along the bone to the elbow where they were cut out by a surgeon." In the years that followed, Pinkerton never alluded to the outrage, nor did he appear to have suffered any lasting damage from the wound, which is curious considering its severity and the primitive nature of frontier medicine at the time. In 1868 another attempt was made on his life, but the "gunman" revealed later that it was all a publicity stunt concocted by Pinkerton, who was "rather fond of sensations." The 1853 attempt on Pinkerton's life certainly brought his new business some publicity, but did it actually take place, or had Pinkerton planted the story with the newspaper in return for subsequent scoops?

20 "an out-and-out Abolitionist": PLM, 2.

20 "in the vigor of early manhood": Ibid., xi.

20 "Procure it, and read it": Ibid., 1.

21 "had come to regard him as a man of original": Ibid.

21 "fascinated by the descriptive analysis": Ibid.

22 "murdered in the most shocking manner": *New York Times*, February 14, 1859.

22 "Two or three leaves": Ibid., 1.

22 "and stopped at the principal hotel": PLM, 2.

22 "He reviews the life of the man": Letter from G. H. Bangs to Pryce Lewis, Pryce Lewis Collection, St. Lawrence University Library.

23 "fire-eating Southerners boasted": PLM, 2.

23 "he readily fell in with the ways": Ibid.

Chapter Four: "A Plan Had Been Laid for My Assassination"

25 Which left only Abraham Lincoln: The nickname rail-splitter was born during a political rally in 1860 when one of Lincoln's managers showed a crowd a pair of fence rails that his master had reputedly split as a young man, proof that here was a politician who personified the Republican belief that America was a land of opportunity for anyone who worked hard.

25 "From early morning voting": Quoted in Catherine Cooper Hopley, *Life in the South from the Commencement of the War* (Chapman and Hall, 1863).

26 "there is nothing in all the dark caves": *Times* (London), May 28, 1861.

27 "A lady's thimble will hold all": James M. McPherson, *Battle Cry of Freedom* (Penguin, 1990), 238.

27 "detested slavery . . . this institution of human bondage": Allan Pinkerton, *The Spy of the Rebellion* (M. A. Winter and Hatch, 1883), 25.

28 "mute and motionless": *Harper's Weekly*, December 10, 1889.

28 "had it not been for the excessive watchfulness": Pinkerton, *The Spy of the Rebellion*, 26.

29 "worm out secrets in many places": Pinkerton, *The Spy of the Rebellion*.

29 "Her complexion was fresh and rosy": Ibid., 367.

31 "the simple inventions of those who are agents": Edward Stanley Lanis, "Allan Pinkerton and the Baltimore 'Assassination' Plot against Lincoln," *Maryland Historical Magazine* (March 1950).

31 "[Pinkerton] informed me that a plan had been laid for my assassination": Benson J. Lossing, *Pictorial History of the Civil War in the United States of America* (G. W Childs, 1866).

32 "the solicitations of a professional spy": Ward H. Lamon, *The Life of Abraham Lincoln from His Birth to His Inauguration as President* (J. R Osgood, 1872).

32 "not believe the Presidency can ever": *Baltimore Sun*, February 26, 1861.

32 "a gentleman of Vidocquean repute": Eugène François Vidocq was a French criminal turned private detective in the early nineteenth century, the inspiration for Jean Valjean in Victor Hugo's *Les Misérables*.

Chapter Five: "Set a Price on Every Rebel Head and Hang Them"

33 "After the closest observation": PLM, 3.

34 "in a fever of preparation for war": Ibid., 2.

34 He received little help from his cabinet: Seward's deviousness in regard to Fort Sumter is best described by James M. McPherson in *Battle Cry of Freedom* (Penguin, 1990), 268–69.

35 "must be trampled under foot": *New York Times*, April 13, 1861.

35 "convulsion seized the public mind": Quoted in Catherine Cooper Hopley, *Life in the South from the Commencement of the War* (Chapman and Hall, 1863).

36 "that the country will have to pass through": McPherson, *Battle Cry of Freedom*, 281.

36 "be of any service in the way of obtaining information": Allan Pinkerton, *The Spy of the Rebellion* (M. A. Winter and Hatch, 1883), 138.

36 "filled with soldiers, armed and eager for the fray": Ibid., 137.

37 "had for some time entertained the idea": Ibid., 139.

37 "as fully and concisely": Ibid.

Chapter Six: "An English Nobleman Travelling for Pleasure"

39 "great excitement among the people": PLM, 3.

40 "consists in suspending the offender by a rope": *Richmond Dispatch*, May 20, 1861.

40 "the character of an English nobleman": Allan Pinkerton, *The Spy of the Rebellion* (M. A. Winter and Hatch, 1883), 210.

40 "would thus escape a close scrutiny": Ibid.

41 "and a pair of strong gray horses": Ibid.

42 "a handsome segar case": PLM, 8.

43   "carefully destroyed the papers": Ibid., 18.

44   ulcers, sores, swelling stiffness: In *Life at the Springs of Western Virginia*, by Mary Hagner, written in 1839, she reported that the springs were popular with people suffering "hemorrhoidal [*sic*] affections, jaundice . . . long standing dysentery and chronic syphilitic diseases."

45   "a gentlemanly fellow": The encounter with the rebel patrol, and Lewis's interview with George Patton, are described in PLM, 8–13.

48   Then he went on to regale Patton: The storm in November 1854 sent thirty—and not fourteen—British transport ships to the bottom of Balaclava Harbor.

Chapter Seven: "Don't You Know There Is a War in This Country, Sir?"

50   "Charleston is quite a pretty place": *Gallipolis Dispatch*, August 8, 1861.

51   "Men of Virginia! Men of Kanawha!": Granville Davisson Hall, *Lee's Invasion of Northwest Virginia in 1861* (Mayer and Miller, 1911).

52   "blown down over your head": The confrontation between Mrs. Littlepage and General Wise was gleaned from a 1984 application to have the farmhouse included in the National Register of Historic Places. A copy of the application form can be viewed at the West Virginia Division of Culture and History Web site, www.wvculture.org/.

52   "whip the world": Roy Bird Cook, "The Civil War Comes to Charleston," *West Virginia History Journal* 23, no. 2 (January 1962).

52   "sky was clear, the air inspiriting": PLM, 14.

53   "rough-looking men, mountaineers in woolen shirts": Cook, "The Civil War Comes to Charleston."

54   "thin and below the average size": PLM, 16.

55   "I would like to speak to your Excellency": Lewis described his heated exchange with General Wise in ibid., 16–17.

56   "Let's leave everything behind us": Ibid., 17.

56   "was traveling as an inoffensive tourist": Ibid.

56   "if the consul should be suspicious": Ibid., 19.

57   "incipient insanity"; "a more bracing climate": Letter from Consul George Moore to the British Foreign Office, June 11, 1861, document no. FO5/786, National Archives, Kew, UK.

57   "Mr. Cridland begged me to be seated": Catherine Cooper Hopley, *Life in the South from the Commencement of the War* (Chapman and Hall, 1863).

57   "I have waited so long for an opportunity": Ibid.

58   "Look at the paper I am obliged to use!": Ibid.

Chapter Eight: "Grossly Insulting to Some of the Officers"

59   "the grass of the soil we are defending is full": Dispatch from Wise to General Cooper, July 17, 1861, reproduced in *The War of the Rebellion: A Compilation of the Official Records of the Union and Confederate Armies* (Government Printing Office, 1880–1901).

59   "copperhead traitors": James M. McPherson in his excellent *Battle Cry of Freedom* (Penguin, 1990) writes: "Ohio Republicans seem to have used it [the term *copperhead*] as early as the fall of 1861 to liken antiwar Democrats to the venomous snake of that time. By the fall of 1862 the term had gained wide usage and was often applied by Republicans to the whole Democratic party." (494) However, in a dispatch sent by Wise from Charleston on July 17, 1861, to General Samuel Cooper, he refers to Kanawha being "full of copperhead traitors," indicating that the insult was already in use, at least by Wise.

59   "a spy is on every hill top": Dispatch from Wise to General Cooper, July 17, 1861.

60   the right protector to have: The meeting between Lewis and the two rebel officers is described in PLM, 20–21.

61   "more impressed by the exalted position": Ibid., 22.

61   "always careful to avoid details": Ibid., 23.

61   "compared notes and planned modes of escape": Ibid.

62   "cutting chutes through the river's shoals": Ken Sullivan, ed., *The West Virginia Encyclopedia* (West Virginia Humanities Council, 2006), 393.

62   "the rebels have sunk two boats laden with stone": James D. Horan, *The Pinkertons: The Detective Dynasty That Made History* (Crown, 1967), 66.

63   "grossly insulting to some of the officers": PLM, 24.

63   "passed a miserable day reviewing every plan": Ibid., 25.

64   "heard some one ascending the stairs": Ibid.

64   "The Yankees will give him hell!": Ibid.

65   Since the initial order from McClellan: In William Cochran's biography of Jacob Cox, written in 1901, the author said that McClellan's dispersal of Cox's meager force showed that either he "had unbounded confidence in General Cox, or he designed that he should be defeated in order to add luster to his own achievements." (23)

66   "drive Wise out and catch him": Charles Preston Poland, *The Glories of War: Small Battle and Early Heroes of 1861* (Authorhouse, 2004), 337.

Chapter Nine: "I See You Are a Stranger in These Parts"

67   "a fine-looking, middle-aged man": PLM, 26.

68   a total of $35.75: Lewis retained the bill for his stay at the Kanawha House Hotel, and it is among his papers of the Pryce Lewis Collection at St. Lawrence University Library.

68   "a rough road through a hilly country": PLM, 28.

68   the village of Logan Courthouse: Logan Courthouse was named after James Logan, secretary of the province of Pennsylvania in the eighteenth century, although in 1852 Mayor Thomas Dunn English decreed that the village would be renamed in honor of Aracoma, daughter of a famous Indian chieftain. The name failed to catch on, however, and to most it remained Logan Courthouse. In 1907 it underwent its final name change, becoming Logan.

69   "most of whom were rough-looking soldiers": Lewis's overnight stop in Logan Courthouse is described in PLM, 29–35.

70 "had prohibited the slave-trade, and did not mean to revive it": Ephraim Douglass Adams, *Great Britain and the American Civil War* (Russell and Russell, 1924), 55.

71 "Finality John": Ibid.

71 "I will not stop to depict": www.civilwarinteractive.com.

72 "cotton would bring England to her knees": *Charleston Mercury*, June 4, 1861.

74 "England is bound to have the cotton in the south": PLM, 31.

74 Queen Victoria had issued a proclamation against any of her subjects: Ibid., 33.

75 "went over England's history": Ibid., 34.

76 "we had been gone only nineteen days": Ibid., 36.

Chapter Ten: "Do You Mean to Say That You Have Been in Wise's Camp?"

77 "six feet in height, very erect": William C. Cochran, *General Jacob Dolson Cox: Early Life and Service* (Bibwotheca Sacra, 1900), 18.

78 "he might see over the banks of the stream": Charles Preston Poland, *The Glories of War: Small Battle and Early Heroes of 1861* (Authorhouse, 2004), 338.

78 "the landscape seemed more beautiful": Ibid.

79 "At this juncture Col. Norton ordered": *Perrysburg Journal*, August 8, 1861.

80 "front rank were ordered to fire": Ibid.

80 "took off his cap and turning partly around": Ibid.

81 "as was common with new troops": Poland, *The Glories of War*, 350.

81 "From the time the enemy opened fire": *Perrysburg Journal*, August 8, 1861.

81 "Cox checked on the Kanawha": Poland, *The Glories of War*, 351.

82 "in a bullying manner": The encounter between Pryce Lewis and the captain of the ferry is described in PLM, 37.

82 "Do you mean to say that you have been in Wise's camp": Lewis's meeting with General Cox is described in ibid., 37–38.

83 "the remains of Captain Allen": Ibid., 39.

84 "the commander of the rebel forces": Ibid., 40.

84 "whose gentlemanly confidence": Ibid., 41.

85 "found him on the upper deck": Ibid.

85 "ten miles from Charleston I heard that Wise": Ibid., 42.

85 "at a large round table": Ibid.

85 "re-enforce us with men, arms and ammunition": General Wise's dispatches are reproduced in *The War of the Rebellion: A Compilation of the Official Records of the Union and Confederate Armies* (Government Printing Office, 1880–1901).

86 "He is now there, about three thousand": Ibid.

86 "a panic-stricken force running off": Poland, *The Glories of War*, 351.

87 "murdering Yankees": Ibid., 340.

88 "Retreat! Never dare call it a 'retreat' again": Ibid., 356.

Chapter Eleven: "That Is Tim Webster"

89 "discharged for celebrating our safe return": PLM, 44.

90 "Bridgeman directed my attention": Ibid.

90 "a tall, broad-shouldered, good-looking man": Allan Pinkerton, *The Spy of the Rebellion* (M. A. Winter and Hatch, 1883), 110.

91 "The residents of Newhaven are chiefly engaged": Reverend T. W. Horsfield, *The History and Antiquities of Lewes and Its Vicinity* (Baxter, 1824).

92 "men were found dead behind hedges": This quote is attributed to the radical nineteenth-century MP and writer William Corbett, and reproduced in Trevor Wild, *Village England: A Social History of the Countryside* (Tauris, 2004).

92 "about the number of Sussex laborers": Letter from William Coleman to Home Secretary Robert Peel, February 2, 1830, which is held by the Kew National Archives, London.

93 "the thickly-studded drinking shops": Horace Greeley, *Art and Industry of the Crystal Palace* (Redfield, N.Y., 1853).

94 His family remained in New York: This period of Tim Webster's life is best dealt with in Patricia Dissmeyer Goff, *Timothy Webster: The Story of the Civil War Spy and His Family* (Elgin, England: Goff, 2000).

94 "he was of a quiet, reserved disposition": Pinkerton, *The Spy of the Rebellion*, 158–59.

94 "a genial, jovial, convivial spirit": Ibid.

95 "got in conversation with men from Louisville": Report of Timothy Webster to Memphis and Knoxville, written on August 7, 1861, and preserved in the Pinkerton Collection at the Library of Congress.

95 "that there was 3,000 men at Randolph": Ibid.

97 "there was 5 to 6,000 stand of arms in Baltimore": Report of Timothy Webster's trip to Baltimore, Pinkerton Collection at the Library of Congress.

97 "we have leaders enough": Ibid.

Chapter Twelve: "The Most Persuasive Woman That Was Ever Known in Washington"

98 "We are utterly and disgracefully routed": James M. McPherson, *Battle Cry of Freedom* (Penguin, 1990), 347.

99 "be prepared to hear from me": quoted in James D. Horan, *The Pinkertons: The Detective Dynasty That Made History* (Crown, 1967), 78.

99 "procuring from all possible sources": Quoted in ibid., 79.

99 "that the rebels have spies": Allan Pinkerton, *The Spy of the Rebellion* (M. A. Winter and Hatch, 1883), 252.

100 "her love of notoriety and dread of sinking": W. E. Doster, *Lincoln and Episodes of the Civil War* (Putnam, 1915), 81.

100 "she hunted man with that resistless zeal and unfailing instinct": Stephen Mallory's opinion of Greenhow was revealed to Mrs. Clement Clay, the wife of a Confederate politician in Canada. The letter was reproduced in William Tidwell, *April '65: Confederate Covert Action in the American Civil War* (Kent State University Press, 1995), 58.

100 "black eyes, an olive complexion, firm teeth, and small hands and feet": Quoted in Doster, *Lincoln and Episodes of the Civil War*, 79.

101 "after expiating on the injustice of the North": Quoted in General Erasmus Keyes, *Fifty Years' Observation of Men and Events, Civil and Military* (Charles Scribner's Sons, 1885).

101 "was a traitor and met a traitor's doom": Quoted in Ann Blackman, *Wild Rose: The True Story of a Civil War Spy* (Random House, 2005), 14.

101 "McDowell has certainly been ordered to advance on the sixteenth": Quoted in ibid., 6.

102 "Our President and our General direct me to thank you": Quoted in ibid., 45.

102 "movements had excited suspicion": Pinkerton, *The Spy of the Rebellion*, 252.

103 "natural shrewdness, experience and patriotic zeal": PLM, 46.

103 "induced me to remain in a service": Ibid., 47.

103 "this was a subject of amusement to me": Rose Greenhow, *My Imprisonment and the First Year of Abolition Rule at Washington* (Bentley, 1863).

103 "two-storey and basement brick building": Pinkerton, *The Spy of the Rebellion*, 253.

103 "remained a little distance across the street": PLM, 47.

104 "stand under a tree": Ibid.

104 "something that sounded very much like a kiss": Pinkerton, *The Spy of the Rebellion*, 259.

105 "distinguished member of the diplomatic corps": Greenhow, *My Imprisonment*.

105 "a beautiful woman": PLM, 49.

105 "for I knew that the fate": Greenhow, *My Imprisonment*.

105 "conversed on impersonal subjects": PLM, 49.

105 "If I had known who you were when you came in": Ibid.

106 "compared herself to Marie Antoinette": Ibid.

106 "two of the most insolent of these men": Greenhow, *My Imprisonment*.

107 "live to plague mankind a little more": Journal of Mrs. Eugenia Levy Phillips, 1861–62, Phillips papers, Library of Congress.

107 "had been severely scolded for lighting": PLM, 50.

107 "presented a pass signed by Secretary of War": Lewis's war of words with Edwin Stanton is described in PLM, 50–51.

107 "bring down the wrath of the abolitionists": Greenhow, *My Imprisonment*.

108 "lodged a complaint against me": PLM, 51.

Chapter Thirteen: "You'll Have to Be Mighty Careful Now, or You'll Be Arrested"

109 "Hotel Greenhow": *New York Times*, November 5, 1861.

109 "virtuous, refined, pure-minded women": Rose Greenhow wrote in *My Imprisonment and the First Year of Abolition Rule at Washington* (Bentley, 1863) that on September 10, 1861, she had read the editorial in the *Baltimore Exchange*.

110 "untiring energies"; "nothing has been too sacred for her appropriation": Dispatch written by Pinkerton (using the alias E. J. Allen) to Brigadier General Porter in November 1861, reproduced in *The War of the Rebellion: A Compilation of the Official Records of the Union and Confederate Armies*, series 2, vol. 2 (Government Printing Office, 1880–1901).

111 "You'll have to be mighty careful now": Quoted in Allan Pinkerton, *The Spy of the Rebellion* (M. A. Winter and Hatch, 1883), 327.

112 "The Northern press bears testimony": J. B. Jones, *A Rebel War Clerk's Diary* (Old Hickory Bookshop, 1866), 91.

112 "I have declared my purpose to sign no more": Ibid.

112 "it is my belief that they render": Ibid.

113 "miniature world . . . the hum of conversation": Mrs. Fannie Beers, the wife of a Confederate officer, quoted in *Ladies of Richmond*, edited by Katharine Jones (Bobbs-Merrill, 1962), 67.

113 "brothers, husbands, sons, and sweethearts": Alfred H. Bill, *The Beleaguered City* (Knopf, 1946).

113 "perhaps the youngest landlord of a large hotel in the world": *Richmond Whig*, January 3, 1862.

114 "noticed, lying upon the floor"; "the contents of the bundle": Pinkerton, *The Spy of the Rebellion*, 475.

114 "James Howard, a native of the south"; "confessed his treason": Ibid.

114 Tim Webster's report of his trip to Nashville is in the Pinkerton Papers, Library of Congress, Washington, D.C.

115 "a gentleman of about thirty-six": *Richmond Whig*, April 3, 1862.

Chapter Fourteen: "It Would Be Folly for Me to Go to Richmond"

116 "discovered in his conduct"; "to justify harsh measures": PLM, 49.

117 Pryce Lewis gives an account of the investigation of Elizabeth Morton and her children in ibid., 51.

118 "take a musket, join the army": Ibid., 54.

118 "It would be folly for me": Lewis gives an account of his meeting with Pinkerton in ibid., 54–57.

120 "purchased a new suit of clothing apiece": Ibid., 58.

121 "to negotiate with a man": Ibid.

122 "about an hour before sunset": Ibid., 60.

122 "suddenly a pack of hounds came baying toward us"; "noticed McChesney's faded gray uniform": Ibid., 61.

123 "wanted to go to Richmond by the most direct route": Ibid., 62.

123 "in dingy, ill-fitting uniforms": Ibid., 63.

123 "Where did you capture the Yankees?": Ibid., 64.

124 "anxiety to reach Richmond had been very great": Ibid., 66.

Chapter Fifteen: "He Is a Noble Fellow, a Most Valuable Man to Us"

125 Cobb Neck: Situated on the peninsula between the Wicomico and Potomac rivers, Cobb Neck got its name when a seventeenth-century trader called James Neale bought the land with Spanish coins known at the time as "cub dollars." He christened his two thousand acres "Cub Neck," and time distorted this to "Cobb Neck."

126 "a cold rain fell in sheets": Alfred H. Bill, *The Beleaguered City* (Knopf, 1946).

126 "black with spectators": Ibid.

127 "Richmond burst beautifully into view": Emory Thomas, *The Confederate State of Richmond* (University of Texas Press, 1971).

127 "twelve parallel streets, nearly three miles in length": *New York Herald*, July 28, 1862.

128 "the long, gaily-painted buses": Bill, *The Beleaguered City*.

128 "the atmosphere of Richmond is redolent of tobacco": Catherine Cooper Hopley, *Life in the South from the Commencement of the War* (Chapman and Hall, 1863).

129 "gay ladies and grande dames": *Richmond, Virginia, 1861–1865*, published by Richmond Civil War Centenntial Committee 1961.

129 "the merriest little place": Quoted in James Wilson, *Thackeray in the United States, 1852–3, 1855–6* (Dodd Mead, 1904).

130 "During all the night of the arrival": *Richmond Dispatch*, November 12, 1860.

130 "rounds of beef, saddles of mutton, venison": *Charleston Mercury*, January 5, 1865.

131 "by the accuracy of its reporting": Thomas, *The Confederate State of Richmond*, 19.

131 "the qualities of the scimitar of Saladin": Bill, *The Beleaguered City*.

131 "ferocious old Orang-Outang": Ibid.

131 "would find Captain Webster at the Monumental": PLM, 67.

131 "the rough brick walls had been covered": Bill, *The Beleaguered City*.

132 the Monumental Hotel: A hotel had been located at this spot since 1797, when Colonel Parke Goodall opened the Indian Queen Tavern. It was later renamed the Washington tavern, then the Monumental Hotel. Some people called it the Monumental, others the Hotel Monument, and during the war its name changed again, this time to the Central Hotel. Pryce Lewis referred to it as the Monumental.

132 Lewis's initial encounter with the sick Webster is described in PLM, 67–68.

133 "unheralded appearance of his companions": Allan Pinkerton, *The Spy of the Rebellion* (M. A. Winter and Hatch, 1883), 502.

133 "small, handsome man": *Richmond Enquirer*, February 28, 1862.

133 "soldiers, free and easy in their ways": Ibid.

135 Lewis's introduction to McCubbin is described in PLM, 69–70, and in Pinkerton, *The Spy of the Rebellion*, 503–4.

135 "short and compact in frame": William Harris, *Prison Life in Tobacco Warehouse in Richmond* (G. W. Childs, 1862).

136 "a feared and fearful thing": Ibid.

136 "tied up by the thumbs": *Richmond Dispatch*, March 3, 1895.

136 "made by sawing a common flour barrel": Evidence given by T. G. Bland at enquiry into treatment of prisoners at Castle Thunder, April 1863.

136 "petty larceny detectives": J. B. Jones, *A Rebel War Clerk's Diary* (Old Hickory Bookshop, 1866), 39.

137 "seem to be on peculiar terms of intimacy": Ibid.

137 "to resign his commission": Edwin Fishel, *The Secret War for the Union* (Houghton Mifflin, 1998), 98.

137 "very glad to meet any friends": PLM, 71.

138 "perfectly secure from any mishap:" Ibid., 72.

138   "occupied by parties of a dubious and uncertain character": *Richmond Dispatch*, June 20, 1861.

138   "smirks and smiles, winks, and, when occasion served": Ibid., May 13, 1862.

139   "to leave the following day": PLM, 73.

139   Lewis's encounter with Clackner and Morton is described in ibid., 73–74.

Chapter Sixteen: "I Suspected You All Along"

141   "if I ought to know the Lord Mayor": The account of Lewis's interrogation is in PLM, 75–77.

144   "that probably one of them had been placed": Ibid., 83.

146   "John Scully and Pryce Lewis were arrested": *Richmond Enquirer*, March 4, 1862.

146   "snug institution, hitherto known as": Ibid.

147   "the main entrance to the jail": PLM, 85.

148   "could wrench it off": Ibid., 86.

148   "cover himself in the ash heap": Ibid.

148   "a lump of soap mixed with ashes": Ibid., 87.

148   "asserted that if we took them with us": Ibid., 88.

149   "Stanton wrapped himself in a blanket": Ibid., 89.

149   "rigged up a broomstick in blankets": Ibid., 90.

149   "the jailor's eye caught sight of the heap of straw": Ibid.

150   "positively refused to follow his body"; "cursing, intermingled with expressions of disgust": Ibid., 91.

150   "passed the last house in the suburbs": Ibid., 93.

Chapter Seventeen: "Trust for a Favorable Outcome"

153   "secret enemies were endeavoring to prejudice the mind": Allan Pinkerton, *The Spy of the Rebellion* (M. A. Winter and Hatch, 1883), 537.

153   "tortured by the uncertainty of their fate": Ibid., 544.

154   "trust for a favorable outcome": Ibid., 534.

Chapter Eighteen: "We Have All Your Companions"

155   The escape from Henrico County Jail and the subsequent recapture of Lewis and his companions are recounted in PLM, 93–101.

156   "the tall pines": Three months later, on June 13, 1862, the correspondent of the *New York Times* had this to say about the Chickahominy River: "No better defensive line could exist than the Chickahominy swamp. The river flows through a dense forest of pines and underbrush. The river itself is not over sixty or seventy feet wide, but on each side of it, extending beyond the forest, is a deep marshy swamp, heretofore considered as practically impassable."

159   The shoulder wound: George Patton resumed command of his regiment and by May 1864 was leading a brigade under General John Breckinridge. He died of wounds received at the Battle of Winchester in September 1864. He was buried alongside his brother, who had fallen the previous year at Gettysburg.

Chapter Nineteen: "Hanged by the Necks Until We Were Dead"

160 "learned that jailor Staples and keeper Thomas": PLM, 102.

162 Lewis describes his court-martial in ibid., 109–10.

163 "haggard and woe-begone": Ibid., 111.

164 "was always in the company of known Secessionists": Allan Pinkerton, *The Spy of the Rebellion* (M. A. Winter and Hatch, 1883), 535.

164 "suspicion that would naturally attach to Webster": PLM, 116.

Chapter Twenty: "Keep Your Courage Up"

165 "sought and obtained an interview with the officer": Letter from Cridland to Lord Lyons, August 19, 1862, a copy of which is in the Kew Public Records Office, file: F.O 115/328.

165 "in the cases of persons who had evidently violated": Ibid.

166 "their movements very extraordinary and suspicious": Ibid.

166 "Keep your courage up": Ibid.

167 "John Scully and Pryce Lewis acknowledged to me": Letter from Cridland to Lord Lyons, August 19, 1862.

167 "the prisoners had been tried and condemned to death": Ibid.

167 "the brains of the Confederacy": This description is contained in the introduction to J. B. Jones's *A Rebel War Clerk's Diary* (Old Hickory Bookshop, 1866).

167 "intellect, education, and extensive reading": Ibid.

168 "cowardly rout, a miserable, causeless panic": The *Times* description was reproduced in the August 31 edition of *Harper's Weekly*.

168 "the exponent of that British public opinion": *Harper's Weekly*, October 26, 1861.

168 "a profound indignation is felt by the larger part": *New York Times*, August 29, 1861.

168 "The [London] *Times* reflects the sentiment": Mary Chesnut, *A Diary from Dixie* (Houghton Mifflin, 1961), 75.

169 "a hideous black harem"; "holds his head high": Ibid., 114.

169 "increased to an unlimited extent"; "the Nicaraguan Embassador": *Harper's Weekly*, September 14, 1861.

170 The eyewitness account provided by the *Trent*'s purser of the incident with the *San Jacinto* appeared in the London *Daily Telegraph*, November 29, 1861.

171 "the American government are determined": *Manchester Guardian*, November 28, 1861.

171 "the arrest of the rebel Commissioners": *Harper's Weekly*, November 30, 1861.

171 "Wilkes has done the very thing in principle": The comments of the *New York Commercial Advertiser* were reproduced in the *Daily Telegraph*, December 3, 1861.

172 "the fifty-one gun screw frigates": *Blackburn Times*, December 7, 1861.

172 "We are, indeed, too strong a nation": *Daily Telegraph*, November 30, 1861.

173 "Oh, that'll be got along with": "The Trent Affair of 1861," *Canadian Historical Review* 3, no. 1 (1922).

173 "the preparation for war": Ephraim Douglass Adams, *Great Britain and the American Civil War* (Russell and Russell, 1924), 238.

173 "the *Trent* affair has done us incalculable injury": Ibid., 246.

173 "he held him and his Government responsible for this outrage": *Daily Telegraph*, November 29, 1861.

174 "the most worthless booty it would be possible": Quoted in Adams, *Great Britain and the American Civil War*, 146.

174 "three British subjects were at this moment": *Hansard Parliamentary Debates*, vol. 165 (Cornelius Buck, 1862).

175 "the safety of the whole people has become": *Harper's Weekly*, November 2, 1861.

Chapter Twenty-one: "I Have Made a Full Statement and Confessed Everything"

176 "a hole cut in the door about five inches square": PLM, 122.

176 "there is no people in the world": Ibid.

176 "you know nothing beyond the grave": Ibid., 117.

177 "an excellent supper, including": Ibid., 123.

177 "that the physical pain would not be greater"; "believed in a just God": Ibid., 115.

177 "in the public papers": Letter from Cridland to Lyons.

178 "style of his evidence": *Richmond Dispatch*, April 30, 1862.

178 "you can always catch flies with molasses": This description of Philip Cashmeyer comes from George Washington Frosst, a prisoner in Richmond. Frosst's memoirs of his war experiences were published many years later by the Old Berwick Historical Society in a 2001 article titled "Quamphegan Landing."

179 "he was greatly suffering from rheumatic pains in his limbs": Ibid.

180 "Scully had told about my visit": PLM, 125.

180 "my mental suspense was such that"; "to make a statement to the authorities": Ibid., 126.

180 "were a couple of large, leather-bound": The account of Lewis's interview with Crump appears in ibid., 127–28.

182 "an emissary between the Union people": Ibid., 131.

182 "The condemned spies have implicated Webster": J. B. Jones, *A Rebel War Clerk's Diary* (Old Hickory Bookshop, 1866), 119.

Chapter Twenty-two: "I Suffer a Double Death"

183 "lurking about the armies and fortifications": *Richmond Dispatch*, April 30, 1862.

184 "might be termed elegant": PLM, 128.

184 "sitting down on a step": Ibid., 135.

185 "two thirds of the Court concurring": *Richmond Dispatch*, April 30, 1862.

185 RICHMOND PAPERS MENTION THAT TWO MEN: *The War of the Rebellion: A Compilation of the Official Records of the Union and Confederate Armies*, series 2, vol. 3 (Washington: Government Printing Office, 1880–1901).

186 IT IS INDISPENSABLE TO YOU THAT YOU STRIKE A BLOW: Quoted in James M. McPherson, *Battle Cry of Freedom* (Penguin, 1990), 426.

186 "his sympathy and sorrow were as acute as though": Allan Pinkerton, *The Spy of the Rebellion* (M. A. Winter and Hatch, 1883), 545.

187 "plenty of gold and C.S. Treasury notes": *Richmond Dispatch*, April 30, 1862.

189 "white beard, long and flowing": J. Marshall Hanna, "Castle Thunder in Bellum Days," *Southern Opinion*, November 23, 1867.

189 "'I suffer a double death": *Richmond Examiner*, April 30, 1862.

189 "You are going to choke me this time": Ibid.

189 "making use of horrid oaths and treating the subject": Ibid.

190 "read the psalm of David, invoking vengeance on his enemies": *Richmond Dispatch*, April 30, 1862.

190 "endeavors to bring about a pious state of mind": *Richmond Enquirer*, May 3, 1862.

190 "Gentlemen: Will you please allow me to correct": Ibid., May 6, 1862.

Chapter Twenty-three: "It Was Not War, It Was Murder"

191 "What if the federal government should commence": *New York Post*, May 2, 1862.

191 "the report that he had his wife with him": *Burlington Hawk Eye*, May 10, 1862.

192 "they let the cat out of the bag on him": *Richmond Dispatch*, April 30, 1862.

192 A copy of Thomas Lewis's letter to Charles Adams is held in the Pryce Lewis Collection, St. Lawrence University.

192 "inquire into the matter and make a report to me upon it": Lyons wrote to Cridland on April 16, 1862, a copy of the letter being housed at the Kew Archives, London, file F.O. 115/328.

192 "the arduous duties at this office and the innumerable": Ibid.

193 "to make a full confession": PLM, 126.

193 "for it was his downright lack of judgment": Ibid., 116.

194 "The enemy's gun-boats are ascending the [James] River": Varina Davis's recollection, reproduced in *Ladies of Richmond*, edited by Katharine Jones (Bobbs-Merrill, 1962), 111.

194 "The panic began some days later": Ibid., 112.

195 ENCOURAGEMENT FOR THE OPPORTUNITY: Tom Crouch, *The Eagle Aloft* (Smithsonian Institution Press, 1983).

196 On May 28 George Randolph: On May 31 a Richmond woman, Judith Brockenbrough McGuire, one of those gilded ladies who had swapped the splendor of her drawing room for the squalor of an army hospital, finished her shift and wrote in her diary: "The booming of cannon, at no very distant point, thrills us with apprehension. We know that a battle is going on. God help us!" (*Ladies of Richmond*).

197 "we again took the double quick step": The Letters of Lt. Henry Ropes, 20th MA (Boston, 1888), Rare Books and Manuscripts Department, Boston Public Library.

197 "it was not war, it was murder": Quoted in James M. McPherson, *Battle Cry of Freedom* (Penguin, 1990), 470.

198 "Though [the slaves] were incapable of giving realistic information": James D. Horan, *The Pinkertons: The Detective Dynasty That Made History* (Crown, 1967), 117.

198 "the odors of the battlefield were distinctly perceptible": Jones, ed., *Ladies of Richmond*.

198 "by a string of girls, children and Negroes": Judith Brockenbrough McGuire, quoted in Jones, ed., *Ladies of Richmond*, 109.

199 "was taken to the best hotel in the place": Rose Greenhow, *My Imprisonment and the First Year of Abolition Rule at Washington* (Bentley, 1863).

199 "the President did me the honor of calling upon me": Ibid.

199 Instead she began to write a book: Greenhow's book, *My Imprisonment and the First Year of Abolition Rule at Washington*, was published in Britain to widespread praise, and in September 1863 she visited the country as an emissary of Jefferson Davis. On October 1, 1864, upon her return to the United States, Greenhow's steamer ran aground three hundred yards off the North Carolina coast, and she was drowned.

Chapter Twenty-four: "They Held Existence by a Frail Tenure"

202 "are about 70 patients in a garret room": Inspection report written by William A. Carrington, October 3, 1862. Available to view at http://www.mdgorman.com.

202 "as though delivering them through a speaking-trumpet": J. Marshall Hanna, "Castle Thunder in Bellum Days," *Southern Opinion*, November 23, 1867.

202 "There is no use, men": Frances H. Casstevens, *George W. Alexander and Castle Thunder: A Confederate Prison and Its Commandant* (Mcfarland, 2004), 92.

203 "consisted originally of two large rooms": PLM, 141.

203 "squeeze out into the large rooms and enjoy the society": Ibid.

203 "by praising his poetry it was easy to keep": Ibid., 149.

204 "a piece of wheat bread"; "tin can of soup and a piece of bread": Ibid., 142.

204 "two hundred and forty five Abolition prisoners of war": *Richmond Dispatch*, November 29, 1862.

205 "I come to you, a poor weak woman": This letter from Hattie Lawton (aka Mrs. Webster) to President Davis is reproduced in *The War of the Rebellion: A Compilation of the Official Records of the Union and Confederate Armies*, series 2, vol. 4 (Government Printing Office, 1880–1901).

205 "I am requested by Mr. Allen to write you": A copy of Pinkerton's letter to Lewis can be found in the Pryce Lewis Collection, St. Lawrence University.

206 "best illustrates the amount of hellish recklessness": *Richmond Examiner*, January 29, 1863.

206 "marched down into the prison yard": PLM, 147.

206 "most barbarously and inhumanely": "Official Report on the Treatment of Prisoners in Castle Thunder," May 1, 1863, *The War of the Rebellion*, series 2, vol. 3.

207 "embraced among its inmates": Ibid.

207 "subpoenaed as a witness": PLM, 147.

207 "three most powerful pills"; "swallowed only one of them": Ibid.

207 " 'life was slowly ebbing away": Ibid.

207 Pinkerton's letter to Lewis, written on March 23, 1863, can be found in the Pryce Lewis Collection.

208 "to your mind the cases of Lewis and Scully": *The War of the Rebellion*, series 2, vol. 5.

210 "Resolved: that this meeting being convinced that slavery": Ephraim Douglass Adams, *Great Britain and the American Civil War* (Russell and Russell, 1924), 293.

210 "these manifestations are the genuine expression": Ibid.

211 "but regard your decisive utterances": Ibid.

211 "delaying on little pretexts of wanting this and that": James M. McPherson, *Battle Cry of Freedom* (Penguin, 1990), 570.

211 Pinkerton's letter to Lincoln of June 5, 1863, can be found in the Abraham Lincoln Papers, Library of Congress.

212 "he made a present of his new boots to a nephew": PLM, 154.

212 "but it cost so much": Ibid., 148.

212 "what a difference money makes": Ibid.

212 "a different class of prisoner": Unpublished memoirs of William Williams of Waterford, Virginia (1888), available at http://www.waterfordhistory.org.

212 J. T. Kerby: Kerby was never brought to trial and in May 1863 he was sent north on a flag-of-truce boat.

213 "they held existence by a frail tenure": Albert Deane Richardson, *The Field, the Dungeon & the Escape* (Gale Cengage Learning, 1897), 398.

213 "At the head of the Richmond Post they have placed": A copy of "The Castle Song" can be found in the Pryce Lewis Collection.

214 "too heavy to mount a horse"; "suggested to Scully": PLM, 155.

214 "he had seen Commissioner Ould": Ibid.

214 Lewis and Scully's interview with Marshall is described in ibid., 155–56.

215 "said goodbye to our fellow prisoners": Ibid., 157.

215 "got up on a box freight car for fresh air": Ibid., 158.

216 "If before this I had any English feelings left": Ibid.

216 "full-dressed, pompous, heavy official": Ibid., 160.

216 "The bearer Lewis Price": The pass can be found in the Pryce Lewis Collection.

217 "he uttered an exclamation": PLM, 162.

Chapter Twenty-five: *"Lewis Remained Staunch, and Did Not Confess"*

218 "Will you pardon me for asking": James M. McPherson, *Battle Cry of Freedom* (Penguin, 1990), 569.

221 "I can flatter almost anything": Arch Frederic Blakey, *General John Winder* (University of Florida Press, 1990), 266.

221 "energetic and active and wise"; "camp follower": Ibid.

223 "a hot interview": PLM, 163.

223 "because they had betrayed their companion": Allan Pinkerton, *The Spy of the Rebellion* (M. A. Winter and Hatch, 1883), 547.

223 "I hope your situation [at Old Capitol] will be of long continuance": William Pinkerton's January 15, 1864, letter to Pryce Lewis is in the Pryce Lewis Collection, St. Lawrence University.

224 "authorized to arrest deserters": The pass, signed by L. C. Baker, is contained in the Pryce Lewis Collection.

224 He had no contact with John Scully: By the 1880s, John Scully was employed as a guard at Chicago's City Hall, and in December 1894, it was reported that he attended the funeral of Sam Bridgeman in the city. The date of his death is not known.

226 HOW I REGRET THAT I HAD NOT BEEN NEAR HIM: James Mackay, *Allan Pinkerton: The Eye Who Never Slept* (Mainstream, 1996), 176.

227 "from a government by aristocracy to one by democracy": Ephraim Douglas Adams, *Great Britain and the American Civil War* (Russell and Russell, 1924), 400.

227 "My dear wife, don't be discouraged": Undated letter in the Pryce Lewis Collection.

229 "tempted to the recitals which follow": Pinkerton, *The Spy of the Rebellion*, xxiv.

230 "In an article first published in the Chicago Times": The article was reproduced in the following weeks in, among others, Iowa's *Sioux County Herald*, the *Freeborn County Standard* of Minnesota and *Eau Claire News* of Wisconsin.

230 "Yours of the 3rd was received and contents noted": Ibid.

231 "I had informed Mr. Lincoln": Pinkerton, *The Spy of the Rebellion*, 103.

231 "The mouth, almost concealed by": Ibid., 111.

231 "Self was his last and least": Ibid., 577.

232 "with rare grace": Ibid., 228.

232 "without the slightest hesitation": Ibid., 494.

232 "I had made extensive enquiries": Ibid., 496.

233 "I heard the story of your escape from Henrico County Jail!" PLM, appendix 1.

233 "to include a lot of lies about his experiences": Pryce Lewis Collection, folder entitled, "Correspondence of Pryce Lewis and his contemporaries."

233 "was very sorry to learn of ma's relapse": Ibid.

234 "died because he overworked in the printing business": Mary Lewis quoted by Harriet Shoen, among notes in ibid.

234 "I lost my wife 4 years ago and my son nearly 3 years ago": Pryce Lewis Collection, December 11, 1904.

235 "Making allowance for what you have": Letter from Cronin to Lewis, dated February 27, 1905, and contained in the Pryce Lewis Collection.

235 "I have never needed": Letter from Lewis to Cronin, dated May 22, 1905, and contained in the Pryce Lewis Collection.

235 "After considerable discussion the opinion prevailed": Letter from Funk & Wagnalls to Anson Barnes, dated January 5, 1908, and contained in the Pryce Lewis Collection.

235 "I've served this [American] government well": *Harper's Weekly*, January 30, 1912.

236 "Scully made a confession, implicating Webster": The pamphlet *Timothy Webster: Spy of the Rebellion* is among the Pinkerton Papers, Library of Congress. Washington, D.C.

236 "my memoirs will soon be published": Pryce Lewis Collection.

236 "My Dear Mary, Yours of yesterday is recv'd": Ibid.

237 " 'There goes a big slide of snow": *New York Times*, December 7, 1911.

Epilogue: "A Faithful Servant to His Country"

239 "had realized he had outlived his usefulness": *New York Herald*, December 9, 1911.

239 "established a private burial ground near Chicago": *World*, December 10, 1911.

241 "Dear Mr. Editor, As I am always interested in reading": *Montgomeryshire Express*, January 9, 1912.

Appendix 1: The Baltimore Plot

243 "It is perfectly manifest": Ward H. Lamon, *The Life of Abraham Lincoln* (James R. Osgood, 1872), 513.

243 "intensely ambitious to shine in the professional way": Ibid., 512.

243 "a brainless, egotistical fool": Quoted in *Lincoln and the Baltimore Plot, 1861: From Pinkerton Records and Related Papers*, edited by Norma Cuthbert (Huntington Library, 1949), xx.

Appendix 2: The Trial

249 The letter from Louis Sigaud to Harriet Shoen, dated August 1, 1945, can be found in the Pryce Lewis Collection, St. Lawrence University.

Appendix 3: Pinkerton's Military Espionage

251 "not conducted by a recognizable organizational entity": Edwin Fishel, *The Secret War for the Union* (Houghton Mifflin, 1998), 54.

251 "have received reports from the cavalry": Ibid., 55.

INDEX

Double Death is Gavin Mortimer's seventh book. His two most recent are *Chasing Icarus* and *The Great Swim*. He has also written numerous books for children and contributed articles to a wide range of publications. He lives in France.